T0214255

Communications in Computer and Information Science 1153

Commenced Publication in 2007
Founding and Former Series Editors:
Phoebe Chen, Alfredo Cuzzocrea, Xiaoyong Du, Orhun Kara, Ting Liu,
Krishna M. Sivalingam, Dominik Ślęzak, Takashi Washio, Xiaokang Yang,
and Junsong Yuan

More information about this series at http://www.springer.com/series/7899

Héla Fehri · Slim Mesfar · Max Silberztein (Eds.)

Formalizing Natural Languages with NooJ 2019 and Its Natural Language Processing Applications

13th International Conference, NooJ 2019
Hammamet, Tunisia, June 7–9, 2019
Revised Selected Papers

Springer

Editors
Héla Fehri (iD)
University of Sfax
Sfax, Tunisia

Slim Mesfar (iD)
Manouba University
Manouba, Tunisia

Max Silberztein (iD)
University of Franche-Comté
Besançon, France

ISSN 1865-0929   ISSN 1865-0937 (electronic)
Communications in Computer and Information Science
ISBN 978-3-030-38832-4   ISBN 978-3-030-38833-1 (eBook)
https://doi.org/10.1007/978-3-030-38833-1

This Springer imprint is published by the registered company Springer Nature Switzerland AG
The registered company address is: Gewerbestrasse 11, 6330 Cham, Switzerland

Preface

NooJ is a linguistic development environment that provides tools for linguists to construct linguistic resources that formalize a large gamut of linguistic phenomena: typography, orthography, lexicons for simple words, multiword units and discontinuous expressions, inflectional, derivational and agglutinative morphology, local, phrase-structure and dependency grammars, as well as transformational and semantic grammars. For each linguistic phenomenon to be described, NooJ proposes a set of computational formalisms, the power of which ranges from very efficient finite-state automata (that process regular grammars) to very powerful turing machines (that process unrestricted grammars). NooJ also contains a rich toolbox that allows linguists to construct, maintain, test, debug, accumulate, and share linguistic resources. This makes NooJ's approach different from most other computational linguistic tools that typically offer a unique formalism to their users, and are not compatible with each other.

NooJ provides parsers that can apply any set of linguistic resources to any corpus of texts, to extract examples or counter-examples, annotate matching sequences, perform statistical analyzes, and so on. Because NooJ's linguistic resources are neutral, they can also be used by NooJ's generators to produce texts. By combining NooJ's parsers and generators, one can construct sophisticated NLP (Natural Language Processing) applications such as MT (Machine Translation) systems, abstracts and paraphrases generators, etc.

Since its first release in 2002, several private companies have used NooJ's linguistic engine to construct business applications in several domains, from Business Intelligence to Opinion Analysis. To date, there are NooJ modules available for over 50 languages; more than 140,000 copies of NooJ have been downloaded.

NooJ has also been enhanced with new features to respond to the needs of researchers who need to analyze texts in various domains of Human and Social Sciences (history, literature and political studies, psychology, sociology, etc.), and more generally of all the professionals who analyze texts. In 2013, a new version for NooJ was released, based on the JAVA technology and made available to all as an open source GPL project, distributed by the European Metashare platform.

This volume contains 18 articles selected from the papers and posters presented at the International NooJ 2019 conference in Hammamet, Tunisia. The following articles are organized in three parts: "Development of Linguistic Resources" contains six articles; "NLP Applications" contains five articles; and "NooJ for the Digital Humanities" contains seven articles.

The six articles in the first part involve the construction of electronic dictionaries and grammars to formalize various linguistic phenomena:

We would like to thank Ms. Olfa Ben Amor from the University of Monastir for her editing work on this volume.

– In their article "Recognition of Arabic Phonological Changes by Local Grammars in NooJ," Rafik Kassmi, Mohammed Mourchid, Abdelaziz Mouloudi, and Samir Mbarki present a set of local grammars used to recognize Arabic phonological changes.
– In "Lexicon-Grammar Tables Development for Arabic Psychological Verbs," Asmaa Amzali, Asmaa Kourtin, Mohammed Mourchid, Abdelaziz Mouloudi, and Samir Mbarki show how they organized and formalized Arabic psychological verbs using lexicon-grammar tables.
– In "The Identification of English Non-Finite Structures Using NooJ Platform," Ben Amor Olfa and Faiza Derbel present a set of local grammars used to identify non-finite clauses in an English corpus of business-related texts with a impressive recall rate (96%).
– In "Automatic Recognition and Translation of Polysemous Verbs Using the Platform NooJ," Hajer Cheikhrouhou presents the linguistic information associated with communication and movement verbs extracted from Dubois & Dubois-Charlier's LVF (*Les Verbes Français*) dictionary and implements a set of NooJ grammars to identify and disambiguate them. Once disambiguated, they can be safely translated into Arabic.
– In "Negation of Croatian Nouns," Natalija Žanpera, Kristina Kocijan, and Krešimir Šojat present a set of morphological grammars for Croatian that can recognize the various prefixes used to express negation and compute the words polarity accordingly.
– Finally, in "The Automatic Generation of NooJ Dictionaries from Lexicon-Grammar Tables," Asmaa Kourtin, Asmaa Amzali, Mohammed Mourchid, Abdelaziz Mouloudi, and Samir Mbarki present a set of computer tools aimed at helping linguists to implement the wealth of information contained in lexicon-grammar tables in the form of NooJ electronic dictionaries.

The five articles in the second part describe the implementation of spectactular NLP software applications:

– In "The Data Scientist on LinkedIn: Job Advertisement Corpus Processing with NooJ," Maddalena della Volpe and Francesca Esposito present an application capable of parsing a large number of job advertisements collected by LinkedIn to extract skills required by companies and organizations.
– In "Recognition and Analysis of Opinion Questions in Standard Arabic," Essia Bessaies, Slim Mesfar, and Henda Ben Ghezala show how a question/answering system for Arabic can be structured in four processes (Question Analysis, Text Segmentation, Passage Retrieval, and Answer Extraction) and how NooJ can be used to perform tasks in these four processes.
– In "Disambiguation for Arabic Question-Answering System," Sondes Dardour, Héla Fehri, and Kais Haddar focus on the problem of solving ambiguities in Medical Question-Answering systems for Arabic. Both Arabic written texts in general, and medical questions in particular are highly ambiguous; the authors present a set of local grammars used to solve these two types of ambiguity.
– In "A NooJ Tunisian Dialect Translator," Roua Torjmen, Nadia Ghezaiel Hammouda, and Kais Haddar show how they built an automatic Tunisian dialect to

modern standard Arabic translator, using bilingual dictionaries, morphological grammars, and local translation grammars.

- In "Automatic Text Generation: How to Write the Plot of a Novel with NooJ," Mario Monteleone presents a system capable of generating novel plot templates automatically using dictionaries that use narrative-related tags (such as "cloth", "game", "currency") and local grammars.

The seven articles in the last part involve applications of NooJ in the Digital Humanities, three pedagogical applications of NooJ and three analysis of various discourses, university communication, Amazon reviews, and detection of hate crime and terroris threats:

- In "Arabic Learning Application to Enhance the Educational Process in Moroccan Mid-High Stage using NooJ Platform," Ilham Blanchete, Mohammed Mourchid, Samir Mbarki, and Abdelaziz Mouloudi present a pedagogical application that helps students analyze nouns, in terms of linguistic information (e.g. lemma, root, semantic domain, etc.).
- In "Causal Discourse Connectors in the Teaching of Spanish as a Foreign Language (SLF) for Portuguese Learners using NooJ," Andrea Rodrigo, Silvia Reyes, Cristina Mota, and Anabela Barreiro present a pedagogical application that helps teach Spanish causal discourse connectors to Portuguese students.
- In "Construction of Educational Games with NooJ," Héla Fehri and Ines Ben Messaoud present two educational games: ProMoNooJ (a multilingual game in which players must classify terms) and AlphaNooJ (a word-building game). While playing, the users actually learn terms and linguistics concepts.
- In "Mining Entrepreneurial Commitment in University Communication: Evidence from Italy," Maddalena della Volpe and Francesca Esposito process websites of 91 Italian Universities to analyze how they communicate their strategic intentions.
- In "Dealing with Producing and Consuming Expressions in Italian Sentiment Analysis," Nicola Cirillo has parsed a corpus of product reviews from Amazon in order to extract sentiment terms and compute their polarities.
- In "Detecting Hate Speech Online: A Case of Croatian," Kristina Kocijan, Lucija Košković, and Petra Bajac present a system capable of finding and categorizing hate speech in Croatian online texts from Facebook news pages. The crucial issue to solve was to adapt the standard Croatian linguistic resources to parse texts that are not necessarily used in informal communication.
- In "Rule Based Method for Terrorism, Violence and Threat Classification: Application to Arabic Tweets," Elahsoumi Wissam, Boujelben Ines, and Keskes Iskander have parsed tweets in Arabic in order to find inappropriate messages promoting terrorism, violent messages, and threats automatically.

This volume should be of interest to all users of the NooJ software because it presents the latest development of its linguistic resources as well as a large variety of applications.

Linguists as well as Computational Linguists who work on Arabic, Croatian, French, Italian, Portuguese, Argentinian Spanish, or Tunisian dialects will find advanced, up-to-date linguistic studies for these languages.

We think that the reader will appreciate the importance of this volume, both for the intrinsic value of each linguistic formalization and the underlying methodology, as well as for the potential of developing NLP applications along with linguistic-based corpus processors in the Social Sciences.

June 2019

Héla Fehri
Slim Mesfar
Max Silberztein

Contents

NooJ for the Digital Humanities

Development of Linguistic Resources

Recognition of Arabic Phonological Changes by Local Grammars in NooJ

Rafik Kassmi[(✉)], Mohammed Mourchid, Abdelaziz Mouloudi,
and Samir Mbarki

MISC Laboratory, Ibn Tofail University, Kénitra, Morocco
rafik.kassmi@gmail.com, mourchidm@hotmail.com,
mouloudi_aziz@hotmail.com, mbarkisamir@hotmail.com

Abstract. In this paper, we present how to use NooJ in order to recognize all transformations occurring on words following Arabic phonological changes. Our goal is to give the concerned phonological rule, its category, the cause and finally the origin of the word before any transformation. We describe the phonological changes by presenting the three main categories; assimilation, substitution, and weakening. Then, we recall our previous work in this field. We detail all the steps to adopt in order to achieve our goal. We present our classification of word forms, the dictionary, the inflectional grammar, the morphological grammar, and the local grammar. Finally, we present some examples and results.

Keywords: Arabic language · Phonological change · Substitution · Assimilation · Weakening · Local grammar · NooJ

1 Introduction

In the first century of the Hijrah (A. H.), the Arabs began to study phonetics with other branches of linguistics such as grammar, lexicography, and rhetoric. The basis of these studies was drawn from the Quran in order to preserve its text from corruption. It manifested itself at that time mainly in the science of tajwid, which is the correct recitation of the Quran [1]. Ibn Jinni (392 A. H.) was the first Arab linguist interested in phonetics and his best work on the subject was entitled "Sirr ṣināʿat al-iʿrāb" [سِر صِنَاعَة الْإِعْرَاب/the secret of grammatical cases industry] [2].

The Arabs have described Arabic sounds regarding both point of articulation (makhraj/مَخْرَج) and manner of articulation (ṣifah/1] (صِفَة]. Arabic sounds are divided into three groups: the first group is plosive or stop (šadīda/شَدِيدَة) consisting of eight consonants. The second is fricative (riḥwa/رِخْوَة) consisting of 14 consonants. The third group, between plosive and fricative, is resonant (rannāna/رَنَّانَة) and includes nasal, lateral, trill and glide sounds (see Fig. 1).

© Springer Nature Switzerland AG 2020
H. Fehri et al. (Eds.): NooJ 2019, CCIS 1153, pp. 3–14, 2020.
https://doi.org/10.1007/978-3-030-38833-1_1

Point of articulation / Manner of articulation		bilabial	labiodental	interdental n.e.	interdental em.	alveolar n.e.	alveolar em.	alveopalatal	palatal	velar	uvular	pharyngeal	glottal
Plosive	voiceless					ت t				ك k			ء '
	voiced	ب b				د d	ط ṭ	ج ǧ			ق q		
Fricative	voiceless		ف f	ث ṯ		س s	ص ṣ	ش š			خ ḫ	ح ḥ	ه h
	voiced			ذ ḏ	ظ ẓ	ز z	ض ḍ				غ ġ	ع '	
Resonant	nasals	م m				ن n							
	lateral					ل l							
	trill					ر r							
	glides	و w						ي y					

n.e. : non emphatic   em. : emphatic

Fig. 1. Chart of Arabic consonants

Arabic has 28 consonants and six vowels, three of which are short and three are long. The total number of Arabic sounds is 34. The Arabic writing system contains only 32 signs because [و – wa] and [ي – ya] have the same symbol as [و – ū] and [ي – ī] respectively. It is only from the second century A. H. that the short vowels, namely fatḥa (فَتَحة) [ó/a], kasra (كَسرَة) [ọ/ i] and ḍamma (ضَمة) [ó / u], were written in Arabic orthography. But still, remain absent in most Arabic hand-written and printed documents.

2 Phonological Changes

In Arabic, the phonological change is a transformation of a word from one base form to another derived form in order to ease the pronunciation. We can distinguish three main categories [3, 5] (see Fig. 2):

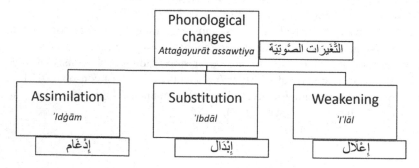

Fig. 2. Categories of phonological changes

2.1 Assimilation

The assimilation [إِدْغَام – 'idġām] is the germination of one letter with another. It's defined as the intensification in pronunciation of two identical sounds and may be written as one letter with the brief vowel šadda (ّ) above it. For example, let's consider the verb abata (أَبَتَ – *heat up*) in the singular first person of the past tense (pattern [فَعَلْتُ – faʿaltu]). According to the phonological rule, for verbs ending with t (ت), if the first t (تْ) is unvowelled followed by a vowelled t (تَ), we keep only one t carrying šadda (تَّ ← تَ + تْ) (see Table 1[1]).

Table 1. Example of assimilation

Root	Pattern	Underlying structure	Phonological rule	Surface structure
ابت	فَعَلْتُ	أَبَتْتُ	تَّ ← تَ + تْ	أَبَتُّ
'BT [Heat up]	faʿaltu	'abat-tu	unvowelled t followed by vowelled t → t carrying šadda	'abattu [I heated up]

2.2 Substitution

The substitution [إِبْدَال – 'ibdāl] is removing a letter and replacing it by another. This phenomenon is seen in verbs representing the pattern [إِفْتَعَلَ – 'iftaʿala] [4, 6] and we have five rules:

- If the first radical of the root is ṣ (ص) or ḍ (ض) or ṭ (ط) or ẓ (ظ), the t (ت) of 'iftaʿala is replaced by ṭ (ط). For example, the underlying structure of the root [صحب – ṣḥb] is [إِصْتَحَبَ – 'iṣtaḥaba] and the surface structure is [إِصْطَحَبَ – 'iṣṭaḥaba – *escorted*] (see Table 2)
- If the first radical of the root is a glide w (و) or y (ي), it is replaced by t (ت) and geminated with the following t (ت) to became tt (تّ). For example, the underlying structure of the root [يسر – ysr] is [إِيْتَسَرَ – 'iytasara] and the surface structure is [إِتَّسَرَ – 'ittasara – *became easy*]
- If the first radical of the root is d (د), the t (ت) of 'iftaʿala is replaced by d (د). For example, the underlying structure of the root [دعى – dʿā] is [إِدْتَعَى – 'idtaʿā] and the surface structure is [إِدَّعَى – 'iddaʿā – *claimed*]
- If the first radical of the root is ḏ (ذ), the t (ت) of 'iftaʿala is replaced by ḏ (ذ). For example, the underlying structure of the root [ذكر – ḏkr] is [إِذْتَكَرَ – 'iḏtakara] and the surface structure is [إِذَّكَرَ – 'iddakara – *remembered*]
- If the first radical of the root is z (ز), the t (ت) of 'iftaʿala is replaced by d (د). For example, the underlying structure of the root [زهر – zhr] is [إِزْتَهَرَ – 'iztahara] and the surface structure is [إِزْدَهَرَ – 'izdahara – *flourished*]

---

[1] The table is designed according to the phonological process suggested by Spencer [9].

Table 2. Example of substitution

Root	Pattern	Underlying structure	Phonological rule	Surface structure
صحب	إِفْتَعَلَ	إِصْتَحَبَ	ط ← ت	إِصْطَحَبَ
ṢḤB [accompanied]	'ifta'ala	'iṣtaḥaba	If the 1ˢᵗ radical of the root is ṣ t → ṭ	'iṣṭaḥaba [he escorted]

2.3   Weakening

The weakening [إعلَال – 'i'lāl] is a transformation that occurs on long vowels ā (ا), ī (ي) or ū (و), glides w (و) or y (ي) or a Hamza letter (glottal stop) ' (ء). It is divided into three sub-categories (see Fig. 3):

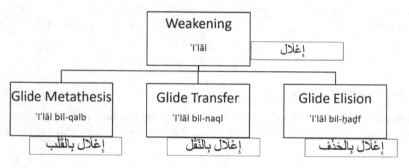

Fig. 3. Categories of weakening

- **Glide Metathesis**

The glide metathesis [إعلَال بالقَلْب – 'i'lāl bil-qalb] is replacing a long or short vowel, a glide or a Hamza letter by either of the two others. For example, let's consider the word 'a'dāwun (أَعْدَاوٌ) derived from the plural 'af'ālun (أَفْعَالٌ) of the root 'dw (عَدَوَ – *to feel hatred*). According to the phonological rule, if the extremity of the word is a glide w (و) after a long vowel alif (ا) with fatha (◌َ), the glide will be replaced by a Hamza ' (ء). So, the structure surface became [أَعْدَاءٌ – 'a'dā'un – *Enemies*] (see Table 3).

Table 3. Example of glide metathesis

Root	Pattern	Underlying structure	Phonological rule	Surface structure
عدو	أَفْعَالٌ	أَعْدَاوٌ	◌َاء ← او	أَعْدَاءٌ
'dw [feel hatred]	'af'ālun	'a'dāwun	The extremity is w or y after an alif with fatha; w → '	'a'dā'un [Enemies]

- **Glide Transfer**

The glide transfer [إعلال بالنقل – 'i'lāl bil-naql] is removing a short vowel from one sound and transfer it to another. For example, let's consider the word yaqwulu (يَقْوُلُ) derived from the pattern yaf'ulu (يَفْعُلُ) of the root qwl (قول – *say*). According to the phonological rule, for the hollow verbs, the short vowel damma (ُ) above the glide w (و) following a vowel sukūn (ْ) is removed and replaced the sukūn. So, the surface structure became [يَقُولُ – yaqūlu – *he says*] (see Table 4).

Table 4. Example of glide transfer

Root	Pattern	Underlying structure	Phonological rule	Surface structure
قول	يَفْعُلُ	يَقْوُلُ	ْوُ → ُوْ	يَقُولُ
qwl *[say]*	yaf'ulu	yaqwulu	Transfer of the damma above the w (و) to the letter before	yaqūlu [*he says*]

- **Glide Elision**

The glide elision [إعلال بالحذف – 'i'lāl bil-ḥadf] is deleting a long or short vowel, a glide, or a Hamza letter. For example, let's consider the word yaw'idu (يَوْعِدُ) derived from the pattern yaf'ilu (يَفْعِلُ) of the root w'd (وعد – *promise*). According to the phonological rule, for assimilated verbs, the glide w (و) with the vowel sukūn (ْ) above it followed by a vowel kasra (ِ) is removed. So, the surface structure became [يَعِدُ – ya'idu – *he promises*] (see Table 5).

Table 5. Example of glide elision

Root	Pattern	Underlying structure	Phonological rule	Surface structure
وعد	يَفْعِلُ	يَوْعِدُ	وْ ِ → ِ Ø	يَعِدُ
w'd *[Promise]*	yaf'ilu	yaw'idu	Deletion of the glide w and sukūn وْ	ya'idu [*he promises*]

3 Previous Works

In [8], we have proposed two solutions to implement Arabic phonological rules in NooJ. As a first solution, we have developed a new java module in NooJ, like a toolbox, which deals with phonological rules. Rules have been grouped by a line in an independent formatted file. A rule is composed of the triplet anomaly, correction, and condition.

We can feed easily this file by adding, replacing and suppressing rules. This module can be used in all generative operations including inflections and derivations. This new transformation process module has been used after the NooJ inflectional process. We have also created and added a new box dialog in NooJ Labs which provides users a tool to perform phonological corrections to the input words and displays all applied rules.

As a second solution, we have used local grammars within the NooJ platform, to locate anomalies in words and to give the appropriate transformations. On the one hand, we have used morphological grammars which allows us to verify the presence of the anomaly and if the condition is verified, it adds a lexical trait that will also include the correction. On the other hand, we have used syntactic grammars which allow us to apply the transformations and add them to annotations for output.

4   Contribution

In the continuity of our previous work, our goal in this study is to recognize all transformations occurring on words following Arabic phonological changes, to give the applied phonological rule and its type, the cause and finally, to give the origin of the word before any transformation.

To achieve this goal and after studying Arabic phonological rules, we need to make a clear and strong classification of all types of word forms (verbs, nouns…), then create a dictionary including special properties (as a result of this classification), then add special tags in inflectional grammar (as a result of the Arabic phonological rules study), then create a morphological grammar and finally create a local grammar.

4.1   Classification

The first step which is the base of our solution is the classification of all types of word forms (verbs, nouns…). Here is an example of classification of hollow verbs (see Fig. 4). The stronger and clearer the classification, the better and more precise the result. For example, the verb [قَالَ – qāla – to say] is classified as HR2AW which means hollow verb with as second radical the glide a (ا) whose origin is w (و).

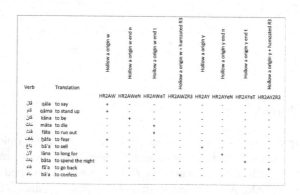

Verb	Translation	Hollow a origin w	Hollow a origin w end n	Hollow a origin w end t	Hollow a origin w + hamzated R3	Hollow a origin y	Hollow a origin y end n	Hollow a origin y end t	Hollow a origin y + hamzated R3
		HR2AW	HR2AWeN	HR2AWeT	HR2AWZR3	HR2AY	HR2AYeN	HR2AYeT	HR2AYZR3
قَالَ	qāla	to say	+	-	-	-	-	-	-	-
قَامَ	qāma	to stand up	+	-	-	-	-	-	-	-
كَانَ	kāna	to be	-	+	-	-	-	-	-	-
مَاتَ	māta	to die	-	-	+	-	-	-	-	-
فَاتَ	fāta	to run out	-	-	+	-	-	-	-	-
خَافَ	ḫāfa	to fear	+	-	-	-	-	-	-	-
بَاعَ	bā'a	to sell	-	-	-	-	+	-	-	-
لَانَ	lāna	to long for	-	-	-	-	-	+	-	-
بَاتَ	bāta	to spend the night	-	-	-	-	-	-	+	-
فَاءَ	fā'a	to go back	-	-	-	-	-	-	-	+
بَاءَ	bā'a	to confess	-	-	-	+	-	-	-	-

Fig. 4. Sample class of classification of hollow verbs

4.2   Dictionary

In the second step, we have created the dictionary including the result of our previous classification as a property of each entry. Figure 5 shows some hollow verb entries of our dictionary, which is based on the root and pattern approach.

```
########### Hollow // الأجوف المعتل ##################
#### Hollow R2 [A] origin [w] // و أصلها ألف با أجوف  ##
قال,قول,V+Tr+HR2AW+FormIau+FLX=V_FormIau_HR2AW
قام,قوم,V+Tr+HR2AW+FormIau+FLX=V_FormIau_HR2AW
## end N
كان,كون,V+Tr+HR2AWeN+FormIau+FLX=V_FormIau_HR2AW
## end T
مات,موت,V+Tr+HR2AWeT+FormIau+FLX=V_FormIau_HR2AW
فات,فوت,V+Tr+HR2AWeT+FormIau+FLX=V_FormIau_HR2AW
```

Fig. 5. Sample of hollow verb entries in our dictionary

4.3   Inflectional Grammar

Then we have created all inflectional grammars by adding special tags as a result of our linguistic study and which represent the phonological rules. Hereafter an example of inflectional sub-graph, in imperative tens, representing inflections of the hollow verbs with as second radical the glide a (ا) whose origin is w (و) (see Fig. 6) [10].

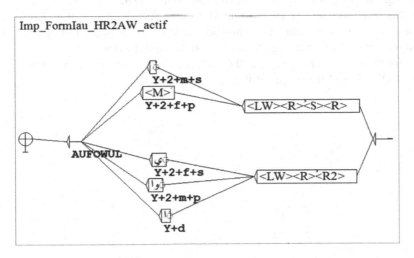

Fig. 6. Sample of inflectional sub-graph

In this example, we have added a special tag AUFOWUL which represent the phonological rule or all phonological rules applied to a word. We must remember that one word can undergo up to four transformations. Table 6 shows all transformations

Table 6. Description of the rule AUFOWUL

Transformation	Detail	Word	Transliteration
Underlying structure		أُقْوُل	'uqwul
Glide transfer	Transfer of the damma (ُ) of w (و) to the previous letter (ق) and change it with sukūn (ْ)	أُقْوْل	'uquwl
Glide elision	Delete the glottal stop (أ)	قُوْل	quwl
Glide elision	Delete the w (و) because we have two followed unvowelled letters	قُلْ	qul
Surface structure		قُلْ	qul

applied to the verb qāla [قَالَ – *to say*] in the second person, singular masculine, of the imperative tense (example of an entry with the tag AUFOWUL) [7].

4.4   Morphological Grammar

In the next step, we have created the morphological graph composed of three main graphs representing the three main categories of Arabic transformations, as mentioned above, namely assimilation, substitution, and weakening. Figure 7 shows a sample of morphological sub-graph dealing with the rule AUFOWUL.

At this level, we can already have an idea of the resulting annotation. NooJ allows us to test the graph by using the command GRAMMAR > Show Debug [11, 12]. It evaluates each path taken and gives corresponding annotations.

So, for the word qul [قُلْ – say!] in the imperative tense, we give as result the applied rule AUFOWUL and the origin of the word 'uqwul [أُقْوُل].

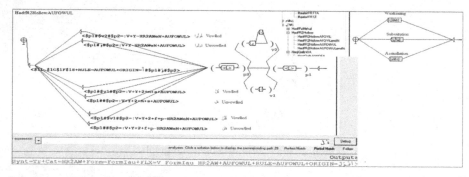

Fig. 7. The morphological sub-graph dealing the rule AUFOWUL

4.5   Syntactic Grammar

Finally, we have created a single syntactic grammar dealing with all types of words and which gives, as a result, the applied rule and the origin of the word (see Fig. 8).

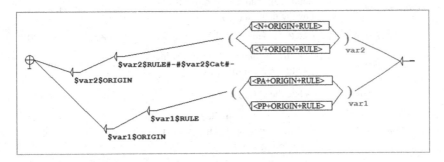

Fig. 8. The syntactic grammar

4.6   Examples and Results

For experimentation of our recognition system, we have used two important functions in NooJ platform; linguistic analysis and concordance [12].

Let's consider the unvowelled word [فت– ft], the linguistic analysis recognize the word as a verb [فَاتَ – fāta – *to run out*] classified as HR2AWeT which means hollow verb with as second radical the glide a (ا) whose origin is w (و) and ending with t (ت) (see Fig. 9).

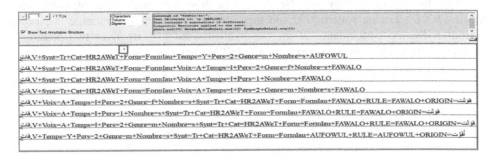

Fig. 9. Annotations of the unvowelled word [فت- ft]

We have four annotations corresponding to four possible inflections:

a. [فُتِّ – futti – *you ran out*]: A + I + 2 + f + s + Tr + HR2AWeT + FormIau + FAWALO/The applied rule is FAWALO (see Table 7) and the origin of the word is [فَوَتْتِ – fawat-ti]

b. [فُتُّ – futtu – *I ran out*]: A + I + 1 + s + Tr + HR2AWeT + FormIau + FAWALO/ The applied rule is FAWALO and the origin of the word is [فَوَتْتُ – fawat-tu]

Table 7. Description of the rule FAWALO

Transformation	Detail	Word	Transliteration
Underlying structure		فَوَتُّ	fawat-tu
Glide metathesis	Replace the fatha (ó) below the w (و) by the damma (ó)	فَوُتُّ	fawut-tu
Glide elision	Delete the fatha (ó) before the w (و)	فْوُتُّ	fwut-tu
Glide transfer	Transfer the damma (ó) below the w (و) to the previous letter	فُوْتُّ	fuwt-tu
Glide elision	Delete the w (و)	فُتُّ	fut-tu
Assimilation.[a]	Assimilate the unvowlled t (ت) with the followed vowelled tu (ت) to ttu (ت) carrying šadda.	فُتُّ	futtu
Surface structure		فُتُّ	futtu

---

[a] We add this transformation because the verb is ending with t (ت)

c. [فُتُّ – futta – *you ran out*]: A + I + 2 + m + s + Tr + HR2AWeT + FormIau + FAWALO/The applied rule is FAWALO and the origin of the word is [فَوَتَّ – fawat-ta]

d. [فُتُّ – fut – *run out!*]: Y + 2 + m + s + Tr + HR2AWeT + FormIau + AUFOWUL/ The applied rule is AUFOWUL and the origin of the word is [أُفْوُتْ – 'ufwut]

After the linguistic analysis in NooJ, we can show the concordance by using the menu TEXT > Locate pattern [12] and then choose our syntactic grammar in NooJ grammar. So, the concordance of the unvowelled word [فت- ft] gives two possible solutions according to the category of verbs HR2AWeT (see Fig. 10):

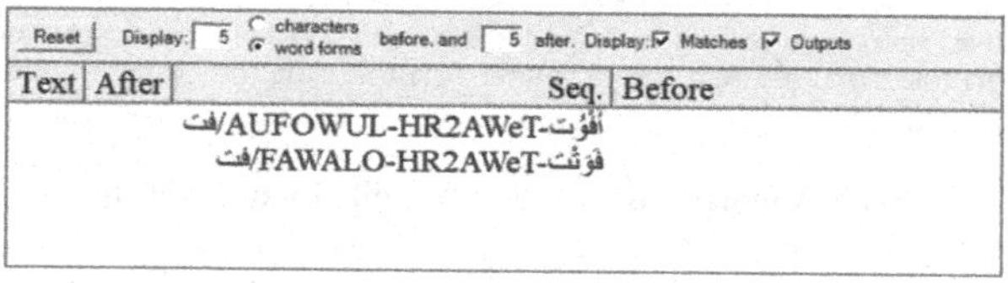

Fig. 10. Concordance of the unvowelled word [فت- ft]

a. [ف/AUFOWUL-HR2AWeT- أُفْوُت]: if the rule is AUFOWUL, the origin of the word is [أُفْوُت – ʾufwut]

b. [ف/FAWALO-HR2AWeT- فَوَتَ]: if the rule is FAWALO, the origin of the word is [فَوَتَ – fawat-t].

Let's consider now an example of substitution in words representing the pattern [إِفْتَعَلَ – ʾiftaʿala]. For the unvowelled word [إِتعظا – ʾitʿẓā], the linguistic analysis in NooJ recognizes the word as the verb [إِتَّعَظا – ʾittaʿaẓā – *they became moralized*] in FormVIIIai form and classified as IFAR1W which means assimilated verb in pattern ʾiftaʿala with the first radical of the root as w (و). The applied rule is IFAR1WY which means that the w (و) is replaced by t (ت) and merged with the following t (ت). The origin of this word is [إِوْتَعَظا – ʾiwtaʿaẓā] (see Fig. 11).

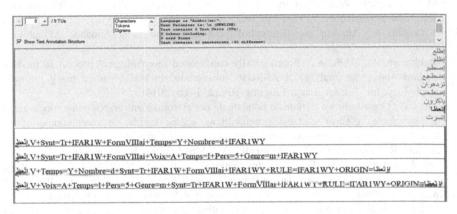

Fig. 11. Annotations of the unvowelled word [إِتعظا – ʾitʿẓā]

5   Conclusion and Perspectives

In this paper, we have presented how to use NooJ in order to recognize all transformations occurring on words following Arabic phonological changes. As a result, we give the concerned phonological rule, its category, the cause and finally the origin of the word before any transformation. So, we have described the phonological changes by presenting the three main categories assimilation, substitution, and weakening. Then, we have reviewed our related previous works. As a contribution, we have detailed all necessary steps adopted to achieve our goal. So, we have presented the classification of word forms, the dictionary, the inflectional grammar, the morphological grammar, and the local grammar. Finally, we have presented some examples and results.

As for perspectives, we aim first to cover all phonological rules and then try to introduce morphological rules to our study. The goal is to recognize Arabic morphophonological changes with NooJ by combining both phonological and morphological studies.

We aim also to create an extra NooJ didactic tool to teach lessons on morpho-phonological rules summarizing all covered rules. Adding also the possibility to generate the surface structure from root or lemma and morphological properties.

References

1. Affozan, A.I.: Assimilation in classical Arabic, a phonological study. Ph.D. thesis, University of Glasgow, Scotland (1989)
2. Jinni, I.: Sirr ṣināʿat al-iʿrāb/ مطبعة البابي الحلبي ,"الإعرَاب" سِر صِنَاعَة, Cairo (1954)
3. Al-Galaayiini, M.: "ǧāmiʿ addurūs alʿarabiyah alǧuzʾ alʾawwal" – "a set of Arabic lessons part one". Al-Maktaba Alʾaṣriya, Beirut (1991)
4. Al-Ilwaani, N.: Alʾibdāl assarfī assawtī fī sīġat ʾftaʿala fī maǧmaʿ albayān" – "morphological and phonological substitution in ʾftaʿala pattern in maǧmaʿ albayān. Majallat Allurra Alʿarabiyah wa ʾadābuhā **9**, 93–120 (2010)
5. Al-Raagihi, A.: Attaṭbīq assarfīʾmorphological application'. Dar Annahda Alʿarabiyah, Beirut
6. Altakhaineh, A., Zibin, A.: Phonologically conditioned morphological process in modern standard Arabic: an analysis of Al-ibdal 'substitution' in Ftaʿal pattern using prosodic morphology. Int. J. Engl. Lang. Linguist. Res. **2**, 1–16 (2014)
7. Bohas, G.: Contribution à l'étude de la méthode des grammairiens arabes en morphologie et en phonologie, d'après certains grammairiens arabes tardifs en morphologie et en phonologie. Atelier de reproduction des thèses, University of Lille 3 (1982)
8. Kassmi, R., Mourchid, M., Mouloudi, A., Mbarki, S.: Implementation of Arabic phonological rules in NooJ. In: 12th International Conference, NooJ 2018, Palermo, Italy, 20–22 June (2018). Revised Selected Papers. https://doi.org/10.1007/978-3-030-10868-7_2
9. Spencer, A.: Phonology: Theory and Description, vol. 9. Wiley-Blackwell, Oxford (1996)
10. Mesfar, S.: Analyse morpho-syntaxique automatique et reconnaissance des entités nommées en arabe standard. Ph.D. thesis, Franche-Comte University, France (2008)
11. Silberztein, M. (ed): Formalizing Natural Languages: The NooJ Approach. Wiley-ISTE, January 2016. ISBN 978-1-84821-902-1
12. Silberztein, M.: The NooJ manual (2003). http://www.nooj4nlp.net/pages/references.html

Lexicon-Grammar Tables Development for Arabic Psychological Verbs

Asmaa Amzali[✉], Asmaa Kourtin, Mohammed Mourchid,
Abdelaziz Mouloudi, and Samir Mbarki

Faculty of Science, MISC Laboratory, Ibn Tofail University, Kénitra, Morocco
asmamzali@hotmail.fr, asmaa.kourtin@yahoo.fr,
mourchidm@hotmail.com, mouloudi_aziz@hotmail.com,
mbarkisamir@hotmail.com

Abstract. The identification of psychological verbs is very important in corpora analyses in order to give the polarity of a given text and define the emotional component. The classification of those verbs represents a challenge for
linguists since they classify them according to their needs and their understanding. The aim of this paper is the identification and classification of Arabic
psychological verbs through lexicon-grammar tables that are well structured,
easy to use for linguists and allow them to describe all the grammatical, syntactic and semantic characteristics of the lexicon. In this work we create lexicon-
grammar tables of Arabic psychological verbs with about 400 verbs entries in
three main classes and subclasses to use them in lexical, syntactic and semantic
analyzers. Using NooJ as an automatic natural language processing platform, we
can automatically recognize Arabic psychological verbs by transforming our
lexicon-grammar tables into NooJ dictionaries and syntactic grammars enabling
the detection of those verbs in texts and corpora.

Keywords: Psychological verbs · Lexicon-grammar · Classification ·
Syntactic and semantic analyses · Dictionaries · Syntactic grammars · NooJ

1 Introduction

Psychological verbs are widely used in various genres such as newspapers, novels,
personal communications. So, their identification is very important in corpus analyses
in order to define the polarity of a given text and detect the emotional component in the
corpus. The syntactic and semantic analyses of those verbs are important for numerous
scientific and literary purposes, where they may be used as a component of greater
systems. For example, in business, we can create a prediction system of the user's
behavior. Customers are usually satisfied when the items that have received very
negative feedback are excluded from the recommendations. In social networks, we can
detect the user's emotions from their comments and publications. This detection in turn
can help uncover users' opinions and orientations, or to predict their desires to satisfy
them.

Henceforth, the design of automatic tools capable to mine the psychology of human
beings over the web in real-time is one of the most active research and development

H. Fehri et al. (Eds.): NooJ 2019, CCIS 1153, pp. 15–26, 2020.
https://doi.org/10.1007/978-3-030-38833-1_2

areas [1]. This impels linguists to study in-depth the psychological verbs [4] and extract all their properties to use them in different steps of the linguistic analysis.

The classification of those verbs represents a challenge for linguists since they classify them according to their needs and their understanding [2–4]. In this paper, we deal with the identification and classification of the Arabic psychological verbs through lexicon-grammar tables. These tables are well structured and allow the description of all grammatical, syntactic and semantic features of the language lexicon. Finally, we implement those tables in NooJ platform.

This article is organized as follows: In the second section, we describe psychological verbs and provide a previous related research. The third section, presents the lexicon-grammar approach; we describe the lexicon-grammar table of classes. The fourth section, gives a brief overview of the Arabic psychological verbs used in this study and we expose our classification of those verbs. The fifth section represents in detail our implementation in NooJ platform, illustrating it with an extract of our lexicon-grammar table for Arabic psychological verbs. Finally, in section six we present our concluding remarks and further perspectives.

2　Related Work

Many studies have been done on the psychological verbs by some researchers. For the Arabic language, Saadia Seghir [4] classified psychological verbs into two semantic classes or fields depending on a set of properties and features. The first class is related to the verb أَحَبُّ (Ahabba – to love) and the second one is related to the verbs كَرِهَ (kariha – to hate), غَضِبَ (ghadiba – to blow up), خَافَ (khafa – to fear), and حَزِنَ (hazina – to sorrow). The author assumes a semantic hierarchical relationship that governs the items construction of each class and the lexicalization of these verbs.

El Hannach [5–8] studied the class of Arabic psychological verbs with their syntactic properties. Also, he did a syntactic analysis of those verbs.

For French language, Yvette Yannick [3, 9] classified psychological verbs into three classes according to their valence: *(i)* the negative polarity classes that describe a quite unpleasant feeling like fear or anger; *(ii)* the positive polarity classes that describe a quite pleasant feeling which contains fourteen classes of this type, such as love, passion, etc., and *(iii)* classes without polarity like the indifference class or with a polarity that will be indicated by the context like the classes of emotion and astonishment. After the construction of a lexical and semantic base of these verbs [1], the author developed a system "FEELING" for the automatic interpretation of psychological verbs.

The objective of the present work is to build a classification of the Arabic psychological verbs. This classification induced the lexicon-grammar tables described in Sect. 3 which are well enriched and more useful in lexical, syntactic and semantic analyses for NLP applications as NooJ linguistic platform.

3 Lexicon-Grammar Approach

Today, the lexicon- grammar approach [10–13] is one of the main sources of syntactic lexical information for French language by covering several lexical categories such as nouns, verbs, adjectives, and adverbs. Their development was initiated in the (1970) [10], by Gross [14, 15], within the Laboratory of Documentary and Linguistic Automation (LADL). The lexicon-grammar approach information is in the forms of classes. Each class is coded in a lexicon-grammar table that groups together a number of entries accepting common properties, whose lines represent lexical entries, the columns represent syntactic and semantic properties of constructions, distributions, morphological, transformational, semantic (ex: Nhum = human name), etc. The cells contain either a lexical element, or ("+" or "−") to specify that an expression has a property or not, or the symbol "∼" if it is not yet coded.

As examples, Figs. 1 and 2, shows an excerpt from a lexicon-grammar table of Maurice Gross and Max Silberztein for French language.

NO= :"Nhum	NO= : Nnr	NO= :"le fait Qu P	NO= :"V1-Ω	verbe	V concret	NO V	Adjectif=ant	Adjectif=able	Adjectif=eux	Adjectif=(E+ateur)	N1= :" Nhum	N1= :"-Nhum	Le fait Qu P	N1 se V de ce que P	N1 se V auprès de Nhum de ce que P	N1 est Vpp de ce que P	[passif par]	[passif de]	NO V N1 contre Nhum
+	+	+	+	calmer	+	+	+	-	-	-	+	-	■	■	■	-	+	-	■
-	+	+	+	captiver	-	+	+	-	-	-	+	-	-	-	-	+	+	-	-
+	+	+	+	cataloguer	+	+	-	-	-	-	+	-	+	-	-	-	+	-	-
+	+	+	+	chagriner	-	+	+	-	-	-	+	+	-	+	-	+	+	-	-
-	+	+	+	chamboule	+	+	-	-	-	-	+	+	-	-	-	+	+	-	-
+	+	+	+	charmer	-	+	-	-	-	-	+	+	-	-	-	+	+	-	-
+	+	+	+	charpenter	+	+	-	-	-	-	+	+	-	-	-	-	+	-	-
+	+	+	+	chatouiller	+	+	-	-	-	-	+	+	-	-	-	-	+	-	-
-	+	+	+	chavirer	+	+	+	-	-	-	+	+	-	-	-	+	+	-	-

Fig. 1. Excerpt of verbs class of Maurice Gross.

NO =:" Nhum	NO =:" Nnc	<ENT>=Ppv	Ppv =:" se figé	Ppv =:" en figé	Ppv =:" Neg	<ENT>V	Aux =:" avoir	Aux =:" être	NO est Vpp W	NO V	Prép1	N1 =:" Qu Pind	N1 =:" Qu Psubj	Tp = Tc	Tc =:" passé	Tc =:" présent	Tc =:" futur	Vc =:" devoir	Vc =:" pouvoir	Vc =:" savoir	Prép V0-inf W = Ppv	NO V Prép N1-hum	NO V Prép N1-hum	NO V Prép N1 = Ppv	NO V dans N1	NO V N1-hum	NO V N1-hum	<OPT>
+	-	◇	-	-	-	achever	+	-	-	-	de	-	-	+	-	-	-	-	-	-	-	-	-	-	-	+	+	Max achève de peindre le mur
+	+	◇	-	-	-	aller	-	-	-	-	◇	-	-	-	-	+	+	+	-	-	-	-	-	-	-	-	-	Le verre va tomber
+	+	◇	-	-	-	aller	+	+	-	-	pour	-	-	+	-	-	-	-	-	-	-	-	-	-	-	-	-	Max allait pour partir quand Marie est arrivée
+	-	◇	-	-	-	aller	-	+	-	-	jusqu'à	-	-	+	-	-	-	-	-	-	-	-	-	-	-	-	-	Max va jusqu'à exiger des dommages
-	+	ne	-	-	+	aller	-	+	-	-	sans	-	-	+	-	-	+	+	+	-	-	-	-	-	-	-	-	Cette mesure n'ira pas sans créer des troubles
∼	∼	s'	∼	∼	∼	apprêter	∼	∼	∼	∼	à	∼	∼	∼	∼	∼	∼	∼	∼	∼	∼	∼	∼	∼	∼	∼	∼	La pluie s'apprête à tomber

Fig. 2. Excerpt of verbs class "V_1" of Max silberztein.

4   Lexicon-Grammar Tables for Arabic Psychological Verbs

4.1   An Overview of the Arabic Psychological Verbs

The Arabic psychological verbs describe the change in the emotional and psychological states of a human being as presented by linguists like saadia sghir [4]. Our work is based on the feelings field: positive and negative, then we have extended this semantic field to a neighboring domain of opinions and thought as illustrated in Fig. 3. These three semantic fields are close, they are both parts of the emotional or intellectual sphere of a person and overlap in part because many opinions or thoughts are the expressions of feelings such as indignation, anger or admiration.

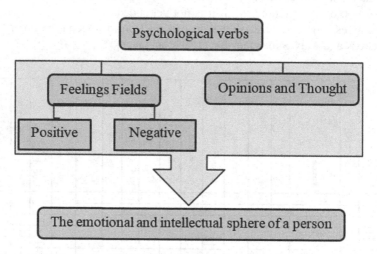

Fig. 3. Proposed classification of Arabic psychological verbs.

4.2   Lexicon-Grammar Tables of Arabic Psychological Verbs

As illustrated in Fig. 3, we focused on the identification of Arabic psychological verbs and we elaborated a classification that is more general and subdivided into three main classes:

✓ أفعال الشعور (Negative feeling verbs)

These verbs are resulting from external circumstances 'e.g.: غَضِبَ (Ghadiba – to blow up)' (see Fig. 4).

✓ أفعال الإحساس (Positive feeling verbs)

They express acts resulting from instinctive emotions 'e.g.: أَحَبَّ (Ahabba – to love)' (see Fig. 5).

✓ أفعال الرأي والتفكير (thought and opinion verbs)

These verbs express an activity of thinking and opinion 'e.g.: فَكَّر (Fakkara – to think)' (see Fig. 6).

At a subsequent stage, we did an extensive research in some Arabic dictionaries like Al-Wassit dictionary (معجم الوسيط) [16] so that we could populate the three classes with all the possible psychological verbs and extract their linguistic properties. These three classes will be in turn subdivided into subclasses where each subclass could contain the entries sharing the same properties. This refined classification makes these lexicon-grammar tables well enriched and more useful in various NLP applications.

<OPT> Explication	<OPT> Exemple	VN0Prép1N1	VN0N1	VN0	Prép1	N1Nhum	N1Hum	N0Nhum	N0Hum	V	<OPT> Catégorie
أبَدَ عليه : غَضِبَ	أبَدَ عليه	+	-	-	على	-	+	-	+	أبَدَ	
أبَى الشيء : كرهه و لم يرضه	أبَتْ نفسُهُ الفَسادَ	+	+	+	<E>	+	-	-	+	أبَى	
أجَمَ : كرِهَهُ .	أجَمَ الطَّعامَ	-	+	-	<E>	+	+	-	+	أجَمَ	
تأجَّمَ : غَضِبَ	تأجَّمَ عليه	+	-	-	على	+	+	-	+	تأجَّمَ	أفعال الشعور
أرِقَ : امتنع عليه النوم ليلا	أرِقَ الرَّجلُ	+	+	+	<E>	+	-	~	+	أرِقَ	
استُوزِقَ على فلان , أزِقَ صَدْرُ..أزِقَ : ضاق (مأزق)	استُوزِقَ على فلان , أزِقَ صَدْر..	+	+	-	<E>	+	-	-	+	أزِقَ	
أزَلَ الرجل : صار في ضيق	أزَلَ الرجل	+	-	+	<E>	+	~	+	+	أزَلَ	
أسِفَ لِرُسوبِهِ، ظَلَّ يأسَفُ لما .أسِفَ : حزن، تألم و ..م	أسِفَ لِرُسوبِهِ، ظَلَّ يأسَفُ لما .	+	-	-	ل	+	+	-	+	أسِفَ	

Fig. 4. Excerpt of class «أفعال الشعور (Negative feeling verbs)».

<OPT> Explication	<OPT> Exemple	VN0Prép1N1	VN0N1	VN0	Prép1	N1Nhum	N1Hum	N0Nhum	N0Hum	V	<OPT> Catégorie
عظَّمَه و فرِحَ به و فخِرَ	بجِحَ بالشَّيء	+	+	-	بـ	+	+	-	+	بَجِحَ	
أفرح	بَجُحَهُ الخَبَرُ	-	+	-	<E>	+	+	-	+	بَجُحَ	
أفرح	~	-	+	-	<E>	-	+	-	+	أبْجَحَ	
بَجِلَ:فرح	~	+	-	+	<E>	-	+	-	+	بَجِلَ	
عظُمَ	~	-	+	-	<E>	-	+	-	+	بَجُلَ	أفعال الإحساس
فرح به	أبْجَلَ الشَّيء	-	+	-	<E>	+	+	+	+	أبْجَلَ	
ابْتَهَجَ بالضَّيْفِ :- ابْتَهَجُ بالتَّأمُّلِ ابْتَهَجَ لَهُ الأهْلُ : فرِحَ وَسُرَّ	ابْتَهَجُ بالتَّأمُّلِ ابْتَهَجَ لَهُ الأهْلُ	+	+	+	<E>	-	+	-	+	ابْتَهَجَ	
بَدَخَ:عظُمَ و افْتَخَر	بدَخَ الشَّخص	+	-	+	<E>	-	-	-	+	بَدَخَ	

Fig. 5. Excerpt of class «أفعال الإحساس (Positive feeling verbs)».

<OPT> Explication	<OPT> Exemple	VN0Prép1N1	VN0N1	VN0	Prép1	N1Nhum	N1Hum	N0Nhum	N0Hum	V	<OPT> Catégorie
بَيْقَرَ:شك في الشيئ و حيره	~	+	+	~	\<E>	+	+	-	+	بَيْقَرَ	
خَتَّمَ:قضى و حكم	~	+	+	+	\<E>	+	+	-	+	خَتَّمَ	
اخْتَتَّنَ الشيئ:لا يخالف بعضه بعضا	اخْتَتَّنَ الشيئ	+	+	+	\<E>	+	+	-	+	اخْتَتَّنَ	أفعال الرأي و التفكير
حَجَا بالشيئ:ظَنَّ	حَجَا بالشيئ	+	-	+	بـ	+	+	-	+	حَجَا	
حَدَسَ:ظَنَّ و خَمَّن	~	+	+	+	\<E>	+	+	-	+	حَدَسَ	
حَزَا:تَكَهَّن	~	+	+	+	\<E>	+	+	-	+	حَزَا	
حَسِبَ:ظَنَّه	~	+	+	-	\<E>	+	+	-	+	حَسِبَ	
أَدْرَكَ:فَهِمَ	~	+	+	+	\<E>	+	+	-	+	أَدْرَكَ	

Fig. 6. Excerpt of class «أفعال الرأي واتفكير (thought and opinion verbs)».

5   Implementation

As shown in [17], the integration of the lexicon-grammar approach in NooJ is a two-step process. First, we convert the lexicon-grammar tables into NooJ dictionaries then we build grammars that use the linguistic knowledge encoded in the lexicon-grammar tables to identify the sentences, we notify that the dictionary and syntactic grammar should have the same name.

5.1   From Lexicon-Grammar Tables to NooJ Dictionaries

As indicated in the previous section, we started by extracting all psychological verbs and we create our lexicon-grammar tables. Then we will construct the lexical resources (dictionary and grammar) developed on NooJ platform [18].

Our dictionary is developed by a program generating NooJ dictionaries from lexicon-grammar tables, the dictionary saved in the file "PS_2.dic" (see Fig. 7) that is extended by the file "PS_2.nod". The file uses a set of flexional and derivational grammars saved in the file "qualitatif.nof", as shown in, Fig. 8. Accordingly, we can generate from our dictionary a lot of forms as presented in Figs. 9 and 10.

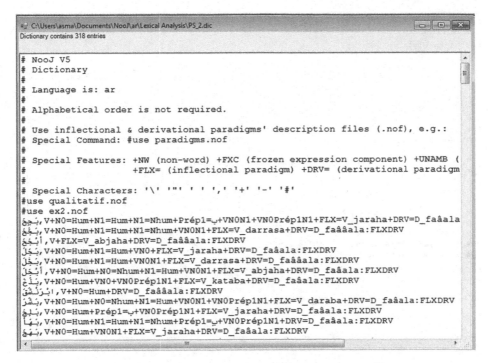

Fig. 7. Excerpt of our dictionary of psychological verbs "PS_2.dic".

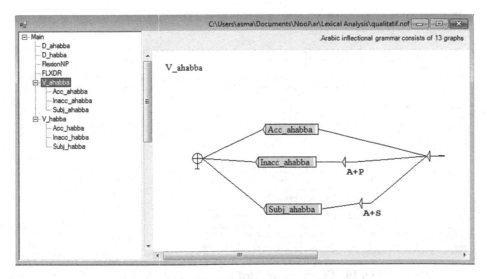

Fig. 8. Excerpt of flexional and derivational grammars.

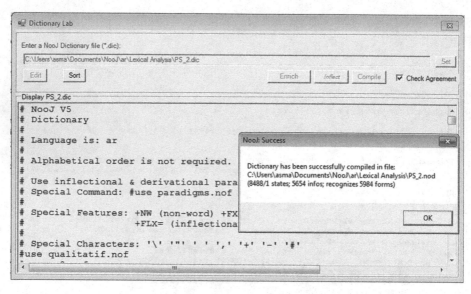

Fig. 9. Dictionary compilation.

```
# NooJ V5
# Dictionary
#
# Language is: ar
#
# Alphabetical order is not required.
#
# Use inflectional & derivational paradigms' description files (.nof), e.g.:
# Special Command: #use paradigms.nof
#
# Special Features: +NW (non-word) +FXC (frozen expression component) +UNAMB (unambig
#                   +FLX= (inflectional paradigm) +DRV= (derivational paradigm)
#
# Special Characters: '\' '"' ' ' ',' '+' '-' '#'
#
# This dictionary was automatically built from C:\Users\asma\Documents\NooJ\ar\Lexica
#
#use qualitatif.nof
#use ex2.nof
#
بَـجِعَ,بَـجِعَ, V+N0=Hum+N1=Hum+N1=Nhum+Prép1=ب+VN0N1+VN0Prép1N1+FLX=V_jaraha+DRV=D_faâala:FL
بَـجِحْنَا, بَـجِعَ,V+N0=Hum+N1=Hum+N1=Nhum+Prép1=ب+VN0N1+VN0Prép1N1+FLX=V_jaraha+DRV=D_faâala:
بَـجِعَا, بَـجِحَا,V+N0=Hum+N1=Hum+N1=Nhum+Prép1=ب+VN0N1+VN0Prép1N1+FLX=V_jaraha+DRV=D_faâala:F
بَـجِعَ,بَـجِخَذ, V+N0=Hum+N1=Hum+N1=Nhum+Prép1=ب+VN0N1+VN0Prép1N1+FLX=V_jaraha+DRV=D_faâala:F
بَـجِعَ,V+N0=Hum+N1=Hum+N1=Nhum+Prép1=ب+VN0N1+VN0Prép1N1+FLX=V_jaraha+DRV=D_faâala:F
بَـجِعَ ا بَـجِحُوا,V+N0=Hum+N1=Hum+N1=Nhum+Prép1=ب+VN0N1+VN0Prép1N1+FLX=V_jaraha+DRV=D_faâala.
بَـجِعَ,بَـجِخْتُم, V+N0=Hum+N1=Hum+N1=Nhum+Prép1=ب+VN0N1+VN0Prép1N1+FLX=V_jaraha+DRV=D_faâala:
بَـجِعَ,بَـجِخْتُن, V+N0=Hum+N1=Hum+N1=Nhum+Prép1=ب+VN0N1+VN0Prép1N1+FLX=V_jaraha+DRV=D_faâala:
```

Fig. 10. Excerpt of inflected forms of our dictionary.

5.2 From Lexicon-Grammar Tables to NooJ Grammars

As we have already shown in Subsect. 5.1, the process of integrating the lexicon-grammar with NooJ dictionary entries is automatic, but the process of creating the grammar that uses knowledge formalized in the lexicon-grammar tables is manual.

So we have created the syntactic grammar as shows in Fig. 11, based on the information of the lexicon-grammar tables.

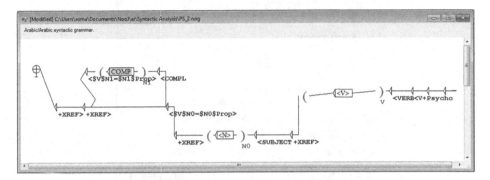

Fig. 11. Syntactic grammar.

To evaluate our dictionary and grammar, we tested the Arabic novel of "منى حارس" named "وجع الفراق وجمال اللقاء". Figure 12 shows the annotations of the Arabic sentence "أحبت علا حساما" 'ahabbat ola hosaman' (olaa loves hosam) that were added to NooJ text annotation structure after doing the linguistic analysis included in the grammar as shown in Fig. 11.

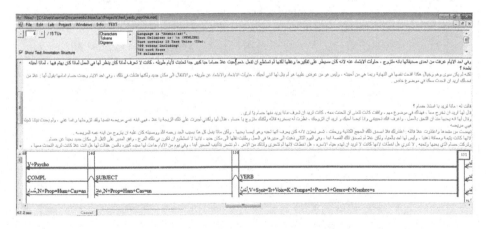

Fig. 12. Annotation of phrase content psychological verbs.

The platform NooJ offers the patterns localization in the corpus and allows, for example, to locate all different morphological and derivational forms of the verbs e.g.: أَحَبَّ "ahabba" (to love).

We choose a NooJ regular expression and we write the expression <V> as mentioned in Fig. 13.

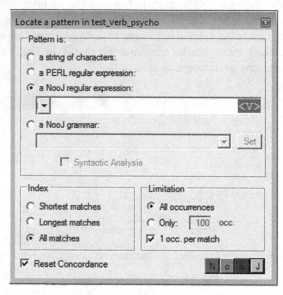

Fig. 13. Example of locate pattern.

The result of this localization is presented in Figs. 14 and 15.

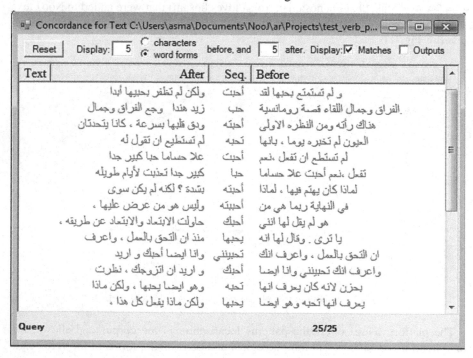

Fig. 14. Result of locate pattern (a).

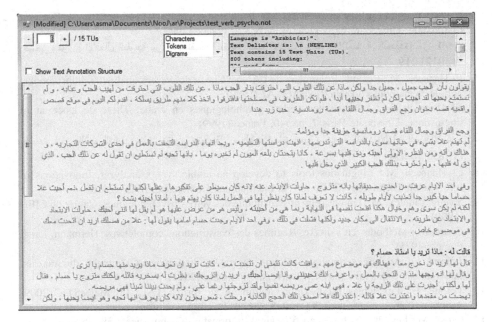

Fig. 15. Result of locate pattern (b).

6   Conclusion and Perspectives

The lexicon-grammar tables play a very important role in NLP applications, even though we notice the dearth of research in this area in Arabic language, especially on psychological verbs. So, in this paper, we have first presented an identification and classification of Arabic psychological verbs into three main classes: أفعال الشعور (Negative feeling verbs), أفعال الإحساس (Positive feeling verbs) and أفعال الرأي والتفكير (thought and opinion verbs), then we create the lexicon-grammar tables of those classes of verbs.

Furthermore, we have presented our dictionary set up automatically by a program generating NooJ dictionaries from lexicon-grammar tables. Then, we constructed the syntactic grammar based on the information of the lexicon-grammar tables.

With regard to perspectives, we plan to implement an application predicting emotions. We will also expand the coverage of our dictionaries and we will treat other grammatical categories, e.g. nouns.

References

1. Yvette Yannick, M.: Interprétation par prédicats sémantiques de structures d'arguments. FEELING, une application aux verbes psychologiques. Thèse de Doctorat en Informatique fondamentale. Université Paris 7, France (1994)
2. Rozwadowska, B.: Psychological verbs and psychological adjectives. In: The Wiley Blackwell Companion to Syntax, 2nd edn. pp. 1–26 (2017)

3. Yvette Yannick, M.: Des descriptions linguistiques à leurs représentations. Doctoral dissertation. Université Paris-Diderot-Paris VII. France (2009)

4. صغير، س. : الأفعال النفسية بين الوصف والتنظير. كلية الآداب والعلوم الإنسانية. الجديدة، ص. 199- 219 (2012).

5. El Hannach, M.: Lexique-grammaire de l'Arabe: Classe des verbes qualitatifs. https://books.google.co.ma/books?id=Nn7IjwEACAAJ (1989)

6. El Hannach, M.: Syntaxe des verbes psychologiques en arabe. Thèse de Doctorat in linguistique. Université Paris 7, p. 540, France (1999)

7. الحناش، م. : النحو التأليفي مدخل نظري وتطبيقي. مجلة دراسات أدبية ولسانية. العدد الأول، السنة الأولى، ص. 58 (1985).

8. El Hannach, M.: Linguistics tools to develop an arabic syntax analyzer, Innovations in Information Technology (IIT). In: 9th International Conference. IEEE (2013)

9. Yvette Yannick, M.: Un classement sémantique des verbes psychologiques. Cahier du CIEL (1999)

10. Gross, M.: Méthodes en syntaxe: Régimes des constructions complétives. Hermann, Paris, France (1975)

11. Tolone, E.: Analyse syntaxique à l'aide des tables du Lexique-Grammaire du français. Informatique et langage [cs.CL]. Université Paris-Est (2011)

12. Tolone, E.: Les tables du Lexique-Grammaire au format TAL. In: MajecSTIC 2009, Avignon, France, November 2009, p. 8 (2009). Electronic version

13. Gross, M.: Les phrases figées en français. L'Information Grammaticale **59**, 36–41 (1993)

14. Gross, M.: La construction de dictionnaires électroniques. Annales des Télécommunications. **44**(1–2), 4–19 (1989)

15. Gross, M.: Une grammaire locale de l'expression des sentiments. Langue française, Armand Colin **105**(1), 70–87 (1995)

16. معجم الوسيط. مجمع اللغة العربية. القاهرة، مصر، ص. 1095 (1960)

17. Silberztein, M.: Complex Annotations with NooJ. In: Proceedings of the 2007 International NooJ Conference. Jun 2007, p. 214. Cambridge Scholars Publishing, Barcelone (2008)

18. Silberztein, M.: La formalisation des langues: l'approche de NooJ. ISTE Editions, London (2015)

The Identification of English Non-finite Structures Using NooJ Platform

Olfa Ben Amor[1](✉)(iD) and Faiza Derbel[2](iD)

[1] University of Monastir, FSEG Mahdia, Monastir, Tunisia
olfa.bamor05@hotmail.com
[2] Manouba Faculty, University of Manouba, Manouba, Tunisia
fderbel26@gmail.com

Abstract. Non-finite clauses, clauses that have a non-finite verb phrase, have proven to be frequent and complex features of the structure of academic discourse in English. They are also indicators of writers' good mastery of academic discourse structures [5, 20, 22]. Therefore teaching non-finite clauses using specifically compiled and selected corpora is believed to have the potential of enhancing the teaching of these problematic structures. The purpose of this paper is to present the application of NooJ software in the automatic detection and extraction of English non-finite clauses occurring in a business English corpus compiled from a student's master dissertation, business editorials, and business academic research articles. We develop for the purpose of the pedagogical application an annotation framework based on syntactic, semantic and discoursal patterns using NooJ platform. Having implemented the annotation in NooJ platform and obtained satisfactory results, the syntactico-semantic and discoursal analysis of the target structure would be expected to facilitate the autonomous discovery of the rules of use governing English non-finite clauses in the English classroom with the ultimate aim of enhancing students' mastery of the elaborate and variant use of non-finite clauses in academic writing.

Keywords: English non-finite clauses · NooJ · Annotation · Data-Driven Learning · ESP

1 Introduction

This paper reports on an attempt to explore the possibility of using NooJ platform (http://www.nooj-association.org/) as an environment to create a tailor-made corpus to be used as a prospective teaching resource in a Data-Driven Learning (DDL) English for Specific Purposes course with university-level students majoring in Business Management and Administration. The paper is a description of the processes and procedures followed during the exploration of the affordances in the NooJ environment which facilitate the creation of such concordance data focusing on phrasal structures as linguistic targets.

NooJ was considered with the conviction that it is a promising option to carry out the annotation process and automatic extraction of the target linguistic items out of the

© Springer Nature Switzerland AG 2020
H. Fehri et al. (Eds.): NooJ 2019, CCIS 1153, pp. 27–38, 2020.
https://doi.org/10.1007/978-3-030-38833-1_3

selected materials from various Business English publication sites. More details will be provided about the selection process in Sect. 2.1.

1.1   Background

As a teaching approach, DDL, consists in designing a course (or a series of lessons) involving learners in exploration, prediction, hypothesis-testing and formulation of rules by directing them to observing the concordance data specifically-compiled and displayed for their convenience on screen or on printed paper. Learners are typically guided through the process of exploration via the teacher's instructional design of classroom activities which may consist of a series of tasks focusing learners 'attention on the instances of occurrence of a specific linguistic item found in the concordance data.

DDL rests on assumptions that the learner is an active participant in the learning process and capable of processing autonomously the primary data presented to them on screen and to generate knowledge and awareness about the language they are learning [17]. Depending on the situation, different corpora may be compiled to teach specific target features and emphasize specific skills such as reading and writing and sub-skills related to them. DDL is used in foreign language teaching to compensate for lack of exposure and to counter the artificial nature of synthetic syllabi [7]. This approach is attractive in instructed second language acquisition (ISLA) contexts within the framework of the focus-on-form movement [10], which rests on reinforcing the teaching of grammar within a communicative orientation. DDL is also appreciated in second and foreign language learning contexts seeing that corpora provide instances of authentic language use and the necessary technical affordances to enhance the input. It can be organized in patterns so that the salient features can be noticed by learners. Technically, the linguistic items and patterns can be highlighted (made salient) in order to trigger noticing. Noticing is viewed as an essential step on the way to acquisition [25]. That is, by harnessing the technical affordances of concordancing, it is possible to envision creating a specifically designed corpora to be used as teaching resources which may not be available in the learners' immediate physical environment. As for the role of the teacher who is attracted to engaging with DDL pedagogy, the first step is the creation of the corpus to be used as teaching aid and then design an instructional plan around the target items and structures available in the corpora. This process consists in the selection, compilation, sorting/parsing, chunking and organizing authentic linguistic data and annotating the features of interest for later use in instruction.

1.2   Previous Studies

A quick overview of the emerging DDL research studies, it can be noted that the overall conditions of integrating corpus linguistics into language learning and teaching has flourished over the last decade [7]. This development coincides with the availability of large-scale corpora, sophisticated software programs and more user-friendly technological tools for corpus analysis and information retrieval. Consequently, a substantial number of empirical studies of corpus applications in language learning and teaching, not only recorded positive results about in-class corpus use, but also contributed to the development of teaching materials and the design of corpus-based syllabi [4, 6, 8, 12], and [18]. Among the studies that reported hands-on concordancing is [12]'s study which reported positive results of adapting concordances for lower-level learners' grammar development. The concordance data were mainly used as feedback to sentence-level written errors. In this line of corpus application, [30] have investigated learners' actual use of corpora and their attitudes of such use. Their findings revealed that L2 learners have improved their writing thanks to an increased awareness of lexico-grammatical patterns fostered by an inductive learning mode. Other studies [9, 13, 20] report similar positive results consisting in improving the scores of the participants' writing skill.

When examining these research studies more closely, the common thread uniting them is their focus on written corpora and lexico-grammatical patterns as resources in order to improve the learners' writing skills. Another common thread is the inductive approach to DDL they adopted. Many other studies have, in the same vein, attempted to investigate the effect of applying DDL for enhancing writing skills through a process of induction in other languages such as French in [8]'s study; or Italian in [18]'s.

Overall, the inductive approach has been predominantly adopted in the aforementioned DDL studies claiming that the central, didactic notions of DDL hinges on an inductive approach to language teaching which, it is claimed, consolidates autonomous learning, learner motivation and language awareness-raising. Although this approach has been the mainstay in DDL [11], research by [9] indicated that improvement in target language performance among their participants did not prove to be statistically significant.

It is worth pointing out that under the DDL inductive approach, learners are required to infer the rule or pattern from the vast number of examples displayed in the concordances, whereas in the deductive approach learners have prior access to the rule or pattern and use the corpus in order to exemplify it [6]. Pedagogically speaking, there seems to be consensus around the idea that both approaches are equally necessary for an effective DDL instruction, as language learning is not entirely based on induction [3]. Yet, little research has tried to investigate which instructional method best enhances students 'learning of grammatical patterns. In this respect, researchers are still enquiring about the relative value of the two approaches within DDL pedagogy.

2   Objectives of the Study

This study is part of an on-going project which focuses on the direct use of DDL with a deductive/inductive approach for the teaching of English non-finite clauses to the students of business in Tunisia. For the purpose of this paper, we focus on the direct application of NooJ Software for the creation of materials to be used in a deductive approach to DDL. To do this, an automatic processing of these structures is necessary for their identification and extraction.

The non-finite clauses, as defined by [19, p71], are clauses that have a non-finite verb phrase: infinitive, gerund or participle and are prevalent in written discourse. Recently, [21] showed that academic English indicates a trend towards a non-finite mode of expression. In addition to their high frequency in written discourse [5], non-finite clauses are considered as good indication of writing proficiency. However, non-finite structure can be challenging for the learners due to the intricate linguistic complexities they carry, such as the grammatical distinction between gerunds and infinitives (such as the difference between "he forgot to take off the lock" and "he saw him taking off the lock"). The latter can cause stumbling blocks for the learners, given the sheer number of verbs followed either by an infinitive or a gerund, and thus leaving students with the overwhelming task of remembering which verb triggers which construction.

Non-finite clauses as attested by [16] were found to be either inexistent or underused by Arab-speaking learners. The non-finite clauses have verbs that are not marked for person, number or tense, as illustrated in examples 1 and 2

Example 1: For her to walk down the road is tiring. (The non-finite verb "to walk" is not marked for number or person
Example 2: To walk down the road is/was tiring. (Only the finite verb in the main clause "is/was determines the tense).

These uninflected verbs do not exist in the Arabic language and therefore can be problematic for Arab-speaking learners. Researchers [1, 2] demonstrated that Arab-speaking learners encounter difficulties in the acquisition of English infinitival sentential complementation and fail to provide an accurate translation of non-finite clauses because of their inability to understand them.

As exemplified below, non-finite clauses can be of three types as can be gleaned from an exploration of the British National Corpus:

Type 1 Infinitive clauses
Example: It is necessary **to obtain** certain information about them
Type 2 ING clauses
Example: A company **obtaining** a route franchise might well invest in new station building
Type 3 Past participle clauses
Example: Information **obtained** during an interview is about assessable but unquantifiable attributes.

For the infinitive clauses, the bare infinitive ("infinitive without to") would be excluded from this study. This is because the bare infinitive clauses do not contain complementizers [22]. In order to explore the pattern of occurrence of, frequency and type of non-finite clauses in academic discourse, a corpus of Business English Texts will be submitted to annotation and analysis using Nooj.

Relying on Nooj for the automatic processing of these target structures, this study adopts a phraseological approach to the analysis of non-finite clauses. It focuses on investigating the co-occurrence of the grammatical categories and their combinational patterns, that [28, p. 65] calls "colligational patterns", and the lexico-grammatcal variations that come with different non-finite complementation patterns. The procedure followed consisted in identifying non-finite complements headed by four targets: adjectives, adverbs, nouns/pronouns, and conjunctions/ subordinators. These targets are chosen in order to give better chance of finding variant categories of non-finite complements and their colligational patterns. These intensively probed non-finite clauses that include the following:

(1) Noun/pronoun + non-finite clause
(2) Adjective + non-finite clause
(3) adverb + non-finite clause
(4) Subordinators/conjunction + non-finite clause

We will begin by explaining how the corpus we intend to use as DDL resource was selected and compiled.

2.1 Compiling a Corpus

For the purpose of teaching non-finite clauses within a data-driven approach, a small corpus is compiled from publications learners are likely to encounter in the business environment. As demonstrated in Table 1, the corpus includes three subsections based on a student's master dissertation, business editorials from The Financial Times and The Economist, and academic research articles from the Journal of Financial Economics, the Journal of Monetary Economics, The Quarterly Journal of Economics and the Journal of International Management. Table 1 shows the number of texts from the three sections of the corpus as well as the total number of words.

Table 1. Business corpus texts

Corpus genres	Source	Number of texts	Number of words
Genre 1: Journal articles	The Journal of Financial Economics The Journal of International Management The Journal of Monetary Economics The Quarterly Journal of Economics	20	268, 908
Genre 2: Editorials	The Economist Financial Times	20	63,720
Genre 3: Student's MA dissertation	Banking and International Finance	1	22, 285
Total number of words = 354,913			

The next step, which is the main focus of this paper, is to report on the attempt to employ Nooj Software to extract the co-patterning structures of the non-finite complements in the corpus, and investigate their semantic preferences and discourse functions. Similar studies have employed NooJ for the automatic treatment of other linguistic items in different languages including the nominal sentence case in Arabic [15], adjectives and adverbs in Spanish [24] and phraseology in French [29].

3   Procedure with NooJ Software

NooJ, created and developed by Silberstein [26, 27], is a freeware language-engineering development environment that automatically annotates texts and performs statistical analyses. This software is capable of providing essential textual statistics of a corpus including the overall number of tokens, word forms, digits, annotations and text units. In addition, it parses texts and takes a sentence as input altogether with its parts of speech. The main difference between NooJ software and other corpus tools is that NooJ can parse the non-finites treating the latter as single units as it is primarily informed (in electronic dictionaries and local grammars) by the various lexico-grammatical units that collocate to form them (see Fig. 1).

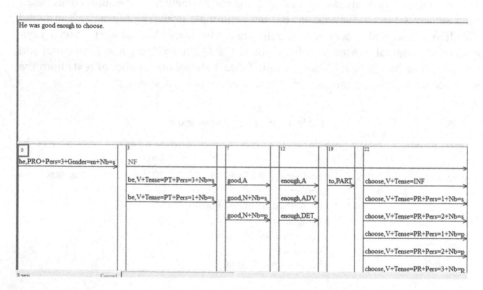

Fig. 1. Recognizing the non-finite (NF) as a single unit

As a Natural Language Processing (NLP) complex tool that automatically locates and retrieves non-finite complement patterns, NooJ also parses ambiguities, which can be a thorny problem in extracting non-finite clauses due to the inherent linguistic complexities in these structures.

For the purpose of this study, a system that recognizes non-finite complements headed by nouns/pronouns, adjectives, adverbs, conjunctions and subordinators is built and implemented in the local grammar of NooJ. More clearly, the non-finite complements are represented with specific composition operations of automata in graphs (i.e. transducers) involving lexical, syntactic, semantic and discoursal elements. With regard to the semantic categories, these would be classified drawing on the taxonomy designed by [5]. The taxonomy proposed by the researchers covers several categories of stance including evaluation, personal affective stance, necessity or importance, degree of certainty, and ease or difficulty among others.

The framework proposed in this study distinguishes between two main categories: the EPISTEMIC which comprises five subcategories (certainty, doubt, actuality, precision, and limitation), and the EVALUATION one which encompasses two subcategories (attitudes and emotion). As for the discoursal functions proposed in this study, they are mainly based on the work of a number of researchers [14, 23], who agree on the syntactic condensation feature of non-finite clauses and the role they play in discourse when positioned initially or at the end of the sentence. Two main discourse functions are proposed in this study. First, information flow management, through which information could be pre-posed or post-posed and second, syntactic condensation, which can be imposed by reduced adverbial clauses or reduced relative clauses.

4   Implementation and Results

The whole procedure was implemented through three main stages. In the first stage, 18 graphs were built on NooJ local grammar to extract the phraseology pertinent to the syntactic structure of the non-finite patterns. Each graph includes the structure of one pattern. The extraction was executed employing one of the 18 patterns (NF1P2) as shown in Fig. 2.

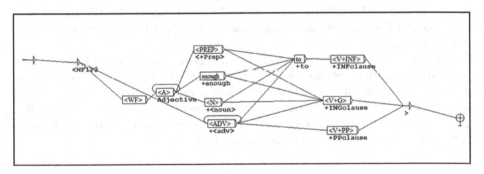

Fig. 2. Grammar pattern 2 of non-finite 1

At this stage, hundreds of unwanted sequences were extracted as non-finites (see Table 2). In order to improve the success rate of the extraction, disambiguation was necessary. For instance, a disambiguation task was carried out on ING words and phrases (gerundial nouns, present participle as adjectives and gerund participle). Other disambiguation tasks were performed on "to" (as a particle or preposition) and other frequent linguistic items that carry different annotations. In addition to disambiguation, NooJ also offers the "EXCLUDE" operator to reject irrelevant sequences by imposing relevant syntactic constraints. Hence, we have added to the main graph other constraints to reject nominal structures with ING (such as adjective + noun) and finite verbs (such as the preterit) as illustrated in Fig. 3.

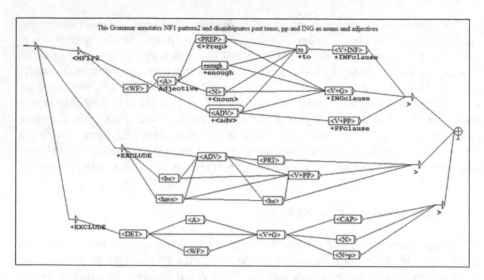

Fig. 3. Grammar pattern 2 of non-finite 1 with exclude operator

As a result, the findings in the first stage are obtained with an accuracy of 80%, precision at 81% and recall with 97%. Table 2 presents the results of the extraction before and after implementing the disambiguation and "EXCLUDE" operator on one of the non-finite patterns.

In the second stage, 499 entries were added to NooJ dictionary in addition to two graphs which were built on NooJ local grammar to extract the semantic categories of the adjectives and adverbs heading the non-finite patterns. The graph in Fig. 4 illustrates one of the semantic categories that extracts non-finite clauses with EPISTEMIC meaning. The graph shows how the EPISTEMIC meaning of adjectives and adverbs can be automatically identified with non-finite clauses.

Table 2. Primary results

Corpus genres	Number of non-finites without disambiguation/ EXCLUDE	Number of non-finites with disambiguation	Number of non-finites with EXCLUDE
Editorials 20 texts 63,720 words	1075	603	490
Journal articles 20 texts 248,578 words	1556	859	703
One Dissertation 63,720 words	138	130	110
Total number	2769	1592	1303

The grammar in the graph was applied on the three sections of the corpus and yielded significant results in terms of accuracy (81%), and recall (90%).

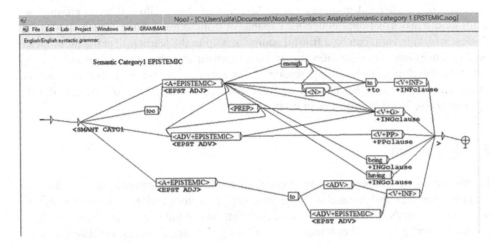

Fig. 4. Screenshot of the semantic category graph

As for the third stage, three graphs were implemented in NooJ grammar in order to proceed with the automatic recognition of the different discourse functions served by non-finites in the corpus. Section two of the editorials was used as a sample to test the success rate of the extraction. The results obtained are significant in terms of the accuracy (80%), precision (72%) and recall (96%).

Finally, to show the complex dynamics of both finite and non-finite structures, a transformation grammar was built (see Fig. 5). Indeed, students may understand further the grammatical constraints in non-finite clauses by applying the transformation grammar (transforming finite clauses into non-finites).

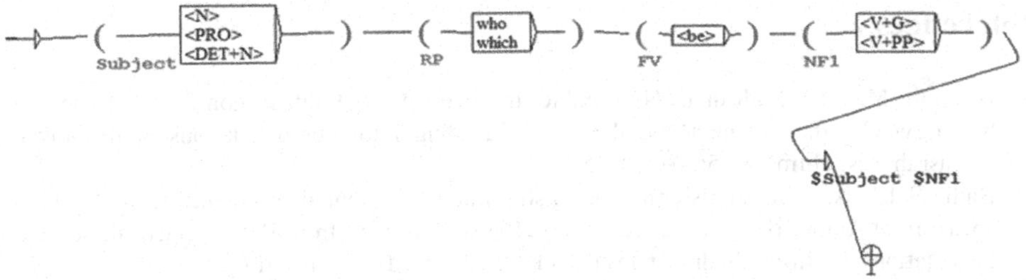

Fig. 5. Screenshot of the transformation grammar graph

So far, NooJ was successfully applied on the three genres of texts (editorials, journal articles and a student's dissertation) in a 354,913-word corpus in order to identify and extract English non-finite clauses. Not only were the syntactic structures detected, but also the semantic categories and discoursal functions. Following the automatic extraction procedures, disambiguation and the EXCLUDE operator were implemented to resolve the problem of noise by applying syntactic constraints that were defined with local grammar rules. Add to that, NooJ allowed us to employ an automatic transformational generator capable of transforming finite clauses into non-finites, which, in turn, can be a fruitful source of help to the learners. Taking all of these performances into consideration, it can be confirmed that the potential of employing NooJ to develop corcordancing resources for subsequent use in DDL activities is promising. In fact, the list of language items which can be object of material development using NooJ platform is unlimited.

5   Conclusion

In this paper, we adopted a phraseological approach in the identification of non-finite variant categories and focused on the four targets (adjectives, adverbs, nouns/pronouns, and conjunctions/subordinators) as head complements of the non-finite clauses for their automatic processing and extraction. The investigation and extraction of English non-finite clauses in a corpus compiled from texts in Business English described in this paper confirmed the prominence of these structures in business written discourse and their relevance for exploitation in DDL. The procedures described above afforded by NooJ as a corpus processing tool are undoubtedly efficient ways to fulfill several requirements including the automatic recognition of non-finites, the implementation of disambiguation rules and the creation of grammatical transformation. Therefore, it can be confirmed that the automatic processing of non-finite clauses can confidently be done with NooJ and that the satisfactory results obtained in this attempt to extract the grammatical categories and their combinational patterns are attributed to the good performance of NooJ. The next step is to take further advantage of the options and possibilities offered by NooJ with a larger corpus in order to create the materials for an instructional plan with Tunisian business students in mind.

References

1. Alasadi, M., Abdul Ridha, N.: Arabic translations of English non-finite clauses in hemingway's "the old man and the sea": a reading into four translations of the novel. J. Basrah Res. Hum. **40**, 55–80 (2015)
2. Badia Saleh, N.: The acquisition of English infinitival sentential complementation by adult speakers of Arabic (Doctoral dissertation) (1983). Retrieved from Retrospective theses and dissertations 33. http://lib.dr.iastate.edu/rtd/33. Accessed 27 Feb 2017
3. Barlow, M.: Corpora for theory and practice. Int. J. Corpus Linguist. **1**(1), 1–37 (1996)
4. Bernardini, S.: Exploring new directions for discovery learning. In: Ketteman, B., Marko, G. (eds.) Teaching and Learning by Doing Corpus Analysis, pp. 165–182 (2002)
5. Biber, D., Johansson, S., Leech, G., Conrad, S., Finegan, E.: Longman Grammar of Spoken and Written English. Longman, London/New York (1999)

6. Boulton, A.: Applying data-driven learning to the web. In: Leńko-Szymańska, A., Boulton, A. (eds.) Multiple Affordances of Language Corpora for Data-Driven Learning, pp. 267–295. John Benjamins, Amsterdam (2015)
7. Boulton, A., Cobb, T.: Corpus use in language learning: a meta-analysis. Lang. Learn. **67**(2), 348–393 (2017)
8. Chambers, A., O'Sullivan, Í.: Corpus consultation and advanced learners' writing skills in French. ReCALL **16**, 158–172 (2004)
9. Chan, T., Liou, H.: Effects of web-based concordancing instruction on EFL students' learning of verb-noun collocations. Comput. Assist. Lang. Learn. **18**, 231–250 (2005)
10. Doughty, C., Williams, J.: Focus on Form in Classroom Second Language Acquisition. Cambridge University Press, Cambridge (1998)
11. Flowerdew, L.: Data-driven learning and language learning theories: whither the twain shall meet. In: Leńko-Szymańska, A., Boulton, A. (eds.) Multiple affordances of language corpora for data-driven learning, pp. 15–36. John Benjamins, Amsterdam (2015)
12. Gaskell, D., Cobb, T.: Can learners use concordance feedback for writing errors? System **32**, 301–319 (2004)
13. Gilmore, A.: Using online corpora to develop students' writing skills. ELT J. **63**, 363–372 (2009)
14. Granger, S.: On identifying the syntactic and discourse features of participle clauses in academic English: native and non-native writers compared. In: Aarts, J., de Mönnink, I., Wekker, H. (eds.) Studies in English Language and Teaching, pp. 185–198. Rodopi, Amsterdam (1997)
15. Hammouda, N.G., Haddar, K.: Arabic NooJ parser: nominal sentence case. In: Mbarki, S., Mourchid, M., Silberztein, M. (eds.) NooJ 2017. CCIS, vol. 811, pp. 69–80. Springer, Cham (2018). https://doi.org/10.1007/978-3-319-73420-0_6
16. Hinkel, E.: Second Language Writers' Text, 1st edn. Erlbaum, London (2002)
17. Johns, T.: Micro-Concord: A Language Learner's Research Tool. System **14**(2), 151–162 (1986)
18. Kennedy, C. and Miceli, T.: The CWIC project: developing and using a corpus for intermediate Italian students. In: Kettemann, B., Marko, G. (eds.) Teaching and Learning by Doing Corpus Analysis. Proceedings of the Fourth International Conference on Teaching and Language Corpora, Graz, 19–24 July. Rodopi, Amsterdam (2002)
19. Leech, G.: A Glossary of English Grammar, 1st edn. Edinburgh University Press, Edinburgh (2006)
20. Lee, D., Swales, J.: A corpus-based EAP course for NNS doctoral students: moving from available specialized corpora to self-compiled corpora. Engl. Specif. Purp. **25**, 56–75 (2006)
21. Malà, M.: A corpus-based diachronic study of a change in the use of non-finite clauses in written English. Prague J. Engl. Stud. **6**(1), 151–166 (2017)
22. Muslih Shwaysh, A., Sinjar, H.H.: Sentential complementation in Standard English. J. AlAnbar, [Univ. Lang. Lit.] **8**, 222–244 (2012)
23. Quirk, R., Greenbaum, S., Leech, G., Svartvik, J.: A Comprehensive Grammar of the English Language. Longman, London (1985)
24. Rodrigo, A., Reyes, S., Bonino, R.: Some aspects concerning the automatic treatment of adjectives and adverbs in spanish: a pedagogical application of the NooJ platform. In: Mbarki, S., Mourchid, M., Silberztein, M. (eds.) NooJ 2017. CCIS, vol. 811, pp. 130–140. Springer, Cham (2018). https://doi.org/10.1007/978-3-319-73420-0_11
25. Schmidt, R.: The role of consciousness in second language learning. Appl. Linguist. **11**, 129–158 (1990)
26. Silberztein, M.: Dictionnaires électroniques et analyse automatique de textes. Le système INTEX. Collection "Informatique Linguistique". Masson, Paris (1993)

27. Silberztein, M.: NooJ Manual (2003). www.nooj4nlp.net
28. Stubbs, M.: Words and Phrases: Corpus Studies of Lexical Semantics. Oxford University Press, Oxford (2001)
29. Yang, T.: Automatic Extraction of the Phraseology Through NooJ. In: Mbarki, S., Mourchid, M., Silberztein, M. (eds.) NooJ 2017. CCIS, vol. 811, pp. 168–178. Springer, Cham (2018). https://doi.org/10.1007/978-3-319-73420-0_14
30. Yoon, H., Hirvela, A.: ESL student attitudes toward corpus use in L2 writing. J. Second Lang. Writ. **13**(4), 257–283 (2004)

Automatic Recognition and Translation of Polysemous Verbs Using the Platform NooJ

Hajer Cheikhrouhou[✉]

University of Sfax, LLTA, Sfax, Tunisia
cheihkrouhou.hager@gmail.com

Abstract. In this work we study the phenomenon of verbal polysemy which poses a big challenge in the domain of automatic treatment of languages. This verbal polysemy constitutes not only a constraint to the automatic linguistic recognition, but also a hurdle in the French-Arabic automatic translation, especially in detecting the exact and precise equivalent in the target language. We will try to find solutions in the process of automatic translation to solve the problem of verbal polysemy using the NooJ platform.

Keywords: Communication verbs · Movement verbs · LVF · Verbal polysemy · Automatic recognition and translation · NooJ

1 Introduction

The most recurrent problem in the automatic treatment of languages and even in linguistics is polysemy, where one word can mean different concepts. Georges Kleiber defines polysemy as the association of different meanings for a single lexical form. This phenomenon, existing in mother languages, indicates that the meaning of a single unit, the verb in our case, depends on the context in which it is used, which leads us to say that the verbal construction determines the meaning of the verb. Verbal polysemy is one among the obstacles facing TAL.

For example, the meaning of the verb "toucher" (to touch) can vary according to context:

- L'armoire touche le lit. The armchair touches the bed.
  Toucher (01): Etre en contact (be in contact)
- Paul est touché par ce cadeau. Paul is touched by this gift.
  Toucher (02): Emouvoir (affect)
- La flèche touche la cible. The arrow touches the target.
  Toucher (03): Atteindre (attain, reach)

To solve this ambiguity, Dubois and Dubois-Charlier [1] created a well-detailed treasury where each verbal entry receives only one usage. Indeed, in LVF, the number of entries of each verb equals the different possible meanings where each verbal use varies from other uses by distinctive criteria such as the syntactic construction, domain, the syntactic and semantic class... In our study of verbs of communication (2012) and of movement (2013), when the subject is human, we met different polysemous

H. Fehri et al. (Eds.): NooJ 2019, CCIS 1153, pp. 39–51, 2020.
https://doi.org/10.1007/978-3-030-38833-1_4

predicates where one predicate can have two, four, five uses and even eleven polysemous uses like the verbs: parler/to speak (11 uses), dire/say (9 uses), aller/to go (5 uses), entrer/come in (7 uses) …

This verbal polysemy constitutes a constraint at the level of the linguistic automatic recognition; yet it becomes a big obstacle at the level of the French-Arabic automatic translation particularly when seeking the exact equivalent in the source language.

In this study which pertains to applied linguistics, we intend to:

- Produce a system to analyse and recognize the syntactic patterns of communication and movement verbs [2].
- Find linguistic solutions for the disambiguation of verbal polysemy.
- Provide adequate and reliable French - Arabic automatic translation for polysemous verbs using the NooJ platform.

2   The Polysemy of Communication Verbs

The class of communication verbs C contains 2039 verbal entries and is subdivided into four subclasses. This class contains many polysemous predicates such as: to show, to cry, to say, to reveal… (see Fig. 1) (Table 1).

Table 1. Class C.

Generic Class C (2039 verbal entries)	
C1 (1059 entries): "s'exprimer par un son, une parole" (expressed by a sound, speech) 10 subclasses: C1a → C1j	**C2** (688 entries): "dire/demander qc" (to say/ask for s.thg) 11 subclasses: C2a → C2 k
C3 (172 entries): "montrer qc" (to show sb sthg) 3 subclasses: C3a → C3f	**C4** (120 entries): "dire ou montrer qc" Figurative of C1 and C3 (to say or show sb sthg) 4 subclasses: C4a → C4d

	B	C	D	E	G	H	I	J	K	L	M
16	censurer 01	PRE	presse, journalisme		C3d.2	(#) [ind] nég texte	ne laisse s'exprimer	On c~ l'article du rédacteu	1aZ	T1308	11- -D ---
17	censurer 02	LIT	littérature	littéraire	C1.3	(#) [loq.mvs] qc/qn	blâmer, condamner	On c~ P pour ses initiative	1aZ	T1907	--- -D ---
18	censurer 03	PSY	psychologie		C4d.1	(#) [ind] nég sent	réprimer	Le sujet c~ ses pulsions.	1aZ	T1306	--- -D ---
19	censurer 04	DRO	droit, administration		C1.3	(#) [loq.mvs] qc/qn	condamner	L'assemblée c~ le gouvern	1aZ	T1907	--- -D ---
20	confesser 01	CHR	christianisme		C2c	(#) [dic] fautes A qn	avouer péchés	Le fidèle c~ ses péchés à	1bZ	T13a8 - P30a0	--- D RARA
21	confesser 02	LAN	langue, parole		C2a.1	(#) [dic] aveu A qn	avouer	On c~ à P son erreur, qu'i	1bZ	T14a8	-- -- RA--
22	confesser 04	CHR	christianisme		C1e.1	(#) [loq] sa foi	professer religion	Le chrétien c~ sa foi en D	1bZ	A16	-- -- --
23	confesser 05 (se)	CHR	christianisme		C1d.4	(#) [loq] confesse A qn	se confier	On se c~ à un prêtre.	1bZ	P10a0	--- D RA--
24	déclarer 01	LIT	littérature		C2d.1	(#) [dic] QUE/soi tal	affirmer, proclamer	On d~ sa satisfaction, qu'o	1aZ	T14B - P15a0	111 -- RB-- --
25	déclarer 02	LIT	littérature		C2a.1	(#) [dic] qc A qn	faire savoir	On d~ ses intentions, son	1aZ	T14a8	-1-- RB-- --
26	déclarer 03	DRO	droit, administration		C2c	(#) [dic] officiel qc A qn	dire devant autorités	On d~ ses impôts, le vol a	1aZ	T13a8	-1-- RB-- --
27	déclarer 04 (se)	LIT	littérature		C1d.4	(#) [loq] franc A qn	se prononcer pour	On se d~ sur ce sujet, pou	1aZ	P10a0	-- RB-- --
28	dire 01	LAN	langue, parole		C21.1	(#) [dic] mots	prononcer	On d~ "pallier un défaut".	6fZ	T1306	-- RP-- --
29	dire 02	LIT	littérature		C2a.1	(#) [dic] information A qn	communiquer	On d~ à P un secret, la dé	6fZ	T14a0	-- --RG --
30	dire 03	LIT	littérature		C2b.2	(#) [dic] ordre A qn DE	ordonner	On d~ à P de venir, qu'il s	6fZ	T15a8	--- -- --
31	dire 04	LAN	langue, parole		C2c	(#) [dic] mot A qn	raconter	On d~ des bêtises à P. Ce	6fZ	T13a8 - P30a0	--- -- --
32	dire 05	LIT	littérature		C2a.1	(#) [dic] énoncé auprès	énoncer	On d~ une évidence, une	6fZ	T1306 - P3000	--- -- --
33	dire 06	LIT	littérature		C2d.1	(#) [dic] QUE/soi tal	prétendre	On d~ que P est bon, aim	6fZ	T14B - P15a0	--- -- --
34	dire 07	ENS	enseignement, pédagogie		C2c	(#) [dic] récit A qn	réciter	On d~ des poèmes à l'ass	6fZ	T13a8	--- -- --
35	dire 08	PSYt	psychologie	littéraire	C4b.3	(qc) [ind] abstrait	montrer, manifester	Ses yeux d~ sa fatigue, sa	6fZ	T3300	--- -- --
36	dire 10	PSY	psychologie		C4a	(qc) [ind] sent A qn	faire penser, évoquer	Ce visage ne d~ rien à P	6fZ	T33a0	--- -- --
37	dire 11	LIT	littérature		C2d.1	(#) [dic] qc/QUE auprès	raconter	On d~ que P est fassassin	6fZ	T14B	--- -- --
38	dire 13	LITt	littérature	littéraire	C4c.2	(#) [ind] abstrait par qc	exprimer, décrire	L'écrivain d~ la tristesse d	6fZ	T13f8 - P3008	--- -- --

Fig. 1. Sample of predications of polysemous communication verbs.

The predicate «prononcer» (to pronounce) is a communication verb that has four verbal entries: prononcer 1, 2, 3 and 5 (see Fig. 2).

	B	C	D	E	G	H	I	J		L
1	prononcer 01	DRO	droit, administration		C1a.3	(#) [loq] sentence	annoncer sentence	Le juge a p~. Le tribunal p~ un jugement.		A16 - T1306
2	prononcer 02	LAN	langue, parole		C2e.1	(#) [dic] à voix haute	dire, lire à haute voix	On p~ un discours, une allocution devant une assistance.		T13l0 - P3000
3	prononcer 03	LAN	langue, parole		C1a.4	(#) [loq] mots/phonèmes	articuler	On p~ ce mot ainsi. On p~ les "r" en roulant.		T1300
4	prononcer 05	LIT	littérature		C1f.3	(#) [loq] POUR/CONTRE	conclure en faveur de	On ne s'est pas encore p~ pour P. Le juge s'est p~.		P10k0

Fig. 2. The polysemous predicate "to pronounce".

Prononcer 01 (to pronounce): means "to announce sentence". It can have two constructions: intransitive A16 or direct transitive T1306 with a circumstance of modality.

Example: Le juge n'a pas encore prononcé son jugement.
The judge has not yet pronounced his judgment.
→ [A16]+ AR=   "حَكَمَ" to judge

Le juge a prononcé son jugement. The judge pronounced his judgment.
→ [T1306] + AR = " نَطَقَ" to pronounce

Prononcer 02: It belongs to the subclass C2e.1 of type «dire qc auprès de qn» (say something to someone).
This verb expresses "say, read out loud" and its syntactic construction [T13l0] is direct transitive with a nominal direct object expressing the content of the verb and a complement "In front of/near someone" which indicates the interlocutor.

Example : Le président prononce son discours devant les membres du parlement.
The President delivers his speech to the members of parliament.
→ [T13l0]+ AR = " ألْقى " made statements

Prononcer 03: The syntactic construction of this usage is [T1300] direct transitive with a direct semantic type object "loq mots/phonèmes". This verbal entry means "to articulate" «articuler».

Example : L'enfant prononce ce mot correctement.
The child pronounces this word correctly.
→ [T1300] + AR = " نَطَقَ "   to pronounce

Prononcer 05(s): The pronominal construction [P10k0] with a complement "for/against" means "to conclude in favour of".

Example : Le juge s'est prononcé contre l'accusé.
The judge ruled against the accused.
→ [P10k0] +AR = "حَكَمَ "

⇒We notice that the syntactic constructions of the verb «prononcer» "to pronounce" are very similar and the distinction between them is slightly difficult especially between direct transitive constructions.

3 The Polysemy of Movement Verbs

The class of movement verbs E contains 2444 verbal entries which are subdivided into four subclasses. In this class, we find many polysemous predicates such as: to come in, to go, to come down, to pass, come back … (see Fig. 3) (Table 2).

Table 2. Class E.

Generic Class E (2444 verbal entries)	
E1 (698 entries): "sortir, venir de qp", "aller, entrer qp" sujet humain: "faire sortir, aller, entrer qn qp" ("to go out, to come from a place", "to go, to come in" human subject: "to lead sb") 7 subclasses: E1a → E1 g	**E2** (440 entries): figurative of E1 5 subclasses: E2a → E2e
E3 (984 entries): "(faire) sortir/venir de qp", "(faire) aller/entrer qp" ("to lead sb to a place, to guide" "to show sb in") 6 subclasses: E3a → E3f	**E4** (322 entries): figurative of E3 6 subclasses: E4a → E4f

MOT	DOMAIN	MAINE en o	N LANGUE	CLASSE	OPERATEUR	SENS	PHRASE	CONSTRUCTION	DERIVATIO
54 aller 01	LOC	locatif, lieu		E1d.1	(#) [ire] qp	venir	On a~ à Paris, dans un musée.	A12	--1 -A --- -A
55 aller 02	LOC	locatif, lieu		E1d.1	(#) [ire] qp pour action	se déplacer	On a~ pour chasser. On a~ à la chasse, à la recherche de P.	A12	--- --- ---
56 aller 03	COM	commerce		E1d.1	(#) [ire] qp comme client	se rendre chez	On a~ chez le boucher, le médecin, le coiffeur.	A12	--- --- ---
57 aller 12	TPS	temps		E2c.4	(#) [ire] SUR temps/âge	être proche d'atteindre	On a~ sur ses cinquante ans.	N1g	--- --- ---
58 aller 15 (s'en)	LOCt	locatif, lieu	littéraire	E1a.2	(#) [ex] DE lieu qp	aller de/à, sortir de.	On s'en est a~ de Paris à Lyon.	P1030	--- --- ---
463 déplacer 01	MAN	manutention		E3c	(#) [f.ex] qc DE place	retirer de place	On d~ un vase de la cheminée.	T13b0 - P30b0	---1 --- --
464 déplacer 02 (se)	LOC	locatif, lieu		E1b.2	(#) [ex] DE place	changer de place, bouger	On se d~ de son siège. On d~ un spectateur de son siège.	P1030 - T1138	---1 --- --
465 déplacer 04	TPS	temps		E4d.1	(#) [f.ire] qc à temps autre	décaler, différer de	On d~ une réunion, un rendez-vous. Le cours ne peut pas se	T1905	---1 --- --
466 déplacer 05	LOC	locatif, lieu		E1f.1	(#) [f.ire] qn chez qn	amener vers soi	On d~ le médecin. Le chanteur d~ la foule.	T1102	---1 --- --
467 déplacer 06	DRO	droit, administration		E1b.1	(#) [f.ex] qn DE lieu	changer de poste, muter	On d~ un fonctionnaire de son poste.	T1138	-1--1 --- --
468 déplacer 07	LIT	littérature		E4e.3	(#) [f.ire] abstrait SUR	orienter autrement	On d~ le sujet, la difficulté. Le problème est seulement d~.	T13g0 - P30g0	---1 --- --
469 déplacer 08	SOC	sociologie		E1e.1	(#) [f.ire] qp qn	déporter, transporter	On d~ la population dans un camp. Ce sont des personnes d~	T1120	-1- -1 --- --
519 descendre 01	LOC	locatif, lieu		E1a.3	(#) [ex] DE lieu	dégringoler	On d~ du premier. On d~ les escaliers, un chemin en pente.	A13 - T1300	--1 -A --RA --
520 descendre 02	VEH	véhicule motorisé		E1b.2	(#) [ex] DE véhicule/bateau qp	débarquer	On d~ de voiture. On d~ les passagers du bateau.	A13 - T1130	--- -A --- --
521 descendre 03	LOC	locatif, lieu		E1d.2	(#) [ire] qp de lieu vers sud	partir vers le midi	On d~ sur la côte pour les vacances.	A14	--- -A --- --
522 descendre 08	LOC	locatif, lieu		E1d.3	(#) [ire] VERS buts	foncer vers	Le joueur de foot d~ vers les buts.	A1g	--- -A --- --
523 descendre 11	PAR	parenté, filiation		E2a.1	(#) [ex] DE famille	être issu de	On d~ d'une famille noble, de paysans.	N1b	--1 --- ---
524 descendre 12	LOC	locatif, lieu		E3a.3	(qc) [ex] DE lieu qp	porter en bas	Les cartons d~ à la cave. On d~ les cartons à la cave.	A33 - T1330	--- -A --AM ---
525 descendre 13	AUT	automobile		E1e.1	(#) [f.ire] qp qn	transporter, conduire	On d~ P à la gare.	T1120	--- --- ---
526 descendre 14	NAV	navigation, bateau		E3e	(#) [f.ire] par rivière	parcourir la rivière	On d~ le torrent jusque dans la plaine.	T1300	--- -A --- --
635 diriger 01	OBJ	objet		E3f.3	(#) [f.ire] qc VERS	orienter, braquer	On d~ la lampe, son arme sur P. L'arme se d~ vers P.	T13g0 - P30g0	2-- -2B2B --
636 diriger 02	PTT	postes		E3f.1	(#) [f.ire] qc VERS	acheminer, diriger	On d~ la lettre vers Paris.	T13g0	--- 2B- --
637 diriger 03	ENS	enseignement, pédagogie		E2d.4	(#) [f.ire] qn VERS abstrait	orienter	On d~ P vers d'autres études.	T11g0	--- 2B- ---

Fig. 3. Sample of predications of polysemous movement verbs.

As a verb of movement, the predicate "entrer" (come in) clusters seven verbal entries where the subject is human [N0hum] (see Fig. 4).

1	entrer 01	LOC	locatif, lieu	E1d.4	(#) [ire] DANS lieu	pénétrer	On e~ dans la maison.	N1j
2	entrer 07	SOC	sociologie	E2c.2	(#) [ire] DANS comme membre	faire partie de	On e~ dans une association, dans la société, dans le syndicat.	N1j
3	entrer 08	DRO	droit, administration	E2c.2	(#) [ire] DANS fonction	débuter	On e~ dans le professorat, comme instit dans l'enseignement.	N1j
4	entrer 09	TPS	temps	E2c.2	(#) [ire] DANS temps	commencer temps	On e~ dans l'année nouvelle, dans sa quinzième année.	N1j
5	entrer 15	LOC	locatif, lieu	E3f.4	(#) [f.ire] qc DANS lieu	faire pénétrer	On e~ le bateau au port. Le tenon e~ dans la mortaise.	T13j0 - N3j
6	entrer 16	PSY	psychologie	E4e.4	(#) [f.ire] idée DANS pensée	enfoncer	On e~ cette idée dans sa tête. Ceci n'e~ pas dans sa tête.	T13j6 - N3j
7	entrer 17	LOC	locatif, lieu	E3f.4	(#) [f.ire] qc DANS som	enfoncer	On e~ ses ongles dans la chair.	T13j0 - P30j0

Fig. 4. The polysemic verb "entrer".

Use 01 belongs to the sub-class E1d.4 and the uses 07, 08, 09 belong to E2c.2.

The entries 15 and 17 are integrated in the sub-class E3f.4 and finally «entrer 16» is classified in sub-class E4e.4. These different verbal entries are distinguished by three syntactic constructions and consequently by different translations:

N1j: indirect transitive with a complement introduced by the preposition «dans» (in): entrer 01, 07, 08, 09.

Example: *Entrer 01:* Il entre au cinéma. +N1j+AR = دَخَل : daḫala
He comes in/enters the cinema.

Entrer 07: Il entre dans une association culturelle.
+N1j + AR = اِنْخَرَطَ :'inḫara a
He enters / joins a cultural association.

Entrer 08: Il entre dans sa nouvelle fonction. +N1j + AR = بَاشَرَ : bāšara
He enters on / embarked on a new post.

Entrer 09: Nous entrons dans l'année nouvelle. +N1j + AR = بَدَأَ :bada'a
We enter a new year.

T13j0: direct transitive with a complement introduced by «dans» (in): entrer 15 and 17.

Example : *Entrer15*: Il entre la voiture au garage. +T13j0 + AR = أَدْخَل :'adḫala
He puts the car in the garage.

Entrer17: Il entre ses ongles dans la chair. +T13j0 + AR = غَرَزَ: ġaraza
(+sens figuré/ figrative meaning) He enters / clutches his fingers in the chair.

T13j6: direct transitive with a complement introduced by «dans» (in) and a modal verb.

Example : *Entrer16*: Il entre cette idée dans sa tête. +T13j6 + AR = غَرَسَ (+sens figuré/ figrative meaning): ġarassa
He enters / plants this idea in his mind.

We remark that entries (01, 07) and (15, 17) share the same syntactic and semantic features but they have different meanings and thus different translations. For a translator who has language competencies and mental capacities and who understands the context of an utterance, they can distinguish between the two uses but the problem stands with the machine: is it able to deduce this problem?

After the definition and the linguistic analysis of different polysemous communication and movement verbs, we move on to the second phase of automatic treatment. In what follows, we have tried to create a process of automatic translation capable of adequately recognizing and translating polysemous predicates using NooJ platform.

4   Automatic Processing of Polysemous Predicates

To translate polysemous predicates of communication and movement verbs, we create a process of automatic translation using NooJ platform (see Fig. 5).

Our process is essentially based on two steps:

- Step of analysis and recognition of syntactic constructions of communication and movement predicates.
- Step of automatic translation.

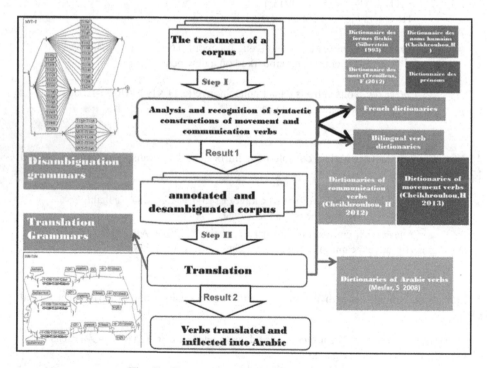

Fig. 5. The processus of automatic translation.

4.1   Analysis and Recognition of Polysemic Predicates

Carrying out this step necessitates the use of:

- Bilingual dictionaries of communication [3] and movement [4] verbs.
- French dictionaries essentially:

- dictionary of formes fléchies (Silberztein. M 1993)
- dictionary of human nouns/noms humains (Cheikhrouhou. H)
- dictionary of words [5]
- dictionary of names

- Formal grammars of disambiguity [6] which can adequately recognize all syntactic constructions of communication and movement predicates. For this reason, we constructed transducers for the following constructions: intransitives (A), direct transitives (T), indirect transitives (N) and pronominals (P) (see Fig. 6).

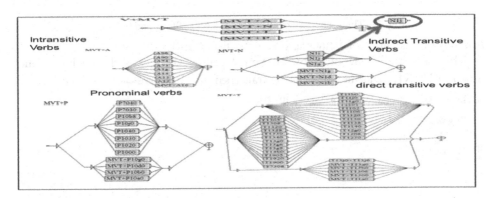

Fig. 6. The transducers of V + MVT.

When applying the grammars of disambiguity on our corpus, we noted that they could solve all syntactic constructions but they analyzed the sentences of indirect transitive construction with all possibilities and even for sentences whose construction is direct transitive (see Fig. 7).

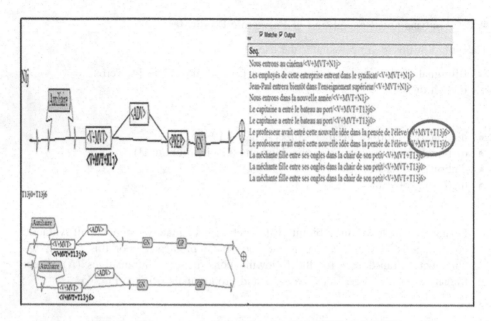

Fig. 7. The grammars of disambiguity N1j, T13j0 and T13j6.

Example: Nous entrons au cinéma. (We enter the cinema.)

This sentence is identified by all verbal entries (1, 7, 8 and 9) whose construction is "N1j" and the verb can be translated as «daḫala: دَخَلَ», «inḫaraṭa: إنْخَرَطَ», «bāšara: بَاشَرَ» et «bada'a: بَدَأ» (see Fig. 8).

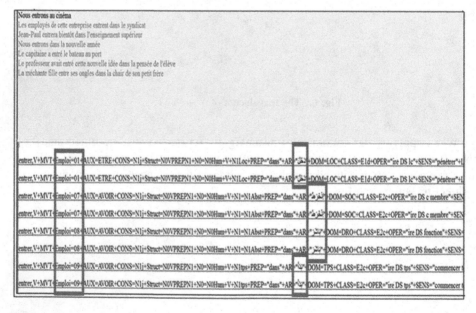

Fig. 8. The semantic-syntactic ambiguities of the polysemic employment of the predicate «entrer» "to enter".

A good analysis of the verb should not be limited only to the detection of its arguments (animate, inanimate, human and abstract) but also to the clarification of their nature and semantic class, especially if we want to produce a correct and adequate translation.

Then what is the solution?

To resolve this ambiguity, Gaston Gross found a solution by providing additional information concerning the arguments. He subcategorizes the characteristics according to semantic sub-classes, which he labelled objects classes [7]. His objective was to discriminate the meaning of the predicate from the required precision for automatic treatment.

In this case, to achieve results compatible with the meaning of the verb, which is conditioned by the semantic class of its complement, we must rewrite the argumentative schemes of these verbs in dictionaries and grammar, while specifying the semantic nature of the arguments to remove all inappropriate annotations.

entrer +N1loc + AR = دَخَل: daḫala ;   *entrer* +N1Abst:groupe + AR = اِنْخَرَط :
'inḫarata ; *entrer* +N1Abst:fonction + AR = بَاشَر : bāšara ;
entrer +N1Conc + AR = أَدْخَل: 'adḫala ;
entrer +N1Abst : idée dans N2Abst:pensée + AR = غَرَس : ġarasa (+sens figuré) ;
entrer +N1Abst dans N2Conc:som + AR = غَرَز : ġaraza (+sens figuré).

→ This information is added to the description of verbs in dictionaries and in grammar.

Example: entrer,V+MVT+Emploi=07+AUX=AVOIR+FLX=AIMER+CONS=N1j+
N0VPREPN1+N0Hum+V+N1Abst:grpe+PREP="dans"+AR="اِنْخَرَط"

→ This step is conditioned by another one, that of defining the names, registered in the "dm.dic" dictionary, by the appropriate semantic features.

Example : syndicat,N+Sem=Abst:grpe+FLX=M_S
enseignement,N+Sem=Abst:fct+FLX=M_S
chair,N+Sem=concret:som+FLX=F_S

Concerning the transducers, we modified the filter to restrict the field of analysis such as: <V + MVT + T13j0 + N2Loc>, <V + MVT + N1j + N1tps> … (see Fig. 9) which will be followed by the compatible argument <N + Loc>, <N + pensée>, <N + temps> (see Fig. 10).

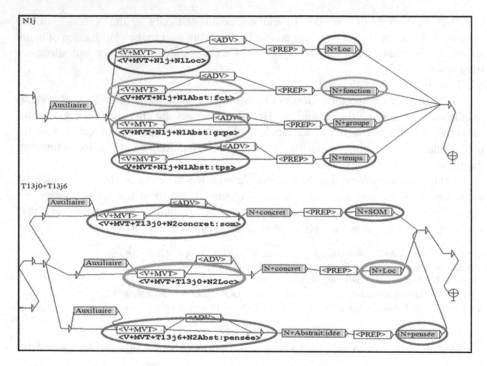

Fig. 9. The modification of transducers.

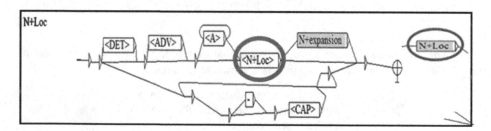

Fig. 10. The transducer of argument N + Loc.

After making the necessary modifications to the verbal entries in dictionaries and syntactic diagrams of our grammar, we reapplied the grammar to our corpus and found the following results (see Fig. 11):

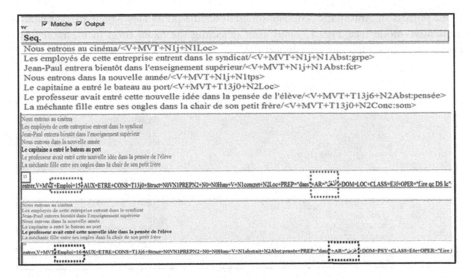

Fig. 11. The removal of unacceptable annotations after the application of semantic disambiguation grammar.

The semantic details we added could remove all ambiguities and also annotations incompatible with the filter, which leads to the resolution of all syntactic analysis and translation ambiguities.

We deduce that this semantic-syntactic method of analysis and recognition guarantees not only a disambiguation of polysemous usage but also an adequate and reliable translation.

The step of analysis and recognition of syntactic patterns is the first phase in our MT process. In fact, the results of this phase are the entries of the second step, which is the translation phase.

4.2 The Automatic Translation

In this phase, we used the same bilingual and French dictionaries but we added also Arabic dictionaries of Slim [8]. For syntactic analysis, we created grammars of translation for communication and movement predicates which can be used in affirmative or negative sentences (see Fig. 12).

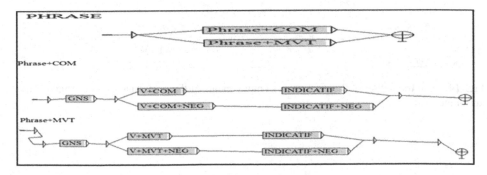

Fig. 12. Local translation grammars.

Our process of Automatic-Translation analyses the predicates which are conjugated in indicative mode (see Fig. 13) and after detecting the exact form in the target language, it provides adequate translation [9].

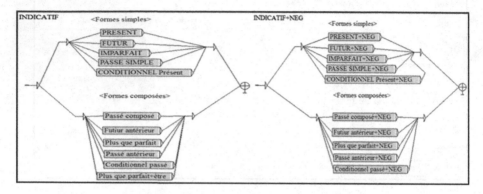

Fig. 13. The transducers of indicative mode.

Applying the grammars of translation on polysemous predicates "entrer/to enter" and «prononcer/to pronounce», the system puts up only necessary annotations and adequate translations which respect the rules of the Arabic language (see Fig. 14).

Example: Nous entrons au cinéma. We enter the cinema.

The verb «entrer/to enter» is conjugated in the present with the affirmative mode and the first plural personal pronoun/the second plural personal pronoun in English. We found that it is translated in nominative «muḍāra': مضارع مرفوع» which corresponds to the indicative present with the first plural personal pronoun «naḥnu نَحْنُ».

TEXT CONCORDANCE	
other. Display	☑ Matche ☑ Output
Seq.	
Nous entrons au cinéma/<V+MVT+N1j+N1Loc>نَدْخُلُ	
Les employés de cette société entrent dans le syndicat/<V+MVT+N1j+N1Abst:grpe>يَنْخَرِطُونَ	
Ils sont entrés dans l'année nouvelle/<V+MVT+N1j+N1tps>دَخَلُوا	
Jean-Paul entrera bientôt dans l'enseignement supérieur/<V+MVT+N1j+N1Abst:fct>سَيُبَاشِرُ	
Le mécanicien a entré la voiture au garage/<V+MVT+T13j0+N2Loc>أَدْخَلَ	
Le professeur avait entré cette bonne idée dans la pensée de l'élève/<V+MVT+T13j6+N2Abst:pensée>كَانَ قَدْ غَرَسَ	
La méchante fille a entré ses ongles dans la chair de son ami/<V+MVT+T13j0+N2Conc:som>غَرَزَتْ	
Le juge n'a pas encore prononcé/<V+COM+A16+N:Mod>لَمْ يَحْكُمْ	
Le juge aura prononcé son jugement/<V+COM+T1306+N1Abst:sentence>سَيَكُونُ قَدْ نَطَقَ	
Le président prononça son discours devant les membres du parlement/<V+COM+T13l0+N1Abst:parole>ألْقَى	
Le garçon aurait prononcé ce mot correctement/<V+COM+T1300+N1Abst:mot>يَكُونُ قَدْ نَطَقَ	
Le juge s'est prononcé contre l'accusé/<V+COM+P10k0>حَكَمَ	

Fig. 14. The translation of the polysemous employments of the predicates «entrer» "enter" and «prononcer».

→ This method shows its effectiveness since our machine translation system was able to analyse the polysemous employments of the verb "entrer/to enter" and "prononcer/to pronounce" by displaying the right annotations, and produced suitable and accurate translations according to the grammatical standards of the target language.

5 Conclusion

In this work, we tried to create a system for automatic translation of polysemous verbs based on two phases: the recognition and disambiguation phase of the different syntactic constructions and the translation phase.

The application of Gaston Gross' theory of object class theory has enabled us to refine recognition grammars and subsequently find encouraging results where verbs of communication and polysemous movement are translated and inflected into Arabic while respecting the rules of conjugation of the target language.

However, we still have a lot to do. As a follow-up to this work, we will consider the automatic translation of other verbal classes into Arabic and the creation of other bilingual French-Arabic dictionaries.

References

1. Dubois, J., Dubois-Charlier, F.: Les verbes français. Larousse, Paris (1997)
2. Silberztein, M.: La formalization du dictionnaire LVF avec NooJ et ses applications pour l'analyse automatique de corpus. Langages 3(179 180), 221-241 (2010)
3. Cheikhrouhou, H.: recognition of communication verbs with NooJ platform. In: Formalising Natural Languages with NooJ 2013, pp. 155–169. Cambridge Scholars Publishing, British (2014)
4. Cheikhrouhou, H.: The Formalisation of movement verbs for automatic translation using NooJ platform. In: Formalising Natural Languages NooJ 2014, pp. 14–21. Cambridge Scholars Publishing, British (2015)
5. Trouilleux, F.: Le, D.M.: A French dictionary for NooJ. In: Proceedings of the 2011 International NooJ Conference (2011)
6. Silberztein, M.: La formalization des langues, l'approche de NooJ. ISTE, London (2015)
7. Gross, G.: Les classes d'objets. Lalies, Presses de l'ENS, Editions rue d'Ulm, pp. 111–165 (2008). https://halshs.archives-ouvertes.fr/halshs-00410784
8. Mesfar, S.: Analyse morpho-syntaxique automatique et reconnaissance des entités nommées en arabe standard. Thèse de doctorat à l'Université de Franche-Comté (2008)
9. Cheikhrouhou, H.: The automatic translation of French verbal tenses to Arabic using the platform NooJ. In: Mbarki, S., Mourchid, M., Silberztein, M. (eds.) NooJ 2017. CCIS, vol. 811, pp. 156–167. Springer, Cham (2018). https://doi.org/10.1007/978-3-319-73420-0_13

Negation of Croatian Nouns

Natalija Žanpera[1], Kristina Kocijan[2]([✉]) [iD], and Krešimir Šojat[1]

[1] Department of Linguistics, Faculty of Humanities and Social Sciences,
University of Zagreb, Zagreb, Croatia
{ntunjic,ksojat}@ffzg.hr
[2] Department of Information and Communication Sciences,
Faculty of Humanities and Social Sciences, University of Zagreb,
Zagreb, Croatia
krkocijan@ffzg.hr

Abstract. The purpose of this paper is to describe a morphological grammar for recognizing negation of a noun and annotating its polarity accordingly. Not all nouns can be negated on the morphological level. For example, nouns like 'activity' and 'knowledge' (*aktivnost, znanje*) can have negatives (*neaktivnost, neznanje* respectfully), but the same is not the case for nouns such as 'battle' or 'table' (*bitka* or *stol*). The most common and frequent Croatian prefix for negation of nouns is '*ne-*' although several more are used either of Slavic ('*be-*', '*bez-*') or Latin origin ('*anti-*', '*dis-*'). In some cases, negated nouns actually denote positive concepts, whereas their non-negated counterparts are used for expressing concepts with negative connotations. For this purpose, all the nouns in NooJ dictionary, that may have nouns in both polarities, are provided with [Polarity = pos] or [Polarity = neg] marker. This information is used in the grammar to switch the polarity of the opposite noun after the insertion of a negative prefix. The grammar is tested on different types of corpora and results are discussed.

Keywords: Negation · Nouns · Prefixes of negation · Morphological grammar · Natural language processing · Croatian · NooJ

1 Introduction

Negation is a phenomenon present in all human languages. The extensiveness of this term can be seen in the definition found in Cambridge Encyclopedia of the Language Sciences that finds negation to be not only linguistic but also "*cognitive and intellectual phenomenon*" [1]. Moreover, Horn [2] points out that "*all human systems of communication contain a representation of negation*". It is a phenomenon that has been discussed by numerous philosophers, logicians and semanticists.

In classical two-valued logic, negation is an operation on one logical value that generally changes the value of an entire proposition. In other words, if a proposition P is true, then ¬ P is false; and conversely, if ¬ P is true, then P is false. Despite the simplicity of negation in prepositional logic, the form and interpretation of negative statements in ordinary language are far from simple and unambiguous.

© Springer Nature Switzerland AG 2020
H. Fehri et al. (Eds.): NooJ 2019, CCIS 1153, pp. 52–64, 2020.
https://doi.org/10.1007/978-3-030-38833-1_5

In many cases, the symmetry between affirmative and negative propositions in logic is not reflected in natural language structures. Negation in a natural language is a complex mechanism that operates on various linguistic levels [3, 4]. Trask [5] defines negation as "*the presence of a negative in a sentence or constituent, or the addition of such an element, or the effect of such an element when present*". A negative is described as "*a grammatical element which, when added to a sentence expressing a proposition, reverses the truth value of that proposition.*" It is pointed out that a negative element is an operator which takes some part of its sentence as its scope and that scope may be the entire proposition or only some part of it. Crystal [6] defines negation as "*a process or construction in grammatical and semantic analysis which typically expresses the contradiction of some or all of a sentence's meaning*".

Negation can also be described as a way that grammar encodes negative polarity, i.e. a relation between semantic opposites. Negation and negative polarity are closely related, but different concepts. Israel [7] stresses that "*polarity encompasses not just the logical relation between negative and affirmative propositions, but also the conceptual relations defining contrary pairs like hot–cold, long–short, and good–bad [...].*" Klenner and Petrakis [8] have experimented with polarity tagged German verbs trying to determine if the polarity of a noun, serving as an object, can be predicted. Their approach, using Naïve Bayes, is reported to have 81% to 92% precision.

Sentences can be negated by adding negative particle to verbal predicates. Note that in Croatian, as in many Slavic languages, multiple negations within one sentence are possible. Unlike in truth tables, double negatives do not exclude each other, thus making the recognition and analysis of such expressions is very difficult. For example, the sentence 'I have never visited China' is translated in Croatian as *Nikada nisam posjetio Kinu* (literally: **Never have I not visited China*). English sentence 'I have never visited any foreign country' is translated as *Nikada nisam posjetio nijednu stranu zemlju* (literally: **Never I have not visited no foreign country*).

On the level of derivational morphology, a set of negative affixes can be attached to stems thus producing lexemes of opposite meanings [9] and usually affecting the interpretation of sentences as affirmative or negative. Negation can also be expressed by various lexical choices, for example by using the opposites like *hot-cold* or *happy-sad*.

In this paper, we focus on negation of nouns in Croatian language and discuss how this issue is dealt with from a computational perspective. Thus, we have designed a grammar for recognizing negation of nouns and annotating its polarity accordingly. For this purpose, we have prepared a prior-polarity marked lexicon of common Croatian nouns to help us determine polarity of unseen negations of nouns. The structure of the paper aims to give a brief theoretical overview of Croatian negations of nouns in Sect. 2 and analysis of nouns in NooJ dictionary in Sect. 3. In Sect. 4 we show and explain the logic behind the algorithm used in morphological grammar, whereas in Sect. 5 we discuss our results on the test corpus. The paper concludes with an outline of the future work.

2 Theoretical Overview of Negation of Nouns

As already stated, in this paper we focus on **prefixal negation of nouns** in the Croatian language. More precisely, we focus on the recognition and annotation of nouns that can be described as mutual opposites in terms of their lexical semantics. Negation on sentential level is out of our scope, i.e. we do not deal with interpretation of sentences as affirmative or negative or as expressing positive or negative attitudes and opinions, at this time.

Oppositeness is usually regarded as a cover term for various and numerous subtypes of opposite relations [10]. One categorization of lexical opposition into direct and indirect negation, with their subtypes (diminution, lack, absence, inferiority, reversal, etc.) is found in Joshi [11]. Lyons [12] distinguishes four major types of lexical opposition: antonymy, converseness, complementarity and directional opposition.

The relation of antonymy is narrowly defined in terms of gradability. Further on, we refer to all types of opposites as *antonymys* taking into account different subtypes of antonymy. Gradable antonyms include opposites like: *beautiful-ugly*, *expensive-cheap* or *fast-slow*. Generally, they represent a 'more-less relation' and comparison of lexical items is possible (e.g. My nose is longer/shorter than yours.) Converse (or relational) antonyms express reciprocal relationships between two (or more) entities, e.g. *borrow-lend*, *buy-sell*, *wife-husband*. **Complementary antonyms** include absolute opposites, i.e. they are based on 'either-or relation', e.g. *dead-alive*, *asleep-awake*, *legal–illegal*. In further discussion we focus on complementary antonyms in Croatian.

Apart from semantic classification into major subtypes (complementaries, gradables and converses), antonyms can be analyzed on the basis of their morphological structure. In other words, antonyms can be classified into those that have identical roots (lexical morphemes) and into those with different roots. Antonyms with different roots are characteristic for all major parts-of-speech: nouns, verbs, adjectives and adverbs, e.g. *visok – nizak* (high – short), *pametan – glup* (clever – stupid), *početak – kraj* (beginning – end), but also for pronouns, particles, and prepositions (e.g. everybody-nobody, yes-no, up-down). This type of antonyms is also referred to as morphologically unrelated antonyms, or 'real' antonyms [13] and they are language universals. Since there is no available large-scale antonymic lexicon for Croatian, this type of antonyms is very difficult for automatic recognition and processing.

Antonyms with **identical roots** are generally derived by prefixation. This word formation process never changes the POS of derivatives in Croatian. Such antonyms are formed by attaching various derivational affixes to stems. Although negation is usually realized by adding a (negative) prefix, there are languages where suffixal word formation is preferred (e.g. *–less* for English, *–talan* for Hungarian, *-ton* for Finnish) [4, 14].

Croatian is a South Slavic language that may produce negations of nouns by bound morphemes. For example, nouns *aktivnost, znanje* (activity, knowledge) can have negatives *neaktivnost, neznanje* (unactivity, unknowledge -> *meaning:* ignorance) respectfully. But, not all nouns can be negated on the morphological level, like *bitka* (battle) or *stol* (table). Although some research states that only positive roots can have negative affixes [2, 15], Zimmer (according to [4]) disagrees and refuses to make this a language universal characteristic. Although he acknowledges that there are languages with tendency to pair negative prefix with positive root, he believes that adding negative prefixes to negative roots does not, by default, makes the construct ungrammatical (e.g. *sad – non-sad*).

Horvat and Golub [14] have observed and reported that the most common and frequent Croatian prefix for negation of nouns, similar to adjectives, is the particle '*ne-*'. In the second position there is the preposition '*bez-*' characterized by the number of realized allomorphs (*be-/bes-/beš-/bez*) due to specific sound changes found in Croatian language [4, 16, 17] that can be observed in examples like *bezub (bez + zub), bespolnost (bez + spolnost), bešćutnost (bez + ćutnost)* and *beživotan (bez + životan)*. These sound changes were taken into consideration during the design of the morphological grammar. There are also nouns that are found with both prefixes like *bezakonitost /nezakonitost*, both denoting negatives of *zakonitost*. On the other hand, there are nouns that already start with prefix '*ne*' but they are not considered negatives of another noun. This is the case for nouns like *neman* (beast) or *nešpula* (type of fruit) for which there are no nouns '*man*' or '*špula*' that might be on the opposite polarity (actually, the word '*špula*' exists in Croatian language but in another meaning then the one that may be inferred from '*nešpula*'). Apart from prefixes of Slavic origin, some prefixes of foreign, mostly Latin origin are used for expressing negation or opposition, e.g. *anti-* or *dis-* (*antialkoholičar – antialcoholic*). Other prefixes are also used (*a-, ab-, de-, i-/im-/in-, kontra-, protu-, sub-*) but they are not as productive as '*ne-*' or '*bez-*' [13, 17]. In some cases, negated nouns actually denote positive concepts, whereas their non-negated counterparts are used for expressing concepts with negative connotations. This is true for e.g. *infekcija* (infection) that has a negative polarity, while, by adding the negative suffix '*dis-*', produces a noun *dezinfekcija* (disinfection) with a positive polarity.

The central point of this research are antonyms with identical lexical morphemes (roots) i.e. nouns derived from other nouns via prefixation (e.g. human – non-human). This area of research has not been sufficiently covered for Croatian [18]. In grammar books and language manuals it is mainly referred to as transformations of grammatical structure of a sentence [19, 20] or as a part of prefixal derivations in the context as understood in Subandowo [9] and Zovko Dinković [18]. Kovačević [4] takes this research a bit further stating that the negation is explicitly expressed with negative prefixes and some POS (adverbs, prepositions, conjunctions etc.) and it is realized at several levels (morphological, syntactic, sentential, discourse).

Our aim is to work on the morphological level in order to extend and enrich existing lexica, i.e. resources for NooJ [21–23] as well as to enable the creation of new ones. The main objective is to automatically recognize noun-noun antonyms with NooJ, using rule-based approach [24]. This procedure relies on morphological rules containing a list of single derivational affixes as well as combinations of affixes in Croatian. Results are manually checked and evaluated. In the following section, the analysis of nouns in NooJ dictionary is presented including the list and distribution of prefixes used to change the polarity of a word. This step was important to provide us with a comprehensive list of prefixes that should be included in the morphological grammar (cf. Sect. 4).

3   Analysis of Nouns in the Dictionary

When there is a negative prefix at the beginning of a word, it is to be expected that the word caries a negative meaning. In Croatian, those prefixes make up a very short list with the prefix 'ne-' at the top, while other usual suspects line up as 'a-, ab-, anti-', 'be [s|š|z|<E>]-' 'de-', 'dis-', 'i[m|n]<E>]-', 'kontra-', 'protu-' and 'sub-'.

We have tested this hypothesis by performing analysis on nouns in the NooJ dictionary. A small morphological grammar was constructed with a purpose to recognize if a noun is composed of a prefix and another noun already present in the dictionary, and to mark these sections accordingly via two attributes (+Prefix = prefix + Noun = noun). The list of prefixes in this case was not pre-prepared. The grammar would find the noun part and the string of letters that precedes that noun is marked as a prefix. A list of 26 179 nouns produced 10 878 annotations that the algorithm believes to be compounds made of a prefix and another noun. Detailed analysis of data has identified a list of 5 322 unique strings that the algorithm marked as a prefix. If sorted by the number of occurrences, among the first fifty are also five negative prefixes (*ne, de, i, dis, a*) (Fig. 1).

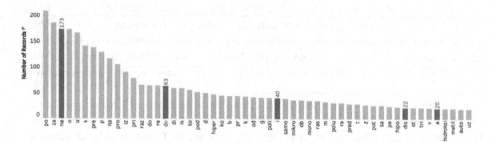

Fig. 1. List of first fifty prefixes sorted by the number of occurrences (*negative prefixes are marked with the number of occurrences*)

Among these prefixes, 4 391 appear only once in the dictionary, 473 twice and 154 three times, and they are mostly false positives (Fig. 1). Distribution of remaining suggested prefixes is as follows: there are 70 suggested prefixes that occur 4 times in the dictionary, 36 occur 5 and 6 times, 22 occur 7 times, 25 occur 8 times, 11 occur 9 times. There are 55 prefixes that occur between 10 and 20 times in the dictionary, 29 occur between 21 and 50 times, 10 occur 52 to 90 times, and the top 10 occur in the range from 105 to 208 times. Some of the incorrect examples with strings falsely marked by the algorithm as prefix include:

- *ambar* → *Pref = am*   *Noun = bar*   * [barn   →   am + pub]
- *arkada* → *Pref = ar*   *Noun = kada*   * [arcade   →ar + tub]
- *brak*   → *Pref = b*   *Noun = rak*   * [marriage →b + crab].

If we extract only negative prefixes, their distribution in the dictionary is shown in Fig. 2. (allomorphs for *bez-* and *i-* are set apart for better acuity). However, not all of these prefixes negate the noun that is found with them, as the following examples illustrate.

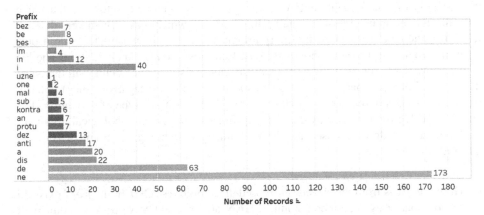

Fig. 2. Distribution of negative prefixes in the dictionary

Some of the incorrect examples with true negative prefix are:

- *antikvar* → *Pref* = *anti*   *Noun* = *kvar*   * [antiquary   →anti + defect]
- *dekada*   → *Pref* = *de*   *Noun* = *kada*   * [decade   → de + tub]
- *kontraadmiral* →*Pref* = *kontra* *Noun* = *admiral*   * [rear admiral →kontra + admiral].

A special type of negation occurs when negative prefix *ne-* is inserted between another prefix and the main noun. Such examples are:

a. *onečišćenje* = o+ne+čišćenje

- noun *čišćenje* exists & *očišćenje* exists

b. *oneraspoloženje* = o+ne+raspoloženje

- noun *raspoloženje* exists but **oneraspoloženje* **does not** *exist*

c. *onemogućavanje* = o+ne+mogućavanje

- noun **mogućavanje* **does not** exist but *omogućavanje exists*

d. onemoćanje = o+ne+moćanje

- noun **moćanje* **does not** exist & **omoćanje* **does not** *exist*.

In order to recognize examples **a**, **b** and **c**, the grammar is designed to account for both possibilities i.e. if the noun exists with or without the prefix *o-* and in some cases with prefix *u-*. However, examples like in **d** are not recognized with the proposed grammar (Fig. 4).

4 Morphological Grammar

In the center of our interest are opposite nouns that share the identical root and fall into the category of non-gradable antonyms, as opposed to gradable antonyms that have irregular formation patterns and usually different roots which makes them very difficult for automatic detection. Thus, the morphological grammar is constructed with a purpose of recognizing unknown nouns derived from other nouns via prefixation. The list of nouns available for derivation are from the closed list of nouns defined in the NooJ dictionary. They are marked with tags for positive (+pos) or negative (+neg) polarity that serve as class descriptors of nouns that may be used in this type of derivation. The list of available prefixes is provided directly from within the morphological grammar.

The original algorithm used for the preliminary morphological grammar (Fig. 3.) had the following steps:

a. Split the word in **prefix + word**
b. **IF** the **prefix** is from the closed set of predefined prefixes **AND IF** the **word** exists in the dictionary as a common noun, **THEN** annotate entire word as a noun with negative polarity.

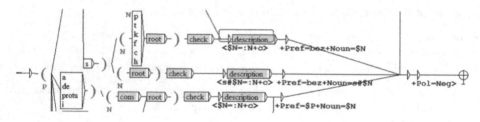

Fig. 3. An excerpt of preliminary morphological grammar

However, in order to raise the precision of this grammar, we have decided to change the second IF statement to:

b. [...] **AND IF** the **word** exists in the dictionary as a common noun **with Polarity attribute value = pos**, **THEN** annotate entire word as a noun with negative polarity".

This modification made sure that nouns that may not produce the negative pairs are excluded from the results (see cf. Sect. 5.2 for examples). Figures 3 and 4 show the introduced change inside the rounded rectangle. Each path in the final grammar (Fig. 4) consists of three sections. The first one parses the word and places a prefix in variable **P** and a noun in variable **N**. The multiple realization of prefix *bez-* (without-) had to be solved separately. For example, if '*bez-*' 'is realized as '*bes-*', the root word may start with any letter. However, if it does not start with letters '*c, f, h, k, p, t*', we need to add the '*s*' at the beginning of the root section when we check against the dictionary if it has the root noun <s#$N = :N + c+pos>, but also to the annotation tag of the derived noun via transducer <$P#$N, N + Pref = bez + Noun = s#$N +Pol = Neg>. This is maybe best shown via an example. Two nouns, *svijest* and *kraj*, both use prefix *'bez-'* to derive the negatives, *besvijest* and *beskraj* respectfully. However, unlike the second noun that may be split into *bes + kraj*, where *bes* is one of the realizations of prefix *bez*, the first noun cannot be split into *bes + svijest* since we are missing a letter. This dropped 's' still needs to be provided to the grammar if we want to keep the same logic of the algorithm, i.e. check that the root noun, found in variable **N**, exists in the dictionary as a common noun with positive polarity tag.

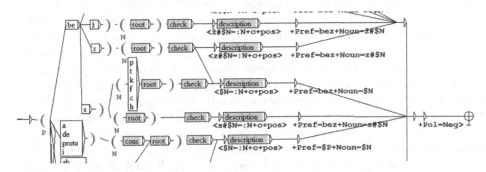

Fig. 4. An excerpt of enhanced morphological grammar for recognition of negative nouns

There are also some special cases where negative prefix *'ne-'* is added between another derivational prefix *'o-'* or *'u-'* and a root noun like in the following examples:

- *one*čišćenost → neg. of *očišćenost* *ones*posobljenost → neg. of *osposobljenost*
- *une*srećivanje → neg. of *usrećivanje* *une*ravnoteženost → neg. of *uravnoteženost*.

Since the negative prefix in these cases negates the derived noun and not its root noun, it is important to include this in the sections of the graph where check against dictionary and final description of a noun are performed.

The second section of the path consists of two checks. With the first one, we want to make sure that the string we are recognizing, i.e. the content of variable **P** followed by the content of variable **N**, does not already exist in the dictionary. This check is provided within the subgraph: **check**. The second check passes only those entries that have a root noun, i.e. the content of variable **N** that may start with an additional letter, in the dictionary marked as a common noun with positive polarity attribute. The last section of the path has a task to annotate the derived noun with all the lexical tags found in the dictionary for the root noun. In addition, its polarity attribute is set to negative and data on prefixes and root nouns are provided.

5   Results

5.1   Test Corpora

To test the morphologic grammar but also to see the distribution of negation usage across two different types of corpora, we have built Sub-Corpus 1 and Sub-Corpus 2 with the help of SketchEngine platform using Croatian corpora hrWaC and Riznica respectfully as sources. The main reason for this was to check if some types of texts more than others are inclined to use specific prefixes for negation of nouns.

HrWaC [25] is the Croatian web corpus consisting of texts collected from the Internet, more specifically from '.hr' domain. The corpus was created in January 2014 and it has over 1.2 billion words. Riznica [26] is Croatian Language Corpus (CLC) built between 2007 and 2011 at the Institute of Croatian Language and Linguistics. It contains texts collected from various text sources such as online articles but also printed books, transcripts of recordings, etc. Overall, it consists of 28% of fiction texts and 72% of specialized texts. It was annotated in 2017 and it has about 85 million words. Since hrWaC and Riznica mainly contain different types of texts, the intention was to note what those differences were regarding negation of nouns using prefixes, making it comparable corpora – the same parameters and principles were used for searching both corpora. Overall, the corpus collected from hrWaC has 2000 concordances i.e. keywords in context, and the corpus collected using Riznica as a source has 1923 concordances. Negation prefixes used in collecting the corpora are: *a-, ab-, an-, anti-, bes-, beš-, bez-, bež-, de-, dez-, dis-, im-, in-, ir-, izne-, kontra-, mal-, ne-, one-, protu-, une-, uzne-*. Both corpora were prepared using regular expressions in CQL with negation prefix and noun as main conditions of the search. CQL is a corpus query language and it is used to set conditions of the search. Regular expressions are used in CQL and they condition the search to character sequence like in the following example:

- [lemma = "ne.*" & tag = "N.*"] filters out the words that start with prefix '*ne-*' and that are tagged as nouns.

  Also, more precisely to avoid results that are not negation:

- [lemma = "bez.*" & lemma= ".*ost" & tag = "N.*"] filters out the words starting with '*bez-*', ending with '*-ost*' that are tagged as nouns, such as *bezosjećajnost* (insensitivity).

The other key condition was that the words included must be negation in its literal meaning – *before adding prefix something is, after the prefix something isn't, or it gets the opposite meaning.* For example, *sreća* (luck, fortune) by adding the prefix '*ne-*'becomes *nesreća* (bad luck, misfortune) which gives it the opposite meaning.

On the other hand, there are words in Croatian language that consist of negation prefixes but cannot be considered as negation in described sense. For example, word *nevolja* (trouble) has a prefix '*ne-*' and word *volja* (will) exists on its own, but is not the opposite of the word *nevolja*. Such words only have negative meaning or negative connotation in Croatian language but are not the opposites of the same word without the prefix. Collected corpora contains such examples because the query could not generate with 100% efficiency.

Our grammar did not recognize these cases. In Table 1 we list all the negative derivations recognized by our grammar and their usage across the two corpora. As the rows in Table 1 demonstrate, this distribution is not equitable and some terms are more likely to be found in one rather than in the other corpus. This list suggests that the root nouns mostly prefer one negative prefix. In our test corpus, this is true for all but three root nouns that each makes derivations with two different prefixes:

- *'menoreja'* with prefixes **a** and **dis**: *'amenoreja'* [3 occ.] and *'dismenoreja'* [1 occ.]
- *'tijelo'* with prefixes **anti** and **protu**: *'antitijelo'* [10 occ.] and *'protutijelo'* [198 occ.]
- *'napad'* with prefixes **kontra** and **protu**: *'kontranapad'* [3 occ.] and *'protunapad'* [6 occ.].

Top ten nouns by the number of occurrences (ranging from 75 down to 14) found in hrWac are *abnormalnost, protutijelo, protuvrijednost, malformacija, ateizam, antidepresiv, malapsorpcija, onešićenost, kontraindikacija* and *uneređivanje*. Similarly, ten most occurring nouns (ranging from 130 down to 25) are *protutijelo, malformacija, kontraindikacija, malapsorpcija, abnormalnost, ateizam, beskonačnost, besmrtnost, neprijatelj* and *antiteza*. Four nouns that are different on these two lists can be explained by the time-period and the source of each corpus but more thorough examination may find some additional explanations for such distributions. However, this topic is far beyond the one intended for this article and it will not be discussed further at this time.

Table 1. Distribution of prefixes and root nouns across the *hrWac* and *Riznica* corpora

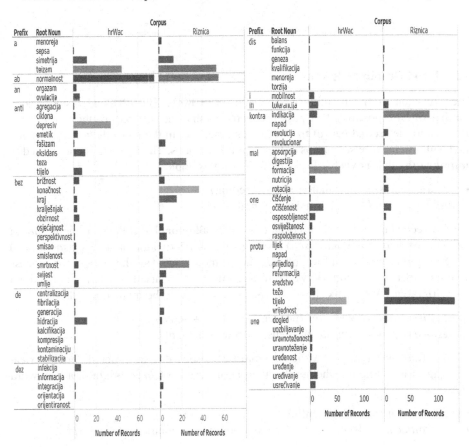

(continued)

Table 1. *(continued)*

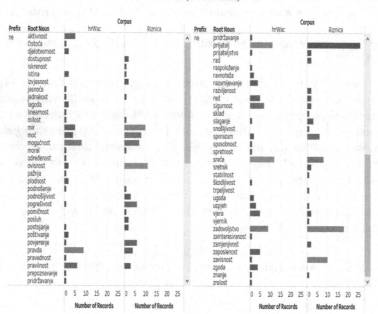

5.2   NooJ Grammar Results

The precision of the preliminary algorithm was 80%. The obtained results had a number of false positives that passed constraints that the first part of the word was a prefix, and the second part of the word was a noun from the NooJ dictionary. Among the results were three subgroups of falsely marked nouns. The first one is contributed to **homography** that is visible from the following examples:

- *analog* ≠ *a* + *nalog* [analog ≠ a + account]
- *malarija* ≠ *mal* + *arija* [malaria ≠ mal + aria].

The second reason for false positive is due to **allomorphy**. If the word *besmisao* (in the sense of *nonsense* or *unreason*) is recognized as a derivation of noun *smisao* (*sense*) to which prefix 'be-' (as a form of 'bez' i.e. without) is added, the recognition process should be marked as good. However, if the same word is parsed as a derivation of noun *misao* (*thought*) and prefix 'bes-', the recognition should be marked as false.

- *besmisao* = *be(s)* + *smisao* [nonsense = no(n) + sense]
- *besmisao* ≠ *bes* + *misao* [nonsense ≠ non + thought].

The third group makes various **semantic** reasons due to either different lexical meaning of a root noun, whether the noun is of Croatian (*zbroj*) origin or a loan word (*dikcija*).

- *bezbroj* ≠ *be(z)* + *zbroj* [infinite ≠ without + sum]
- *kontradikcija* ≠ *kontra* + *dikcija* [contradiction ≠ contra + elocution].

To raise the precision, we have added semantic annotation for polarity of nouns directly to the dictionary for the cases where such polarity was justified, i.e. where both positive and negative polarities exist for a noun, and included it in the graph (Fig. 4). The enhanced graph now checks if the second part of the word is a noun with marked polarity. If this constraint is passed, the entire word is annotated with the semantic annotation of opposite polarity. Thus, if the root noun is marked as a positive noun, the grammar will mark the derived word as a negative noun and vice versa. With introduced changes, the precision was raised to 99.88%. The comparison of results is presented in Fig. 5 i.e. before and after the grammar was augmented with additional tag in the constraint <$N = :N + c+pos> and the polarity attribute is added directly to the dictionary entries. Both results (Fig. 5) depict the examples found in the test corpus.

Prefix	False / True			Prefix	False / True		
	0	1	☲		0	1	☲
ne	17	300		ne		312	
protu	20	278		protu		298	
Mal	7	273		mal		288	
ab		131		bez		144	
A	14	129		a		131	
bez	34	112		ab		131	
anti	66	93		kontra		115	
kontra	13	60		anti		95	
one		42		one	2	62	
de	28	35		une		53	
in	68	27		de		29	
Dez		13		in		27	
i	59	13		dez		14	
dis	48	12		dis		13	
an	2	9		i		12	
im	1			an		9	
une	1						
uzne	1						

Fig. 5. Number of false vs true annotations for each prefix with <$N=:N+c> (left) vs <$N=:N+c +pos> (right) constraints

6 Conclusion

The morphological grammar proposed here lays down the grounds for future work in the domain of word and sentence oriented research. The list of false negatives also needs to be revisited in search of new patterns that can be used to tune up the presented algorithm. With slight modifications, the algorithm can be further checked against other POS, including mainly verbs and adjectives, which in return may result with a full dictionary of Croatian antonyms.

It will be interesting to test if same nouns occur more frequently in positive or negative form in corpora and if there is a pattern in that behavior. In addition, we can test how the polarity of a noun influences the polarity of a noun phrase, but also how it influences the polarity in the interaction with the verb, depending on its position in the sentence.

References

1. Colm Hogan, P.: The Cambridge Encyclopedia of the Language Sciences. Cambridge University Press, Cambridge (2011)
2. Horn, L.R.: A Natural History of Negation, University of Chicago Press (2001)
3. Barić, E., et al.: Hrvatski jezi-čni savjetnik. Institut za hrvatski jezik i jezikoslovlje, Pergamena, Školske novine, Za-greb (1999)
4. Kovačević, A.: Negacija od čestice do teksta: Usporedna i povijesna raščlamba negacije u hrvatskoglagoljskoj pismenosti. Staroslavenski institut, Zagreb (2016)
5. Trask, R.L.: Language and Linguistics: The Key Concepts. Routledge, London (2003)
6. Crystal, D.: A Dictionary of Linguistics and Phonetics. Blackwell Publishing, Oxford (2008)
7. Israel, M.: The pragmatics of polarity. In: Horn, L.R., Ward, G. (eds.) 701–723. Blackwell, Oxford (2004)
8. Klenner, M., Petrakis, S.: Polarity preference of verbs: what could verbs reveal about the polarity of their objects? In: Bouma, G., Ittoo, A., Métais, E., Wortmann, H. (eds.) NLDB 2012. LNCS, vol. 7337, pp. 35–46. Springer, Heidelberg (2012). https://doi.org/10.1007/978-3-642-31178-9_4. https://www.zora.uzh.ch/id/eprint/64977/1/nldb-final.pdf
9. Subandowo, D.: Negation Affixes in English. Premise J. 3(2), 135–144 (2014)
10. Cruse, D.A.: Lexical Semantics. Cambridge University Press (1986)
11. Joshi, S.: Affixal negation. Direct Indirect Their Subtypes. 13, 49–63 (2012)
12. Lyons, J.: Semantics. Cambridge University Press (1977)
13. Šarić, Lj.: Antonimija: Neke značenjske i tvorbene odrednice. Rasprave ZHJ 18, 177–191 (1992)
14. Horvat, M., Štebih Golub, B.: Tvorba riječi u hrvatskim dopreporodnim gramatikama. Rasprave instituta za hrvatski jezik i jezikoslovlje. 38(2), 295–326 (2012)
15. Jespersen, O.: Negation in English and other Languages. A. F. Host, Kopenhagen (1917)
16. Težak, S., Babić, S.: Gramatika hrvatskoga jezika: Priručnik za osnovno jezično obrazovanje. Školska knjiga, Zagreb (1992)
17. Babić, S.: Tvorba riječi u hrvatskome književnome jeziku. HAZU, Nakladni zavod Glo-bus, Zagreb (2002)
18. Zovko Dinković, I.: Negacija u jeziku: Kontrastivna analiza negacije u engleskome i hrvatskome jeziku. Hrvatska sveučilišna naknada, Zagreb (2013)
19. Katičić, R.: Sintaksa hrvatskoga književnog jezika. HAZU, Nakladni zavod Globus, Zag-reb (2002)
20. Barić, E., Lončarić, M., Malić, D., Pavešić, S., Peti, M., Zečević, V., Znika, M.: Hrvat-ska gramatika. Školska knjiga, Zagreb (2005)
21. Vučković, K., Tadić, M., Bekavac, B.: Croatian language resources for NooJ. CIT: J. Comput. Inf. Technol. 18(2010), 295–301 (2010)
22. Kocijan, K., Janjić, M., Librenjak, S.: Recognizing Diminutive and Augmentative Croatian Nouns. In: Barone, L., Monteleone, M., Silberztein, M. (eds.) NooJ 2016. CCIS, vol. 667, pp. 23–36. Springer, Cham (2016). https://doi.org/10.1007/978-3-319-55002-2_3
23. Kocijan, K., di Buono, M.P., Mijić, L.: Detecting Latin-based medical terminology in Croatian Texts. In: Mauro Mirto, I., Monteleone, M., Silberztein, M. (eds.) NooJ 2018. CCIS, vol. 987, pp. 38–49. Springer, Cham (2019). https://doi.org/10.1007/978-3-030-10868-7_4
24. Silberztein, M.: Formalizing Natural Languages: The NooJ Approach. Cognitive Science Series. Wiley-ISTE, London (2016)
25. Ljubešić, N., Erjavec, T.: hrWaC and slWac: compiling web corpora for Croatian and Slovene. In: Habernal, I., Matoušek, V. (eds.) TSD 2011. LNCS (LNAI), vol. 6836, pp. 395–402. Springer, Heidelberg (2011). https://doi.org/10.1007/978-3-642-23538-2_50
26. Ćavar, D., Brozović, R.D.: Riznica: The Croatian Language Corpus. Prace Filo-logiczne. 62, 51–65 (2012)

The Automatic Generation of NooJ Dictionaries from Lexicon-Grammar Tables

Asmaa Kourtin[✉], Asmaa Amzali, Mohammed Mourchid,
Abdelaziz Mouloudi, and Samir Mbarki

Faculty of Science, MISC Laboratory, Ibn Tofail University, Kénitra, Morocco
asmaa.kourtin@yahoo.fr, asmamzali@hotmail.fr,
mourchidm@hotmail.com, mouloudi_aziz@hotmail.com,
mbarkisamir@hotmail.com

Abstract. The syntactic and semantic analyses constitute an important part of the automatic natural language processing field. Indeed, the complexity and the richness of the language make these tasks more difficult since they require the description of all the grammatical, syntactic and semantic features of the language lexicon. It is in this context that the lexicon-grammar approach has been introduced: It consists of describing the lexicon of the language through readable and intuitive tables for manual human editing. On the other hand, NooJ is an automatic natural language processing platform that includes different levels of analysis: lexical, morphological, syntactic and semantic. In order to integrate the lexicon-grammar approach into this platform, the tables must be transformed into dictionaries and syntactic grammars. However, setting up the dictionaries in NooJ through these tables is done manually right now, making it very time-consuming and error-prone. Hence, this work aimed at developing dictionaries automatic generation tool in NooJ from lexicon-grammar tables, ensures time saving and fully exploiting the potentialities of the lexicon-grammar approach.

Keywords: Natural Language Processing (NLP) · NooJ · Lexicon-grammar tables · NooJ dictionaries automatic generation · Syntactic and semantic analyses · Dictionaries · Syntactic grammars · Transformation

1 Introduction

Natural language processing (NLP) is a field of computer science, artificial intelligence, and computational linguistics concerned with interactions between computers and human natural languages. The applications related to the automatic natural languages processing have attracted particular attention for several decades, such as automatic translation, orthographic and grammar correction, corpus analysis, and automatic question answering (QA). These areas represent major challenges.

There are two approaches of the text analysis: statistical and linguistic. The statistical approach is widely used in the applications mentioned above until now, since it needs less time and less work. It allows users to parse the sequence of characters and words in order to find regularities and to be able to predict certain properties without requiring linguistic knowledge, which makes it difficult to give reliable and satisfactory

© Springer Nature Switzerland AG 2020
H. Fehri et al. (Eds.): NooJ 2019, CCIS 1153, pp. 65–76, 2020.
https://doi.org/10.1007/978-3-030-38833-1_6

results. This explains the problems encountered while using existing translation web applications for instance as well as spelling and grammar correctors. That's why the linguistic approach is better than the statistical one despite its difficulties where it needs deeper linguistic skills. To describe the language lexicon we use lexicon-grammar tables that contain all its grammatical, syntactic and semantic characteristics. Those tables play a key role in the syntactic and semantic analyses in order to give powerful results.

On the other hand, NooJ is an automatic natural language processing platform based on the linguistic approach allowing the modeling of linguistic knowledge to make it exploitable by the machine. This platform includes different levels of analysis: lexical, morphological, syntactic and semantic. In order to benefit from the advantages of the lexicon-grammar tables, those tables must be transformed into dictionaries and syntactic grammars [2]. However, those transformations until now are done manually. The manual transformation from lexicon-grammar tables into NooJ dictionaries suffers from several disadvantages that leads to the necessity of the automatization of this process. The objective of this paper is to develop a tool allowing an automatic generation of NooJ dictionaries from any lexicon-grammar table.

This paper is structured as follows: In the Sect. 2, we will begin by reviewing existing works on the lexicon-grammar approach and its implementation. In the Sect. 3, we will give an overview about this approach and state it in the different analysis levels. In the Sect. 4, we will explain how these tables are integrated in NooJ, the problems of the manual transformation of those tables into NooJ dictionaries, and the issues encountered while automating this process. In the Sect. 5, which is the objective of this work, we will explain our proposed algorithm that enables us to automatically obtain dictionaries from lexicon-grammar tables, then we will experiment and evaluate this algorithm for different lexicon-grammar tables. Finally, in the Sect. 6, we conclude this paper with an evaluation and discussion of the benefits of this approach, then we will give some perspectives.

2 Related Work

In this work on the automatic generation of NooJ dictionaries from lexicon-grammar tables, we referred to several studies that have been done, using this approach for several languages, in order to create a tool to generate dictionaries based on lexicon-grammar tables, which is compatible with all languages.

From our research, we found that several researchers have worked on this approach for different languages by creating lexicon-grammar tables.

This theory was initiated in 1975 by Maurice Gross [1–4], who created tables for the French language lexicon, by describing the lexical classification method and the construction principle of these tables, as explained in Sect. 3. Also for this language, Yvette Yannick Mathieu [7–9] built lexicon-grammar tables for psychological verbs, in order to create the feeling system allowing the detection of these verbs in texts. For this, he classified the psychological verbs into three classes according to their polarities: the positive-polarity verbs that describe a pleasant feeling, the negative-polarity verbs that describe an unpleasant feeling, and the verbs that have no polarity that describe an indifference or with polarity that describe a feeling that will be indicated by the context. Subsequently, Max Silberztein [5, 6] extended the work of Maurice Gross by creating other tables to complete the lexicon and grammar of French language, and then he integrated the theory of lexicon-grammar tables into NooJ platform to allow it to benefit from the advantages of this approach, as explained in Sect. 4. In the same context, Elsa Tolone [10, 11] tried to collect previous works on the lexicon-grammar tables of French language by normalizing them to build the LGLex lexicon.

Other studies have been carried out using different languages. For Arabic language, the first who initiated this approach of the lexicon-grammar tables is Mohamed El Hannach [12] who studied the support verbs [13], the qualitative verbs [14] and psychological verbs of this language with their syntactic properties and possible transformations [15]. For the Italian language, Simonetta Vietri created lexicon-grammar tables for idiomatic constructions [16, 17] and integrated them into NooJ by transforming each one into a dictionary associated with a syntactic grammar. In addition, Peter A. Machonis described the neutral phrasal verbs for English language [18] and created lexicon-grammar tables for these verbs. Finally, for Portuguese language, Anabela Barreiro worked on predicate nouns with support verb "fazer" [19], and integrated her lexicon-grammar table in Port4NooJ.

3 The Lexicon-Grammar Approach: Theoretical Study

The lexicon-grammar approach was initiated by Gross and his LADL's team in 1975 [1]. They built a syntactic lexicon for French language by establishing a linguistic classification of the language lexicon. Hence, a lexicon-grammar table is a class that groups together a number of entries sharing the same definitional construction. These tables are represented as matrices where lines depict the lexical entries, the columns depict the syntactico-semantic properties of constructions, distributions, morphological, transformational, semantic features (ex: Hum = Human noun), ...etc. The cells contain either a lexical element, "+" or "−" to specify whether an expression has a property or not, or " ∼ " if the entry is not yet encoded.

For example, Fig. 1 shows an excerpt from the class 1 of verbs that are constructed with an argument introduced by a preposition. If the verb has two distinct meanings, it has two lexical entries since each sense does not accept the same set of properties. One of the examples in the class V_1 is the verb "Aller" (to go) that has four meanings (see Fig. 1): «Le verre va tomber » (The glass will fall), «Max allait pour partir quand Marie est arrivée» (Max was going to leave when Mary arrived), «Max va jusqu'à exiger des dommages» (Max is going to demand damages) and «Cette mesure n'ira pas sans créer des troubles» (This measure will not go without creating troubles).

<ID>	N0 :: Nhum	N0 :: Nnc	<ENT>Ppv	Ppv :: se figé	Ppv :: en figé	Ppv :: Neg	<ENT>V	Neg	Aux :: avoir	Aux :: être	N0 est Vpp W	N0 V	Prép1	Tp = Tc	Tc :: passé	Tc :: présent	Tc :: futur	Vc :: devoir	Vc :: pouvoir	Vc :: savoir	Prép V0-inf W = Ppv	N0 V Prép N1hum	N0 V Prép N1-hum	Prép N1 = Ppv	N0 V dans N1	N0 V N1hum	N0 V N1-hum	<OPT>
1	+	-	<E>	-	-	-	achever	-	+	-	-	-	de	+	-	-	-	-	-	-	-	-	-	-	-	+	+	Max achève de peindre le mur
2	+	+	<E>	-	-	-	aller	-	-	-	-	-	<E>	-	-	-	-	+	+	+	-	-	-	-	-	-	-	Le verre va tomber
3	+	+	<E>	-	-	-	aller	-	+	+	-	-	pour	+	-	-	-	-	-	-	-	-	-	-	-	-	-	Max allait pour partir quand Marie est arrivée
4	+	-	<E>	-	-	-	aller	-	-	+	-	-	jusqu'à	+	-	-	-	-	-	-	-	-	-	-	-	-	-	Max va jusqu'à exiger des dommages
5	-	+	ne	-	-	+	aller	+	-	+	-	-	sans	+	-	-	-	+	+	+	-	-	-	-	-	-	-	Cette mesure n'ira pas sans créer des troubles
6	~	~	s'	+	-	-	apprêter	-	-	+	-	~	à	~	~	~	~	~	~	~	~	~	~	~	~	~	~	La pluie s'apprête à tomber
7	+	+	<E>	-	-	-	arrêter	-	+	-	-	-	de	+	-	-	-	-	-	-	-	-	-	-	-	+	+	Luc arrête de travailler
8	+	+	n'	-	-	+	arrêter pas	+	+	-	-	-	de	-	-	-	-	-	-	-	-	-	-	-	-	-	-	Max n'arrête pas de faire des bétises
9	+	-	s'	+	-	-	arrêter	-	-	+	-	-	à	-	-	+	+	-	-	-	+	-	+	+	-	-	-	Max s'est arrêté à dire une telle chose
10	+	+	s'	+	-	-	arrêter	-	-	+	+	+	de	+	-	-	-	-	-	-	-	-	-	-	-	-	-	Max s'arrête de boire

Fig. 1. Excerpt of the lexicon-grammar table V_1 of Max Silberztein.

4   The Integration of Lexicon-Grammar Approach in NooJ

In order to integrate the lexicon-grammar approach in NooJ platform, the lexicon-grammar tables must be transformed into dictionaries and syntactic grammars that use the linguistic knowledge encoded in the lexicon-grammar tables to identify the sentences. We note that each dictionary and its associated syntactic grammar must have the same name as proposed by Max Silberztein [2]. Each dictionary's entry is related to the properties of the lexicon-grammar table. However, those transformations until now are done manually.

The manual transformation of the lexicon-grammar tables into NooJ dictionaries is a difficult and time-consuming process. This problem leads to the necessity of the automatization of this process. Our objective is to develop and integrate in NooJ a tool to automatically obtain dictionaries from any lexicon-grammar table. This will allow linguists to edit dictionaries through intuitive and readable tables for manual human editing as textual dictionaries.

To set up this automatization, we encountered many issues:

Issue 1: The presence of some entries not yet coded, which are represented by the symbol ' ∼ ' as shown in Fig. 1 for many properties of the entry "apprêter" (to get ready).

Issue 2: The presence of useless columns that should not be in the dictionary such as the columns containing examples, IDs, … etc (see Fig. 2).

<ID>	N0 =: Nhum	N0 =: Nnc	<ENT>Ppv	Ppv =: se figé	Ppv =: en figé	Ppv =: Neg	<ENT>V	Neg	Aux =: avoir	Aux =: être	N0 est Vpp W	N0 V	Prép1	Tp = Tc	Tc =: passé	Tc =: présent	Tc =: futur	Vc =: devoir	Vc =: pouvoir	Vc =: savoir	Prép V0-inf W = Ppv	N0 V Prép N1hum	N0 V Prép N1-hum	Prép N1 = Ppv	N0 V dans N1	N0 V N1hum	N0 V N1-hum	<OPT>
1	+	-	<E>	-	-	-	achever	-	+	-	-	-	de	+	-	-	-	-	-	-	-	-	-	-	-	+	+	Max achève de peindre le mur
2	+	+	<E>	-	-	-	aller	-	-	-	-	-	<E>	-	-	-	+	+	+	-	-	-	-	-	-	-	-	Le verre va tomber
3	+	+	<E>	-	-	-	aller	-	+	+	-	-	pour	+	-	-	-	-	-	-	-	-	-	-	-	-	-	Max allait pour partir quand Marie est arrivée
4	+	-	<E>	-	-	-	aller	-	-	+	-	-	jusqu'à	+	-	-	-	-	-	-	-	-	-	-	-	-	-	Max va jusqu'à exiger des dommages
5	-	+	ne	-	-	+	aller	+	-	+	-	-	sans	+	-	-	+	+	+	-	-	-	-	-	-	-	-	Cette mesure n'ira pas sans créer des troubles
6	~	~	s'	+	-	-	apprêter	-	-	+	~	~	à	~	~	~	~	~	~	~	~	~	~	~	~	~	~	La pluie s'apprête à tomber
7	+	+	<E>	-	-	-	arrêter	-	+	-	-	+	de	+	-	-	-	-	-	-	-	-	-	-	+	+	+	Luc arrête de travailler
8	+	+	n'	-	-	+	arrêter pas	+	+	-	-	-	de	-	-	-	-	-	-	-	-	-	-	-	-	-	-	Max n'arrête pas de faire des bétises
9	+	-	s'	+	-	-	arrêter	-	-	+	-	-	à	-	-	+	+	-	-	-	+	-	+	+	-	-	-	Max s'est arrêté à dire une telle chose
10	+	+	s'	+	-	-	arrêter	-	-	+	+	+	de	+	-	-	-	-	-	-	-	-	-	-	-	-	-	Max s'arrête de boire

Fig. 2. Excerpt of the lexicon-grammar table V_1 of Max Silberztein showing some useless columns.

Issue 3: The major issue encountered is the non-standardization of all the potential lexicon-grammar tables.

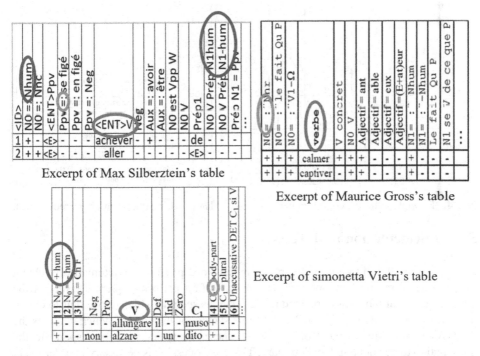

Excerpt of Max Silberztein's table

Excerpt of Maurice Gross's table

Excerpt of simonetta Vietri's table

Fig. 3. Excerpt of some lexicon-grammar tables showing the non-standardization problem.

Figure 3 contains three tables showing the problem of the non-standardization. We can note that in those tables some column headings differ from one table to another although they denote the same property. They do not use the same symbols, also they do not use the same properties codes like the verb property, it differs from one table to another, we have "verbe", "V" and "<ENT>V". The same thing for the Human property, we have "N0 =: Nhum", "N0 = +hum" and "N0 = −hum", etc.

To overcome these difficulties we need to perform a preprocessing of those tables in order to standardize them:

- For the symbol '~' we have to code the entry before executing the program by filling each cell with '+' or '−', or at the runtime if one or more '~' are found, the program will interact with the user such that he will be asking to choose '+', '−' or 'N' to ignore the entry as it is explained in the following section.
- For the useless columns, we can put a code like <OPT> in the header of these columns or delete them manually.
- Finally, for the normalization, all the tables must be standardized, but until now, there is no proposed standard that must be respected when creating any lexicon-grammar table. So, as a solution some preprocessing of the table was undertaken so that the header conforms to the data that must be in the dictionary (see Fig. 4). For example, we have to delete additional informations like <ENT> and any useless information that should not appear in the dictionary.

NOHum	NOnc	Ppv	Ppv=se	Ppv=en	Ppv=Neg	V	Aux=avoir	Aux=être	NOestVppW	NOV	Prép1	Tp=Tc	TcPassé	TcPrésent	VcFutur	Vc=devoir	Vc=pouvoir	Vc=savoir	PrépV0NinfW=Ppv	N0VPrépN1hum	N0VPrépN1Nhum	PrépN1=Ppv	N0VdansN1	N0VN1hum	N0VN1Nhum	<OPT>
+	-	<E>	-	-	-	achever	+	-	-	-	de	+	-	-	-	-	-	-	-	-	-	-	-	+	+	Max achève de peindre le mur
+	+	<E>	-	-	-	aller	-	-	-	-	<E>	-	-	-	+	+	+	-	-	-	-	-	-	-	-	Le verre va tomber
+	+	<E>	-	-	-	aller	+	+	-	-	pour	+	-	-	-	-	-	-	-	-	-	-	-	-	-	Max allait pour partir quand Marie est arrivée
+	-	<E>	-	-	-	aller	-	+	-	-	jusqu'à	+	-	-	-	-	-	-	-	-	-	-	-	-	-	Max va jusqu'à exiger des dommages
-	+	ne	-	-	+	aller	-	+	-	-	sans	+	-	-	-	+	+	+	-	-	-	-	-	-	-	Cette mesure n'ira pas sans créer des troubles
~	~	s'	+	-	-	apprêter	-	+	~	~	à	~	~	~	~	~	~	~	~	~	~	~	~	~	~	La pluie s'apprête à tomber
+	+	<E>	-	-	-	arrêter	+	-	-	+	de	+	-	-	-	-	-	-	-	-	-	-	-	+	+	Luc arrête de travailler
+	+	n'	-	-	+	arrêter pas	+	-	-	-	de	-	-	-	-	-	-	-	-	-	-	-	-	-	-	Max n'arrête pas de faire des bêtises
+	-	s'	+	-	-	arrêter	-	+	-	-	à	-	-	+	+	-	-	-	+	-	+	+	-	-	-	Max s'est arrêté à dire une telle chose
+	+	s'	+	-	-	arrêter	-	+	+	+	de	+	-	-	-	-	-	-	-	-	-	-	-	-	-	Max s'arrête de boire

Fig. 4. Excerpt of the lexicon-grammar table «V_1.xls» of Max Silberztein after pretreatment.

5 Implementation and Tests

In order to develop a tool and integrate it in the NooJ platform to automatically obtain dictionaries from any lexicon-grammar table, we first perform a preprocessing of the lexicon-grammar tables as explained in the previous section, which allowed us to obtain the table we presented in Fig. 4. The first line stands for the header, which contains the properties belonging to the table's entries. These properties must correspond to the information to be added in the dictionary. This preprocessing is necessary in order to get a valid table for our system (see Fig. 4). For this, some conditions must be satisfied:

(a) It is necessary to specify the grammatical category (V, N, ADJ, …) of the entry in the lexicon-grammar table because it will help to determine the location of the column containing the entry and extract its grammatical category.
(b) The header of the useless columns must contain <OPT>, <Opt> or <opt>.

When the preprocessing is done, the table must be saved as an Excel file. Then we process it according to the following algorithm:

Algorithm: Program generating NooJ dictionaries from lexicon-grammar tables

1. **Input**
2.   Lexicon-grammar table in the Excel form
3. **Output**
4.   NooJ dictionary
5. **Begin**
6.   Create a dictionary with the same name of the imported lexicon-grammar table;
7.   Ask the user to choose the language of the table;
8.   Add the header of NooJ dictionaries with the chosen language to the dictionary;
9.   Get the column index of the entry and its grammatical category from the header of the table;
10.   **For** each line **do**
11.   Extract the entry and add it with its grammatical category to the dictionary;
12.   **For** each cell **do**
13.   **If** the column is considered as a useless column
14.   **then** ignore it;
15.   **Else if** the cell contains "+"
16.   **then** retrieve its corresponding property and add it to the dictionary;
17.   **Else if** it contains a lexical element
18.   **then** retrieve its corresponding property and its content, and add them to the dictionary;
19.   **Else if** it contains "-" or <E>
20.   **then** ignore this cell;
21.   **Else if** it contains "~"
22.   **then** ask the user for choosing "+" or "-" or to ignore the entry;
23.   **End if**
24.   **End for**
25.   **End for**
26. **End**

In order to implement this algorithm and incorporate it into NooJ platform, we used Python language (see Fig. 5).

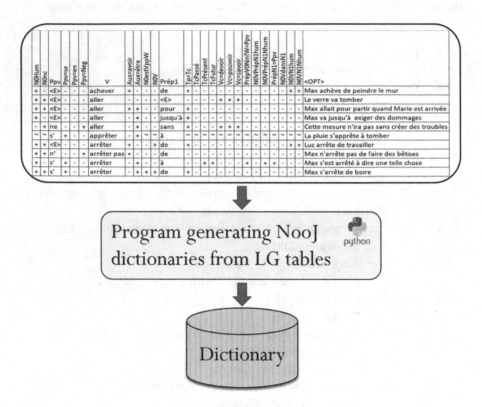

Fig. 5. Execution process.

After executing our program and choosing as input the table V_1 of Max Silberztein (see Fig. 4), we have obtained the following dictionary (see Fig. 6):

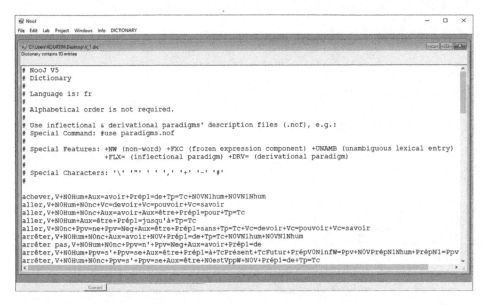

Fig. 6. The dictionary «V_1.dic» generated from the lexicon-grammar table «V_1.xls».

In addition, we tested our tool on other lexicon-grammar tables in the Arabic language. Thus, we transformed into NooJ dictionary the psychological verbs table «PS.xls» that groups three categories: "أفعال الشعور" (Negative feeling verbs), "الإحساس أفعال" (Positive feeling verbs) and "أفعال الرأي والتفكير" (Thought and opinion verbs) (see Figs. 7 and 8).

<OPT> Explication	<OPT> Exemple	VNOPrép1N1	VNON1	VNO	Prép1	N1Nhum	N1Hum	NONHum	NOHum	V	<OPT> Catégorie
بذخ:عظم و افتخر	بذخ الشخص	+	-	+	<E>	-	-	-	+	بذخ	أفعال الإحساس
إبْتهَج لهُ الأهلُ : - : فرِحَ وسُرَّ	إبتهج له الأهل	+	+	+	<E>	-	+	-	+	إنبهَج	أفعال الإحساس
حَمِدَة : رضي عنه وارتاح إليه	حمد الشيء	-	+	-	<E>	+	+	-	+	حمِدَ	أفعال الإحساس
حنّ إليه:اشتاق	حنّ إلى فلان	+	-	+	إلى	+	+	-	+	حنّ	أفعال الإحساس
~		+	-	+	لـ	+	+	-	+		أفعال الإحساس
تَحوّب الأمّ على وَلِدهَا:عطفت	تَحوّب الأمّ على وَلِدهَا	+	-	+	<E>	+	+	-	+	تحوّب	أفعال الإحساس
حامَ على قرابته:عطفَ.	حامَ على قرابته	+	+	+	على	+	+	-	+	حامَ	أفعال الإحساس
تاعَ الى الشيء : تاق و اشتاق	تاعَ الى الشيء	~	+	+	<E>	-	+	-	+	تاعَ	أفعال الإحساس
تامَ (يَتيم) : الهوى	تامَ (يَتيم) : الهوى	~	+	+	<E>	-	+	-	+	تامَ	أفعال الإحساس
أجاد إلى لقائه : أشتاقُ إليه و أساقُ	أجاد إلى لقائه	~	+	+	<E>	-	+	-	+	أجاد	أفعال الإحساس
خَبَت المَكَان : اطمأنّ	خَبَت المَكَان	~	+	+	<E>	-	+	-	+	خَبَت	أفعال الإحساس

Fig. 7. Excerpt of the psychological verbs table of Asmaa Amzali & al. «PS.xls».

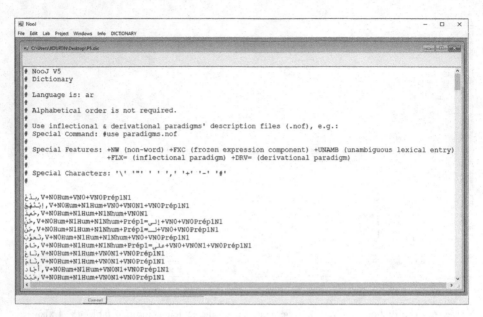

Fig. 8. The dictionary «PS.dic» generated from the lexicon-grammar table «PS.xls».

According to the obtained results (see Figs. 6 and 8), we notice that our proposed program can automatically generate NooJ dictionaries from any lexicon-grammar tables in a very short time. For instance, a table of 118 lines and 27 columns is transformed to an equivalent dictionary in less than one second instead of several hours or days of work for manual transformation, which shows the utility of the automatization. Therefore, we can deduce that the implemented tool allows optimizing time and human effort.

6   Conclusion and Perspectives

The lexicon-grammar tables describe and structure the lexicon of the language through readable and intuitive tables for manual human editing. In order to integrate this lexicon-grammar approach into NooJ platform, the tables must be transformed into dictionaries and syntactic grammars. However, the edition of the dictionaries in Nooj through these tables is manual for now, making it very time-consuming and error-prone. In this work, we have developed an automatic NooJ dictionaries generation tool from lexicon-grammar tables. To do this we encountered many issues, the major was the non-standardization of all the potential lexicon-grammar tables when this approach suffers from the lack of a standard that must be respected when creating those tables. To overcome these issues, we did a preprocessing of the lexicon-grammar tables to obtain valid tables in an Excel file. Our tool gives good results as shown previously in the last section. This automatic generation allows a saving of time and a simple use of the lexicon-grammar tables in NooJ platform, making it possible to exploit the potential of these tables.

Concerning perspectives, we suggest that the NooJ author considers integrating this tool for automatic generation of dictionaries from lexicon-grammar tables in NooJ platform. We therefore propose to add a menu for the processing of lexicon-grammar tables. We can also switch to the automatic generation of lexicon-grammar tables, in the excel form, from the dictionaries, and build syntactic grammars of the generated dictionaries that use the linguistic knowledge encoded in the lexicon-grammar tables to identify the sentences.

References

1. Gross, M.: Méthodes en syntaxe: Régimes des constructions complétives. Hermann, Paris (1975)
2. Gross, M.: La construction de dictionnaires électroniques. Annales des Télécommunications **44**(1–2), 4–19 (1989)
3. Gross, M.: Une grammaire locale de l'expression des sentiments. Langue française, Armand Colin **105**(1), 70–87 (1995)
4. Gross, M.: Les phrases figées en français. L'Information Grammaticale **59**, 36–41 (1993)
5. Silberztein, M.: Complex annotations with NooJ. In: Proceedings of the 2007 International NooJ Conference, June 2007, Barcelone, Spain. Cambridge Scholars Publishing, p. 214 (2008)
6. Silberztein, M.: La formalisation des langues, l'approche de NooJ. ISTE Editions, London (2015)
7. Yvette Yannick, M.: Des descriptions linguistiques à leurs représentations. Doctoral dissertation, Université Paris-Diderot-Paris VII, France (2009)
8. Yvette Yannick, M.: Un classement sémantique des verbes psychologiques. Cahier du CIEL (1999)
9. Yvette Yannick, M.: Interprétation par prédicats sémantiques de structures d'arguments. FEELING, une application aux verbes psychologiques. Thèse de Doctorat en Informatique fondamentale, Université Paris 7, 233 pp. France (1994)
10. Tolone, E.: Analyse syntaxique à l'aide des tables du Lexique-Grammaire du français. Informatique et langage [cs.CL], Université Paris-Est (2011)
11. Tolone, E.: Les tables du Lexique-Grammaire au format TAL. MajecSTIC 2009, Avignon, France, November 2009. Electronic version, pp. 8 (2009)
12. الحناش، م. : النحو التأليفي مدخل نظري وتطبيقي. مجلة دراسات أدبية ولسانية، العدد الأول، السنة الأولى، ص، 58 (1985)
13. El Hannach, M.: Linguistics tools to develop an arabic syntax analyzer. In: 9th International Conference on Innovations in Information Technology. IEEE (2013)
14. El Hannach, M.: Lexique-grammaire de l'Arabe: Classe des verbes qualitatifs (1989). https://books.google.co.ma/books?id=Nn71jwEACAAJ
15. El Hannach, M.: Syntaxe des verbes psychologiques en arabe. Thèse de Doctorat in linguistique. Université Paris 7, p. 540, France (1999)
16. Vietri, S.: The Lexicon-grammar of Italian idioms. In: Proceedings of the Workshop on Lexical and Grammatical Resources for Language Processing (LG-LP 2014), COLING 2014, Dublin, Ireland, August 24, pp. 137–146, August 2014

17. Vietri, S.: Idiomatic Constructions in Italian: A Lexicon Grammar Approch. Lingvisticae Investigationes Supplementa, vol. 31. Amsterdam & Philadelphia, John Benjamins (forthcoming) (2014)
18. Machonis, P.: Neutral phrasal verbs in English. In: Nakamura, T., Laporte, É., Dister, A., Fairon. C. (eds.) Les Tables. La grammaire du français par le menu. Mélanges en hommage à Christian Leclère., Presses universitaires de Louvain, pp. 229–237, Cahiers du CENTAL, 978-2-87463-204-4 (2010)
19. Mota, C., Chacoto, L., Barreiro, A.: Integrating the Lexicon-grammar of predicate nouns with support verb *fazer* into Port4NooJ. In: Mbarki, S., Mourchid, M., Silberztein, M. (eds.) NooJ 2017. CCIS, vol. 811, pp. 29–39. Springer, Cham (2018). https://doi.org/10.1007/978-3-319-73420-0_3

Natural Language Processing Applications

The Data Scientist on LinkedIn: Job Advertisement Corpus Processing with NooJ

Maddalena della Volpe[1]([⊠])[iD] and Francesca Esposito[2][iD]

[1] Department of Business, Management and Innovation System,
University of Salerno, Fisciano, Italy
mdellavolpe@unisa.it
[2] Department of Political and Communication Sciences,
University of Salerno, Fisciano, Italy
fraesposito@unisa.it

Abstract. For organizations using big data, one of the most important element to reach tangible results is exploiting human resources: it is not possible to manage data without using them intelligently. Considering the human intervention in relation to big data, means calling into question the so-called "data scientist". Moving from the above, the main aim of this study is using the linguistic software environment NooJ to process a large corpus of job advertisements for data scientist in Italy collected on the business-networking site LinkedIn. Creating specific linguistic resources with NooJ, we are able to identify the most required skills by companies and organizations.

Searching the ideal candidate to hire, companies pay attention equally to technical skills and soft skills, in particular, as the capacity to work in team and communicate concerns. Finally, our research confirmed that studying the context in which the single words are inserted represents a key step in the process of information extraction by texts.

Keywords: Data scientist · Innovative skills · LinkedIn · Corpus processing · NooJ · Parsing

1 Introduction

To start up big data initiatives, organizations must build infrastructures to manage them, treating big data as a corporate asset [1] and considering that the main goal of big data management is to ensure data that are easily accessible, handy, properly stored and secured [2]. The typical components of a big data infrastructure are: data stacks that consists of structured or unstructured data, big data ecosystem composed of hardware, software, storage and networks, enterprise information management that consists in governance and integration, and finally, data science platforms and tools including a variety of tools for pattern extraction and visualization of results. The implementation of big data infrastructure in companies can be difficult. Moreover, it is highlighted as "available and qualified data scientists who can make sense of big data with a proper understanding of the domain and who are comfortable using analytical tools are not easy to find" [3]. This is also because data scientists should possess numerous skills

© Springer Nature Switzerland AG 2020
H. Fehri et al. (Eds.): NooJ 2019, CCIS 1153, pp. 79–90, 2020.
https://doi.org/10.1007/978-3-030-38833-1_7

that are often provided by a whole team of work. Many guidelines have been suggested in literature on how becoming an ideal data scientist [4–6]. Despite this, it is yet not clear what specific expertise should be met by the candidates responding to the companies' job advertisements, also having regard to the increasing number of individuals that perform such analysis named as data analyst or big data analyst.

Starting from this issue, in our paper we investigate 394 texts of job advertisements for data scientist on the business-networking site LinkedIn to catch the most required personal and technical skills by companies and organizations in Italy. Due to the large amount of textual data, we use the linguistic software environment NooJ to process the corpus. By analysing the linguistic contents with a Natural Language Processing (NLP) software environment, we get a deep mining of texts and a mapping of characteristics of desired applicants across different business sectors. Skills are often implicitly expressed in texts with complex morpho-syntactic and semantic constructs: this information can be extracted or localized in the corpus only through parsing and with the use of local grammars. In fact, lexical items cannot be considered as isolated elements: the local context of the words can modulate the meaning of words and sentences. It is in this respect that we use NooJ lexical parser to annotate expressions in natural language and process the corpus with a local grammar specifically built. When we approach to textual analysis on social media, it can be considered that the first step is certainly represented by the quantitative analysis about single keyword or topics. Moreover, the richness and the heterogeneity of natural language used to discuss on the web drives researchers to make more effort in the process of textual analysis. This could be represented by the semantic analysis [7], which aims to investigate the meaning of words. In this sense, a textual analysis cannot be carried only with traditional statistical techniques, based on keyword occurrences: we must assign a meaning to the element in a certain position of sentence or phrase recognizing who is the subject, object and predicate. Studying the context in which the single words are inserted represents a key step in the process of information extraction.

The paper is structured as follows. After the Introduction, we explored the data scientist profile in literature in the second paragraph highlighting features and definitions. In the third paragraph, we analyse the related works about text mining applied to job advertisements, with particular reference to linguistics. In the fourth paragraph, the research methodology is explained, while in the fifth paragraph we introduce the linguistic analysis of the corpus by means software environment NooJ. Then, conclusions are discussed in the sixth paragraph.

2 Big Data Requires a Big Mind: The Data Scientist

In 2017, the Economist jumped on the "data is the new oil" [8] and business leaders recognized the fact that data-driven management could lead to making better decisions [9, 10]. As a result, nowadays there is a strong demand for data scientists across organizations [11]. Davenport and Patil defined data scientist as a "high-ranking professional with the training and curiosity to make discoveries in the world of big data" [12]. Data scientists want to be autonomous but discussing management issues with executives in real time: they represent a "bridge" between data analysts and managers

[13]. The major tasks performed by this professional figure are identified in: extracting performative knowledge from data to solve business problems, formulating right questions in respect of business goals, meeting the right requirements, recognizing relevant data and using or merging them, selecting fit technologies and tools, exploring solution spaces iteratively without a predetermined end in mind (serendipity), working with domain experts, performing analytics and providing data-driven decision-making [6].

As [4] suggested the ideal data scientist should have five faces: hacker, scientist, adviser, quantitative analyst and business expert. The first face includes both the ability of writing and programming codes and the understanding of big data architectures. As scientist, he takes decisions based on factual elements, owns improvisation, impatience and orientation to the action. The ability to understand decision-making processes and strong communication skills make him a good adviser. To manage big data, the data scientist needs to know the traditional and innovative analytical quantitative techniques as statistical analysis. Finally, the ideal data scientist knows accurately the company in which he is operating, its business goals and how to deploy analytics to reach them. To these skills, [14] one may even add the problem-solving, a real passion for analytics, an applied experience with success stories, and the ability to assess their own salary paid by the company.

As data scientists' job is concerned, [15] interviewed 16 data analysts at Microsoft. The authors describe the workflow of data scientist grouped into five steps: acquiring data, choosing an architecture, shaping the data to the architecture, writing and editing code, reflecting and iterating on the results. Likewise, authors observe as many interviewees emphasize the critical role of visualization: with large data set, it allows identifying patterns over time and "provides a way to maintain context by showing data" (p. 57). Also [16] carried out semi-structured interviews with 35 analysts from several sectors including healthcare, retail, finance, and social networking. They found that analysts generally belong to three different archetypes in terms of skills and typical workflows: hacker, scripter, and application user. Hackers are basically programmers confident in manipulating data. They usually know at least three kinds of programming languages, analysis package (R, Matlab, SAS, Excel), a scripting language (Python, Perl, Java) and a data processing language (SQL, Pig, Hadoop, Hive). Scripters performed most of their analysis within a software package such as R or Matlab. Sometimes the scripters use a separate tool Tableau, to create interactive dashboards for reporting the relevant insights. Application users typically worked on data sets and they typically created illustrations, maps, graphics in Excel to obtain basic visualizations or exported data to put them into a reporting tool. Authors also observed as hackers face much more challenges than application users and the scripters: the latter usually resort to the IT team to perform assured tasks.

However, all of these studies are realized or both with a small number of data scientists and not providing a broader viewpoint. In particular, we refer to the various skills that a person should develop before entering the company. Although sympathetic, the model provided by the investigated literature appears to be ideal and therefore probably not corresponding to the reality. For this reason, we have investigated exactly what requirements in terms of skills must have a data scientist to access a job offer for his professional figure in Italy.

3   Examples of Job Advertisements Corpus Processing

As concerned previous researches, many papers conduct a great quantity of job advertisements analysis to gain insights into employment trends using Text Mining techniques [17–19]. The aspect of job announcements in natural language on the Web needs a deep and sophisticated process of analysis, involving computational linguistic tools. In this respect, [20] used local grammars to extract automatically structured information from the texts of job advertisements on the Web. To retrieve information, the authors collected typical terminology of job offers, frozen expressions and complex phrases. Authors underlined as using local grammars restrict the emergence of certain lexical or syntactical features reducing ambiguities that occur when we consider only a simple keyword.

Another method of analysis is discussed by [21] that, as part of SIRE project, examines a corpus of 200 job ads to understand better how to articulate HR ontologies through a framework of adaptive semantic labeling. They, starting from the idea that categorizing and labeling skills and other characteristics and not only geographical information and business sector, could be made more fit for the match between those who search for a job and those who offer it. Indeed, [22] propose a Latent Semantic Indexing (LSI) model capable of matching job advertisement extracted from the Web with occupation description data in the O*NET, a database of occupational requirements. Their findings reveal that this model of analysis produces much finer and more timely readings of the labour market compare to the common job statistics, over that finding job opportunities transversally for each business sector.

None of the previous studies focused the analysis on a specific professional role or business sector but only described a model useful for every job searching. As new digital jobs are concerned, [23] taking into consideration 173 job advertisements from various sources to understand new professional qualifications and competencies for those who work in the digital curation field in North America. They collected and analysed data from the Web by means of the qualitative analysis software Nvivo and focusing on these six aspects: position title, institution types and location, educational background, experience, knowledge and skills, and duties. He finally divided the found competencies in: communication and interpersonal competency, curating and preserving content competency, curation technologies competency, environmental scanning competency, management, planning and evaluation competency, services competency, systems, models and modeling competency. The authors believe that this set of competencies is also useful for developing educational and training programs that prepare students for the digital field jobs.

Furthermore, [24] explored 1216 job advertisements that contained the word "big data" in the job title published on the website indeed.com. By means a computer-aided content analysis, they used a variation of the pile-sort method to reach common agreement among informants on the concepts expressed in the job ads and the key terms that comprise those concepts. The results revealed as big data job advertisements give importance to technological and analytical skills but also recognize the value of soft skills as communication skills, leadership, problem solving, creativity and entrepreneurship, interpersonal skills, work independently.

Unlike previous studies, our research is focused on a particular professional profile, the data scientists in Italy. The job advertisements typically contain a list of competences declared and explicated by single words but also by expressions that are more complex. Moreover, skills are often implicitly expressed in texts through description, complex morpho-syntactic and semantic constructs: this knowledge can be extracted or localized in the corpus only through parsing and with the use of local grammars. In fact, lexical items cannot be considered as isolated elements: the local context of the words can modulate the meaning of words and sentences. For instance, the competence "problem-solving" is also expressed by the sentence "approccio proattivo alle problematiche" (i.e. proactive approach to problems) oppure "capacità di analisi e risoluzione dei problemi" (i.e. ability to analyse and solve problems) o anche "capacità di proporre approcci innovativi per la soluzione di problemi complessi" (i.e. ability to propose innovative approaches for solving complex problems).

In this respect, to perform our linguistic analysis we applied the Lexicon-Grammar (LG) theoretical and practical framework by Maurice Gross. According to Gross, the description of a language could not be achieved disregarding lexicon, considering only the structural characteristics [25] but it is necessary taking into consideration also the semantic-lexical aspects of a given linguistic system. For Gross, the units of analysis consist of the elementary sentences in which single words occur [26]. We also support the analysis with the creation of local grammars, specifically built for data scientist competences using the NLP software environment NooJ [27, 28]. Our approach uses the tools of computational linguistics for the analysis of business communication and management-related issues [29–32].

4   Methodology

Our research consist of two main steps: at first, we dealt with data collection and created job advertisement corpus. Then, we built specific linguistic resources and processed corpus applying them according to conceptual and practical framework LG [33]. To obtain the corpus, we collected 394 job postings from the business-networking website LinkedIn.com, searching for the word "data scientist". We specifically decided not to expand our search to other professionals that work in the big data sector because our main goal is paying attention to this new and apparently rare professional figure. We grasped the whole text from each advertisement and, where one exists, other information about required skills. As geographical collocation concerns, we choose to limit the research at the national and international companies located in Italy. The investigation was conducted over the period 27 December 2018–15 January 2019.

After regrouping texts in a single corpus within NooJ, we cleaned it recognising and correcting orthographic errors and accents of Italian words. By the end of this process, we created the specific linguistic resources to apply to the corpus. We set up a collection of 265 entries referred to data scientist skills: single words that include 104 Nouns (e.g. "robotics", "linguistics") and 161 multiword expressions. We referred to the multiword expressions when we found sequences of two of more simple words separated by a blank and characterized by a semantic atomicity. These expressions identify a specific concept without ambiguity: for this reason, multiword expressions are frequent in terminology or specialty lexicon. We located and annotated multiword expressions with the Part-of-Speech (PoS) tagging typically used in Italian and English: 67 Adjective + Noun (AN, e.g. predictive analysis); 33 Noun + Adjective (NA, e.g. consulenza manageriale "business consulting"); 50 Noun + Preposition + Noun (NPN, spirito di iniziativa "sense of initiative"); 8 Adjective + Adjective + Noun (AAN, e.g. artificial neural networks) and finally 13 Acronyms (e.g. PhD, NLP, ERP). As the language used for the advertisements is both Italian and English, our resources will be in both languages.

At this point, we created the specific data scientist local grammar. In order to provide a clear mapping of requirements, we considered appropriate inserting into a single graph ten auxiliary nodes, which the general structure is showed in Fig. 1. Therefore, the entries are regrouped in: Analytical skills (e.g. *estrazione di informazioni* "information mining", *sentiment analysis*); Basic skills (e.g. *categorie protette* "sheltered groups", *ambosessi* "of either sex"); Educational requirements (e.g. *Laurea in Economia*, "Degree in Economics", or qualifications as *PhD*); Effective communication (e.g. language skills as *Inglese fluente* "Fluent in English", or *capacità comunicative* "communication capabilities"); Machine learning (e.g. *reti neurali* "neural networks", *robotics*); Management knowledge (e.g. *ricerche di mercato* "market research", *advertising*); Mathematics and Statistics (e.g. *SPSS, Matlab, linear algebra*); Programming and Software development (e.g. programming language as *Python, R, Scala*); Soft skills (e.g. *problem solving, orientamento al risultato* "result-orientation"); and Visualization skills (e.g. *Tableau, interactive dashboards*).

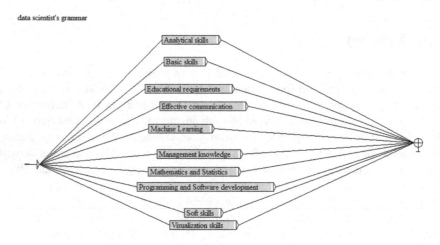

Fig. 1. Data scientist skills local grammar

5   Linguistic Analysis

The linguistic analysis applied to the corpus results in 132,097 tokens including 107, 272 word forms. According to an initial linguistic analysis, the most occurred word in the corpus is "big data": this is probably because the data scientist, as intended in the recent literature, grows with big data explosion [34]. In fact, running the ads texts the data scientist is also named "Big Data Developer", "Big Data Scientist" or "Big Data Analyst", "Big Data Engineer", so it is common to find many times this word in the job advertisements. For this reason, in a later phase of analysis, we decided to inhibit the term "big data" initially contained in the sub-grammar of Analytical skills, assuming that being in confident with big data is a condition to be consider a data scientist.

Therefore, we proceed with concordance analysis by means of NooJ in order to locate patterns gathered in the data scientist local grammar: we extracted 4,077 expressions related to data scientist skills. The list of patterns as they occur in a corpus, allows us to read and verify them in the context in which they occur in the text [35].

Scanning the concordances, we added other 11 patterns to the initial data scientist local grammar (1 single words and 10 multiword expressions) that we had not identified before in the phase of linguistic resources creation. In general, we observed a greater presence of multiword expressions (62%) in the face of fewer single words (38%) to define skills in job requirements. In particular, we found multiword expressions are divided between 24% of AN, 12% of NA, 18% of NPN, 3% of AAN 5% of Acronyms, 37% of single words (N) and 1% monorematic compounds.

Among skills clusters analysis, the most representative is Programming and Software development with 36% of entries. Then, there is the Educational skills cluster with 18% of entries; the Soft skills consists of 13,7% close to the Analytical skills with 13,5%; Machine Learning with 9,8%; Mathematics and Statistics and Visualization skills clusters with the same percentage (5,3%); Effective communication with 4,5%, Management knowledge with 3,2%, and finally, Basic skills with 2,9%. To get an idea of the relevance of each cluster on the entire job advertisement corpus see the tree map in Fig. 2.

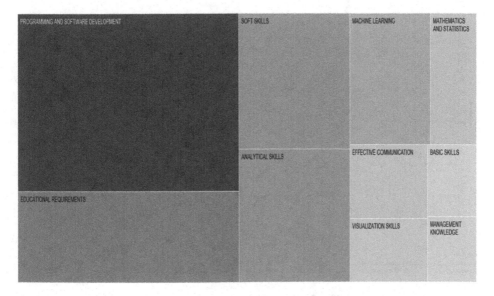

Fig. 2. Treemap of occurrences for clusters

In order to have a clearer picture of word frequency in the corpus, we have put together similar or identical words in terms of meaning. The announcements are written in natural language so that every possible variation must be taken into account. Above all, we analysed the translations from Italian to English and vice versa, such as "Degree in Economics" and "Laurea in Economia" or "Fluent in English" with "Inglese parlato". Considering other forms such as "data warehousing" with "data warehouse": the first identify the storing activity, the second represents the storage. But, if they are considered in terms of required skills, it means the same ability to cope with a data repository. Another issue concerned the difference between capital and small letters in NooJ, which in some cases was essential to disambiguate skills (e.g. SAS or R); in other cases, it appeared as duplicate in statistical analysis (e.g. "protected category" with "PROTECTED CATEGORY" or "Analisi dei dati" with "analisi dei dati").

As a result, the ten most occurred entries in the corpus are: "Python" (213), "SQL" (191), "R" (182), "Laurea in Ingegneria" (148), "algoritmi" (148), "Laurea in Informatica" (137), "Hadoop" (135), "Machine Learning" (124), "Lavoro in team" (112) and "Java" (109). Considering occurrences in each single cluster, the frequent word is *data analytics* for Analytical skills, *esperienza di lavoro* "work experience" for Basic skills, *Laurea in Ingegneria* "Degree in Engineer" for Educational skills, *Inglese* "English" as Effective Communication, a generic *machine learning* in Machine Learning, *Marketing* in Management Knowledge, *Excel* for Mathematics and Statistics, *Python* in Programming and software development, *lavoro in team* "teamwork" as Soft skills and *reports* in Visualization skills. However, the distribution of words extracted for each cluster, are illustrated in Fig. 3. The figure is created and filtered with occurrences and entries: each colour identifies details about clusters and the different size of points shows the number of occurrences, while the marks are labeled by entries.

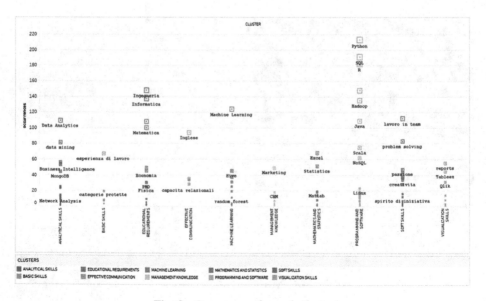

Fig. 3. Occurrences for each cluster

These results highlighted the relevance of considering a word in a local context: for instance, the single world "Ingegneria" identifies a discipline and does not presuppose a formal qualification, while if we locate it in a context as "Laurea in Ingegneria" (NPN) it means that the candidate must be graduated.

If we consider the occurrences in the corpus, we could delineate the profile of ideal candidate for a data scientist position. A solid knowledge in programming languages and relational databases is required. The university background is attributable to a Master degree or a PhD in engineering, statistics or computer science, characterized by quantitative-numerical specialization and tangible expertise in the use of analysis software, creation and optimization of models of machine learning. Problem-solving capacity, passion, creativity and sense of initiative are aspects strongly requested in the profiles. Moreover, the candidate should be actively involved in a project team and be able to interact and communicate in English profitably with co-workers and top management. Another requirement is the ability to create reports and to use visualization software as Tableau. The proven work experience is required both for junior and senior data scientist. Thereby the profile is characterized by a strong propensity for numerical and analytical thinking, with the ability to apply it to concrete and real business problems.

6 Conclusions

Using NooJ software environment, we analyse 394 job requirements extracted by LinkedIn. The main objective of our research is to explore the range of skills required to run as a data scientist in Italy. Even if many general guidelines have been suggested in literature on how becoming an ideal data scientist and they are confirmed from our research, this professional figure would present vague boundaries. This probably happens both for the novelty of profession both for the increasing number of individuals that deal with big data but that they do not necessarily have to possess all the characteristics of a data scientist.

The original feature of this study was creating specific linguistic resources for the data scientist: the use of local grammars enables the description of local context of words and reduce the ambiguity that occur for a simple keyword search. Thus, we built a data scientist local grammar with 10 sub-grammars, each one referred to a skills cluster. Our results suggested that the most required among skill clusters was the Programming and Software development one, followed by Educational requirements, Soft skills and Analytical skills. While the computer knowledge and the university qualifications reveal the highest percentages and seem to be at the base of the profile, the third and fourth clusters present both a similar percentage, so they weight as well in terms of occurrences. This leads to an interesting consideration: for companies, the capacity to analyse data and obtain relevant results equals the ability to explain them clearly. In other words, the ability to access, process and analyse data using new technologies contained in only one person already existed in the past across a wide range of industries. Instead, the innovative aspects of the data scientist of the new millennia are quite linked to the intuitive and communicative capabilities. Written and oral communication skills such as the ability to interact with the own technical and non-technical team, such as the Marketing or Sales departments; the ability to present themselves on a stage, to organize reports, presentations, and interactive dashboards to communicate insights to the managers increase the value that the data scientist provides to the business. In addition, the next step for companies probably could be to recognize also the importance of visualization skills, which are still marginal in our cluster analysis, while they help data scientist in showing outcomes to decision makers and strengthen the communicative abilities.

In conclusion, this analysis confirmed that studying the context in which the single words are inserted represents a key step in the process of information extraction by texts. In this way, we obtain a deep mining and a disambiguation of expressions used in natural language. Thus, we are able to understand better the meaning of each word insert in a sentence. In future research, it would be interesting to apply our linguistic resources created for the data scientist on different types of texts, as for example, universities' study plans to understand the relation between skills developed at universities and what companies search in candidates, matching the job offers and demand. Furthermore, this method could be used to design other innovative professions making an analysis across different business sectors and building local linguistic resources.

References

1. Nalchigar, S., Yu, E.: Business-driven data analytics: a conceptual modeling framework. Data Knowl. Eng. **117**, 359–372 (2018)
2. Oussous, A., Benjelloun, F.Z., Lahcen, A.A., Belfkih, S.: Big data technologies: a survey. J. King Saud Univ.-Comput. Inf. Sci. **30**(4), 431–448 (2018)
3. Storey, V.C., Song, I.Y.: Big data technologies and management: what conceptual modeling can do. Data Knowl. Eng. **108**, 50–67, 52 (2017)
4. Davenport, T.: Big Data at Work: Dispelling the Myths, Uncovering the Opportunities. Harvard Business Review Press, Boston (2014)
5. Van der Aalst, W.M.P.: Data scientist: the engineer of the future. In: Mertins, K., Bénaben, F., Poler, R., Bourrières, J.-P. (eds.) Enterprise Interoperability VI. PIC, vol. 7, pp. 13–26. Springer, Cham (2014). https://doi.org/10.1007/978-3-319-04948-9_2
6. Song, I.Y., Zhu, Y.: Big data and data science: what should we teach? Expert Syst. **33**(4), 364–373 (2016)
7. Goddard, C.: Semantic Analysis: a Practical Introduction. Oxford University Press, Oxford (2011)
8. The economist: the world's most valuable resource is no longer oil, but data. https://www.economist.com/leaders/2017/05/06/the-worlds-most-valuable-resource-is-no-longer-oil-but-data. 6 May 2017
9. McKinsey: The age of Analytics: competing in a data-driven world (2016). https://www.mckinsey.com/ ~ /media/mckinsey/business%20functions/mckinsey%20analytics/our%20insights/the%20age%20of%20analytics%20competing%20in%20a%20data%20driven%20world/mgi-the-age-of-analytics-executive-summary.ashx
10. Gartner: data and analytics leadership vision for 2017 (2017). https://www.gartner.com/binaries/content/assets/events/keywords/business-intelligence/bie18i/gartner_data-analytics_research-note_da-leadership-vision_2016.pdf
11. IBM: The Quant Crunch. How the demand for data science skills is disrupting the job market (2017). https://www.ibm.com/analytics/us/en/technology/data-science/quant-crunch.html

12. Davenport, T.H., Patil, D.J.: Data scientist. Harv. Bus. Rev. **90**(5), 70–76, 72 (2012)
13. Agasisti, T., Bowers, A.J.: Data analytics and decision making in education: towards the educational data scientist as a key actor in schools and higher education institutions. In: Handbook of Contemporary Education Economics, p. 184 (2017)
14. Granville, V.: Developing Analytic Talent: Becoming a Data Scientist. Wiley, Hoboken (2014)
15. Fisher, D., DeLine, R., Czerwinski, M., Drucker, S.: Interactions with big data analytics. Interactions **19**(3), 50–59, 57 (2012)
16. Kandel, S., Paepcke, A., Hellerstein, J.M., Heer, J.: Enterprise data analysis and visualization: an interview study. IEEE Trans. Vis. Comput. Graph. **12**, 2917–2926 (2012)
17. Balbi, S., Di Meglio, E.: A text mining strategy based on local contexts of words. In: Proceedings of the JADT, vol. 4, pp. 79–87 (2004)
18. Iezzi, D.F., Mastrangelo, M., Sarlo, S.: Text clustering based on centrality measures: an application on job advertisements. In: 11es Journées Internationales d'analyse statistique des données textuelles, pp. 515–524 (2012)
19. Amato, F., et al.: Challenge: processing web texts for classifying job offers. In: 2015 IEEE International Conference Semantic Computing (ICSC), pp. 460–463. IEEE (2015)
20. Bsiri, S., Geierhos, M., Ringlstetter, C.: Structuring job search via local grammars. Adv. Nat. Lang. Process. Appl. Res. Comput. Sci. (RCS) **33**, 201–212 (2008)
21. Loth, R., Battistelli, D., Chaumartin, F.R., De Mazancourt, H., Minel, J.L., Vinckx, A.: Linguistic information extraction for job ads (SIRE project). In: Adaptivity, Personalization and Fusion of Heterogeneous Information, pp. 222–224. Le centre de hautes etudes internationales d'informatique documentaire (2010)
22. Karakatsanis, I., et al.: Data mining approach to monitoring the requirements of the job market: a case study. Inf. Syst. **65**, 1–6 (2017)
23. Kim, J., Moen, W., Warger, E.: Competencies required for digital curation: an analysis of job advertisements. Int. J. Digit. Curation **8**(1), 66–83 (2013)
24. Gardiner, A., Aasheim, C., Rutner, P., Williams, S.: Skill requirements in big data: a content analysis of job advertisements. J. Comput. Inf. Syst. **58**(4), 374–384 (2018)
25. Gross, M.: On the failure of generative grammar. Language **55**, 859–885 (1979)
26. Gross, M.: Lexicon-grammar: the representation of compound words. In: Proceedings of the 11th Conference on Computational Linguistics, pp. 1–6, 4. Association for Computational Linguistics, August 1986
27. Silberztein, M.: NooJ: a linguistic annotation system for corpus processing. In: Proceedings of HLT/EMNLP on Interactive Demonstrations, pp. 10–11. Association for Computational Linguistics (2005)
28. Silberztein, M.: NooJ Computational Devices. Formalising Natural Languages with NooJ, pp. 1–13 (2013)
29. Elia, A., Monteleone, M., Esposito, F.: Les Cahiers du dictionnaire. Dictionnaires électroniques et dictionnaires en ligne, Les Cahiers du dictionnaire **6**, 43–62 (2014)
30. Esposito, F., Elia, A.: NooJ local grammars for innovative startup language. In: Barone, L., Monteleone, M., Silberztein, M. (eds.) NooJ 2016. CCIS, vol. 667, pp. 64–73. Springer, Cham (2016). https://doi.org/10.1007/978-3-319-55002-2_6
31. Esposito, F.: Semantic technologies for business decision support. Discovering meaning with NLP applications, Ph.D. thesis (2017). http://elea.unisa.it/bitstreamhandle/105562486 tesi%20F.%20Esposito.pdf?sequence=1&isAllowed=y

32. della Volpe, M., Elia, A., Esposito, F.: Semantic predicates in the business language. In: Mbarki, S., Mourchid, M., Silberztein, M. (eds.) NooJ 2017. CCIS, vol. 811, pp. 108–116. Springer, Cham (2018). https://doi.org/10.1007/978-3-319-73420-0_9
33. Vietri, S.: Lessico-grammatica dell'italiano. Metodi, descrizioni e applicazioni. Turin, UTET (2004)
34. McAfee, A., Brynjolfsson, E., Davenport, T.H., Patil, D.J., Barton, D.: Big data: the management revolution. Harv. Bus. Rev. **90**(10), 60–68 (2012)
35. Wynne, M.: Searching and concordancing. Corpus Linguist. Int. Handb. **1**, 706–737 (2008)

Mining Entrepreneurial Commitment in University Communication: Evidence from Italy

Maddalena della Volpe[1]([✉]) [ID] and Francesca Esposito[2] [ID]

[1] Department of Business, Management and Innovation System,
University of Salerno, Fisciano, Italy
mdellavolpe@unisa.it
[2] Department of Political and Communication Sciences,
University of Salerno, Fisciano, Italy
fraesposito@unisa.it

Abstract. In recent years, the study of language has assumed a central role within the representation of complex systems, triggering a greater interdisciplinarity among separate fields. Thus, new perspectives of analysis are stimulated: using computational linguistic tools to evaluate the impact of language in specific contexts and to understand how social and economic phenomena are developed. Adopting the Lexicon-Grammar theoretical framework, we used NooJ Application to process a corpus gathered with free texts from official universities' websites in order to explore the hidden intentions in Italian universities' web communication. Moreover, we created local grammars with single and compound words, associated to different missions of the university: teaching, research and third mission. The outputs demonstrate that teaching topic is the most common emerging from universities' web communication. As well as organizational aspects, renewing universities purpose implies the ability to communicate effectively the strategic goals, defining the university's role in the society and, meanwhile, aiming to engage several players.

Keywords: University mission · Entrepreneurial University ·
Lexicon-Grammar · Corpus processing · NooJ

1 Introduction

In the *learning society* [1] growing abilities to develop and exploit cognitive, creative and ethical potentials become a pin. According to this, universities, as a place of training and research have to face unprecedented challenges in the definition of their role, purpose, organization and scope [2]. The interdependence among economy, culture and communication needs creative, responsible and thinking hubs, places of comparison, open to new challenges and, at the same time, closed to their original but renewed purposes. It is thus necessary to reactivate a deep reflection on the meaning and future of the university, creating a link between research, teaching, and economic development [3]. Becoming an active agent in the social and economic development of a country, the university must interact closely with industries and governments;

© Springer Nature Switzerland AG 2020
H. Fehri et al. (Eds.): NooJ 2019, CCIS 1153, pp. 91–100, 2020.
https://doi.org/10.1007/978-3-030-38833-1_8

pursuing its *third mission,* university is no longer "an ivory tower isolated from society" [4]. Reaching this goal means creating flows, from inside to outside of universities and the other way around, made of knowledge, people, activities; it means managing relationships and communicating with stakeholders; it means to become a driver of innovation [5]; it means to contribute and provide leadership for the creation of entrepreneurial thinking and actions. This imposes an organizational transformation of university. Once defining the aims, it is necessary to communicate them clearly to the stakeholders, stimulating their involvement. Indeed, supported by an effective communication, universities could redesign their role in the society more effectively. Starting from these considerations, we analysed Italian universities' official website grasping the commitment of each university in communicating its missions: teaching, research and third mission.

In the first section of this paper, we present our linguistic approach to corpus processing. Adopting the Lexicon-Grammar theoretical framework, we used NooJ Application to process corpus and to assess universities' dedication in communicating their intentions. We focus our analysis on English compound words, frozen expressions and collocations. In the second section, we deepen the concept of Entrepreneurial University (EU) in the literature analyzing definition, purpose and elements. In the third section, we explain the methodology used for corpus processing and lexical analysis. We gathered 91 texts from the official websites of each Italian universities and we merged them in a unique corpus. In the fourth and fifth sections, we described and collected the results of our research, starting from the lexical analysis. Subsequently, we applied a statistical analysis by NooJ in order to evaluate the frequency and relevance of terms in the texts. Finally, we conclude proposing a reflection on Italian universities moving from communication activities to the real entrepreneurial commitment.

2 Communicating the Entrepreneurial Commitment

The university that involves extension from ideas to practical activities, capitalizing knowledge, organizing new entities and managing risks is an EU [6]. The model of the EU is currently recognized as a major driver for self-development and innovation, and as an appropriate response to succeeding in highly turbulent and unpredictable economies [7]. The EU most representative models, as Stanford University, MIT, Cambridge University, have for years enhanced the role of innovation, commercialization of research results and entrepreneurship education. Over the last years, the consensus on adopting a more entrepreneurial orientation in knowledge producing institutions is growing.

In addition to the organizational and managerial aspects, another element becomes increasingly strategic for universities: communicating their strategic vision in terms of culture, values and mission. Universities have to communicate their intentions positively and enthusiastically [8], according to "their core elements, their adaptation processes and organizational changes, their internal and external strategies, their different types of entrepreneurial activities and academic characteristics, the environmental pressures, and others" [9]. These communication activities, in line with the social Web development, could support not only university's staff, students and researchers, but also build a bridge with external actors. Also in Kirby [10], communication is a strategic action to endorse an entrepreneurial and positive environment. He identifies eight actions corresponding to several activities that the university must carry out to fulfil its role. What emerges strongly from this study is the need to clarify the strategy and communicate it inside and outside the university. However, the university cultural conservatism and the entrepreneurial mindset lack act as barriers to this openness. In our opinion, encouraging a dynamic entrepreneurial environment starts from the communication of intentions. While in literature much evidence evaluates exclusively the organizational renovation and their influence on universities missions, we propose an original method of analysis to understand the universities' ability to transfer entrepreneurial intentions through the universities' website communication.

3 The Lexicon-Grammar Approach to University Communication

Universities commitment in adopting an entrepreneurial approach is often reflected in knowledge transfer activities: spin-offs [11, 12], patents [13, 14], startups [15], science parks [16] and other indicators. Otherwise, university's commitment also consists in the ability to communicate these activities. The language used, oral and written, can inform and hide real intentions, stimulating acting and doing [17, 18]. Some scholars investigated the universities commitment in communicating entrepreneurial intentions.

Riviezzo, Napolitano and Garofano [19] propose an analysis about university communication and, in particular, refer to exploring EU orientation. These authors discuss about the behaviour of Italian universities in communicating their third mission by applying the analytical framework of Critical Discourse Analysis (CDA). Their results suggest that the third mission of the university does not represent a central topic within the discourse; its role is very limited, at least in terms of statistical-lexical results. Loi and Di Guardo [20] focus on the interpretation of the third mission by the universities and analyse the linguistic and semantic content of 75 Italian universities statements, in relation to key words and expressions used. They conclude that the third mission, as referred to the development of an EU, is not embedded in the Italian universities. In order to measure knowledge transfer activities, Woltmann and Alka-ersig [21] propose text mining and statistical learning tools to analyse texts extracted from corporate websites and academic publications. These authors affirm that patents, license agreements or similar represent a small fragment of the knowledge transfer occurring between universities and industries: there are other many occurrences referred to the commercial use of knowledge.

To perform our analysis we applied the Lexicon-Grammar (LG) theoretical and practical framework by Gross [22]. The LG approach was developed at the end of the Sixties. Gross had adopted for a long time the theoretical and methodological positions of the generational-transformational grammar, from which he had distanced himself. In fact, he was convinced that the generational-transformational grammar clearly distinguished between syntactic and semantic component of a linguistic system, neglecting too much the latter to the advantage of the former. On the contrary, according to Gross, the description of a language could not be achieved disregarding lexicon. Hence, the idea of developing a research approach meant to take into consideration the semantic-lexical aspects of a given linguistic system in addition to the structural characteristics. As for the units of analysis, Gross was convinced that one should not take into account the single words, but the elementary sentences in which they occur.

In particular, we focused on compound words: Gross considered them "the bulk of the lexicon of languages" [23]. They are usually built from the vocabulary of simple words by means of grammatical rules that may involve grammatical words. By definition, their meaning is non-compositional. Compound forms have an institutional meaning, established by use of language: differently, if we take their single components, the meaning is not clear and specific. Compound nouns can be described in terms of the sequence of their grammatical categories. With regard to university's missions, we can consider compound, words such as *higher education* (Adj N), *research project* (N N), *spirit of entrepreneurship* (N of N). Such lexical forms define a concept: compounds behave in a very singular way and, probably, each case should be evaluated separately. LG provides a complete description of natural language lexical and grammatical structures, providing high-quality information from texts and understandings of their semantic contexts. This will be applied by the authors of this paper in further studies on business communication. Add to it, its impact on Italian language analysis and classification has already been coped with in several publications [24–27].

4   Methodology

We examined 91 Italian universities, using the list published by the Italian Ministry of Education, through the CINECA website (http://cercauniversita.cineca.it). We analysed 61 public universities, 19 private universities and 11 virtual universities, excluding doctoral schools; 33 universities are in the Northern side of Italy (36%), 32 in the Centre side (35%) and 26 in the Southern side and islands (29%). Using the official website and the dedicated sections, we extracted every text in English used by universities to communicate mission, vision, objectives, profile and history, culture and values. We preferred to analyse English version because we gave more relevance to the international dimension of communication activities.

After choosing the type of texts to analyse, we cleaned and normalized them. Thus, we compiled a corpus composed by the 91 texts, one for each university. In these terms, corpus processing through the NooJ Application [28–30] allows to analyse university language structures and its uses. To perform texts analysis we used the NooJ English Simple Word Electronic Dictionary (NESWED) created for NooJ by Vietri and Monteleone [31]. It contains inflectional tools and dictionaries of single nouns, verbs and other part of speech (such as prepositions, adverb, and others) in English.

In addition, we created local grammars with terms that could occur inside teaching, research and third mission topics. As for teaching, we included all the terms related to competencies, knowledge, abilities and skills gained through education (i.e. transversal skills, cultural skills). Moreover, education programs have been included (i.e. degree courses, study programs). With respect to research, we considered all the terms referring to the generation and developments of new knowledge, the international dimension of research, the scientific community's members (i.e. researchers, research groups) innovation and technological development (i.e. social innovation, innovative proposal). As for third mission, we collected all the terms referring to the commercialization of new knowledge (i.e. technology transfer, knowledge transfer) and the creation of new companies (i.e. startups or spin-off development). Furthermore, we included the contribution by universities to the growth of socio-economic environment (i.e. economic development, local community, local development and civil society) and the link toward the business world (i.e. enterprises, business network).

5   Linguistic Analysis

After creating the corpus, we processed it with NooJ. The first lexical analysis based on English linguistic resources presents these results: 401,297 characters, 72,987 tokens, 60,363 word forms, 56,559 different annotations. The most relevant tokens are: *university* (885), *research* (355), *students* (346), *teaching* (201), *courses* (168), *training* (145), *activities* (144), *education* (143), and *faculty* (122). We immediately notice that the commitment in communicating entrepreneurial intentions is scant: entries as *entrepreneurship* (N), *entrepreneurial* (Adj), *entrepreneurs* (N) appear overall 10 times in the corpus. Discovering the concordances, their compound forms are even less: entrepreneurial orientation (1), entrepreneurial initiatives (1), and entrepreneurial association (1). No more encouraging data came from the frequency of the term spin-off companies (2). Finally, the term startups or start-ups appears in 3 cases.

In this phase of analysis, terms cannot be associated yet to specific contexts, because there is not a NooJ English dictionary of compound words. In fact, when we refer to a technical area, we typically use specific sequence of words as multi-word units or frozen expressions. Using compound words, we are able to recognize more precisely the notions linked to the terms. For this reason, and in order to recognize a special lexicon referred to teaching, research and third mission, we built local grammars. For instance, the single word "development" (N) appears several times in the corpus, but it acquires different meaning if we evaluate all the matches of this word: *economic development* is referred to third mission topic; *technological development* is referred to research activities. Therefore, we associated the first compound word to the third mission semantic field and the second one to the research semantic field. Thus, the variation of forms contained in the grammars were fixed manually and included the plural and singular forms, where needed. Analyzing manually the concordance in the corpus, we found about 151 words: 49 that can be associated to teaching field, 41 to research (of which only one is a single word) and 61 to third mission (of which 4 are single words). According to the concept of semantic expansion, we considered also some *collocations*: engagement with students (teaching), relationship with the students (teaching), collaboration with companies (third mission), and relationship with the business (third mission).

The local grammars are used to capture in a natural way the positional features "such as the place of determiners and adjectives on the left of their noun" [32] in the corpus. Successively, in order to distinguish the three university missions in the corpus, we considered that it is appropriate to group local grammars into three nodes. They are inserted into a single graph, the general structure of which is shown in Fig. 1. The three nodes hide an auxiliary node with single words (N) and compound words (Adj N; NN; N of N; N with N) tracked down in concordance analysis (Figs. 2, 3 and 4).

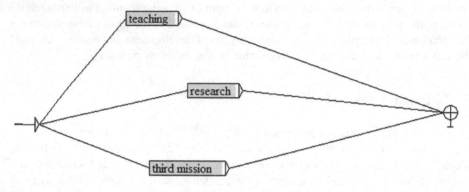

Fig. 1. Local grammars grouping

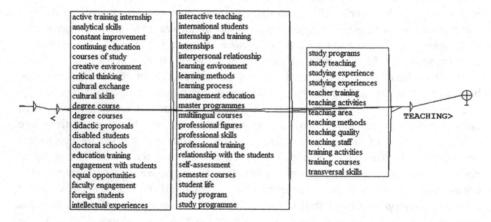

Fig. 2. Teaching local grammar

Once creating the grammars, we proceeded to a descriptive and statistical analysis of the terms distribution within the corpus. First, the occurrences found in the corpus are 656. The outputs reveal that the most relevant topic is teaching with 39.8% of terms occurring in the corpus. The topic research has 33.4%, while third mission has 26.8%. The compound word "degree courses" is the most frequent in the corpus, with 70 occurrences and a 10.7% with reference to all the recognized terms. It appears in 25 texts (27.4%) and is also the most frequent word for the teaching topic. Meanwhile, the

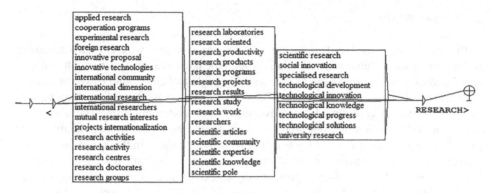

Fig. 3. Research local grammar

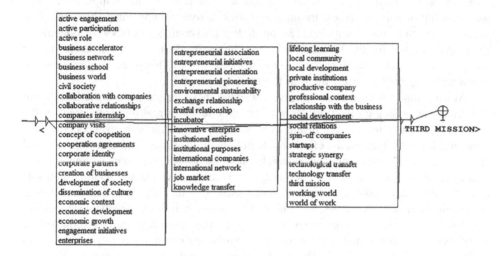

Fig. 4. Third mission local grammar

first term occurring for research topic is the single word "researchers": it occurs 35 times in the corpus (5.4%) and appears in 22 texts (24.2%). Referring to the third mission, the most recurrent word is "world of work" with 20 occurrences (3%); it is present in 16 texts (17.6%). Other most frequent words are: research activities (4.4%), scientific research (3.8%), internships (3.5%), research projects (2.9%), third mission (2.4%), foreign students (2%), international students (2%), teaching staff (1.8%), technology transfer (1.8%), teaching activities (1.7%), enterprises (1.5%), international research (1.5%), private institutions (1.4%), training activities (1.4%), business world (1.2%), equal opportunities (1.2%), international dimension (1.2%).

6   Conclusions

In this paper, using the NooJ linguistic software environment, we analysed a corpus of Italian universities web communication through the texts available on each official web site. Moreover, we created local grammars with single and compound terms, associated to different missions of the university. The output demonstrate that the teaching topic is the most common emerging from universities' web communication. The discussion about the third mission and research is lower. According to occurrences analysis, the most frequent compound word for teaching is *degree courses*. In this sense, the official university websites seem to be mostly useful to engage students and collect matriculations. The word *researchers* represents the research topic, giving more attention to the important role played by human resources in the research activities and research projects development. Then, the third mission is represented by the word *world of work*: as the building of a bridge towards future jobs is considered crucial, we can note that this opens also a channel towards companies. The terms as internships, internships and training, training courses, training activities, active training internships could be placed in the third mission group [33], but Italian universities and ANVUR documents (National Agency for the Evaluation of the University System and Research) do not recognise these activities in relation to the working world. This is the very reason why we were compelled to insert them in the teaching group.

At this point, we could ask ourselves: whether these results witness the inability to communicate strategic intentions or whether they reveal a real disengagement of the university in renewing its role inside society. We believe that both answers conceal a yearning for truth. Despite the efforts made in Italy on the third mission recognition and the redefinition of teaching and research, in order to adopt a more entrepreneurial strategy, universities are far from defining a clear strategic vision and relating their role inside social and economic development. Assuming that the intentions to change academic model are recognized and pursued by universities, the subsequent step should be communicating this commitment clearly to the interested parties (companies, institutions, university staff and others), thus involving them in university activities and stimulating their participation. This is absent in our analysis.

Regarding the limitations of our study, in the construction of the local grammars for the topic recognition, we based ourselves on the lexical resources of the collected texts. Having gathered new textual data and recognizing other forms of linguistic expressions, we could have obtained more precise and complete results. Future research could be focused on the expansion of language entities recognition to deepen other aspects of universities' communication.

References

1. Keep, E., Mayhew, K.: Towards a learning society-definition and measurement. Policy Stud. **17**(3), 215–232 (2007). https://doi.org/10.1080/01442879608423708
2. OECD: Guiding framework for entrepreneurial universities. European Commission, pp. 1–54, 1 (2012)

3. Etzkowitz, H.: The evolution of the entrepreneurial university. Int. J. Technol. Glob. 1(1), 64–77 (2004). https://doi.org/10.1504/IJTG.2004.004551
4. Etzkowitz, H.: Innovation Lodestar: the entrepreneurial university in a stellar knowledge firmament. Technol. Forecast. Soc. Chang. 123, 122–129 (2017). https://doi.org/10.1016/j.techfore.2016.04.026
5. Autio, E., Kenney, M., Mustar, P., Siegel, D., Wright, M.: Entrepreneurial innovation: the importance of context. Res. Policy 43(7), 1097–1108 (2014). https://doi.org/10.1016/j.respol.2014.01.015
6. Etzkowitz, H.: Anatomy of the entrepreneurial university. Soc. Sci. Inf. 52(3), 486–511 (2013). https://doi.org/10.1177/0539018413485832
7. Hannon, P.D.: Why is the entrepreneurial university important? J. Innov. Manag. JIM 1(2), 10–17 (2013)
8. Birley, S.: Universities, academics, and spinout companies: lessons from the imperial. Int. J. Entrepreneurship Educ. 1(1), 1–21 (2002)
9. Guerrero, M., Kirby, D.A., Urbano, D.: A literature review on entrepreneurial universities: an institutional approach. Autonomous University of Barcelona, Business Economics Department, Working Paper Series, No. 06/8, p. 10, SSRN (2006). https://ssrn.com/abstract= 1838615
10. Kirby, D.A.: Creating entrepreneurial universities in the UK: applying entrepreneurship theory to practice. J. Technol. Transf. 31(5), 599–603 (2005). https://doi.org/10.1007/s10961-006-9061-4
11. Link, A.N., Scott, J.T.: Opening the ivory tower's door: an analysis of the determinants of the formation of U.S. university spin-off companies. Res. Policy 34(7), 1106–1112 (2005). https://doi.org/10.1016/j.respol.2005.05.015
12. Walter, A., Auer, M., Ritter, T.: The impact of network capabilities and entrepreneurial orientation on university spin-off performance. J. Bus. Ventur. 21(4), 541–567 (2006). https://doi.org/10.1016/j.jbusvent.2005.02.005
13. Gibb, A., Haskins, G., Robertson, I.: Leading the entrepreneurial university, meeting the entrepreneurial development needs of higher education institutions. Policy paper, National Centre for Entrepreneurship in Education, (2009). Available at http://eureka.sbs.ox.ac.uk/4861/1/EULP_-_LEADERS_PAPER_final_dec_19.pdf
14. Guerzoni, M., Taylor Aldridge, T., Audretsch, D.B., Desai, S.: A new industry creation and originality: insight from the funding sources of university patents. Res. Policy 43(10), 1697–1706 (2014). https://doi.org/10.1016/j.respol.2014.07.009
15. Audretsch, D.B., Lehmann, E.E., Warning, S.: University spillovers and new firm location. Res. Policy 34(7), 1113–1122 (2005). https://doi.org/10.1016/j.respol.2005.05.009
16. Link, A.N., Scott, J.T.: U.S. science parks: the diffusion of an innovation and its effects on the academic missions of universities. Int. J. Ind. Organ. 21(9), 1323–1356 (2003). https://doi.org/10.1016/s0167-7187(03)00085-7
17. Austin, J.L.: How to do things with words. the William James lectures delivered at Harvard University in 1955. J. Symb. Log. 36, 513 (1962)
18. Gee, J.P.: An Introduction to Discourse Analysis: Theory and Method. Routledge, Abingdon (2004)
19. Riviezzo, A., Napolitano, M. R., Garofano, A.: From words to deeds: are Italian universities changing their discursive practices to promote entrepreneurship. Dev. Shap. Grow. Entrepreneurship 126–153 (2015). https://doi.org/10.4337/9781784713584.00014
20. Loi, M., Di Guardo, M.C.: The third mission of universities: an investigation of the espoused values. Sci. Public Policy 42(6), 855–870 (2015). https://doi.org/10.1093/scipol/scv012

21. Woltmann, S., Alkærsig, L.: Tracing knowledge transfer from universities to industry: a text mining approach. In: 77th Annual meeting of the Academy of Management, Atlanta, United States, Academy of Management Annual Meeting, Academy of Management (2017)
22. Gross, M.: On the failure of generative grammar. Language **55**, 859–885 (1979)
23. Gross, M.: Lexicon-grammar: the representation of compound words. In: Proceedings of the 11th conference on Computational linguistics, pp. 1–6, 4. Association for Computational Linguistics, August 1986
24. Elia, A., Monteleone, M., Esposito, F.: Les Cahiers du dictionnaire. Dictionnaires électroniques et dictionnaires en ligne, Les Cahiers du dictionnaire **6**, 43–62 (2014)
25. Esposito, F., Elia, A.: NooJ local grammars for innovative startup language. In: Barone, L., Monteleone, M., Silberztein, M. (eds.) NooJ 2016. CCIS, vol. 667, pp. 64–73. Springer, Cham (2016). https://doi.org/10.1007/978-3-319-55002-2_6
26. Esposito, F.: Semantic technologies for business decision support. Discovering meaning with NLP Applications, Ph.D. thesis (2017). http://elea.unisa.it/bitstreamhandle/105562486t esi%20F.%20Esposito.pdf?sequence=1&isAllowed=y
27. della Volpe, M., Elia, A., Esposito, F.: Semantic predicates in the business language. In: Mbarki, S., Mourchid, M., Silberztein, M. (eds.) NooJ 2017. CCIS, vol. 811, pp. 108–116. Springer, Cham (2018). https://doi.org/10.1007/978-3-319-73420-0_9
28. Silberztein, M.: NOOJ Manual (2003). http://www.nooj4nlp.net/NooJManual.pdf
29. Silberztein, M.: Corpus linguistics and semantic desambiguation. In: Maiello, G., Pellegrino, R. (eds.) Database, Corpora, Insegnamenti Linguistici. Linguistica, 63, Schena Editore/Alain Baudry et C.ie, pp. 397–410 (2012)
30. Silberztein, M.: NooJ computational devices. In: Koeva, S., Mesfar, S., Silberztein, M. (eds.) Formalising Natural Languages with NooJ 2013: Selected Papers from the NooJ 2013 International Conference (Saarbrucken, Germany), pp. 1–14. Cambridge Scholars Publishing, Newcastle (2013)
31. Vietri, S., Monteleone, M.: The NooJ english dictionary. In: Formalising Natural Languages with NooJ 2013 Selected Papers from the NooJ 2013 International Conference 12 BackChapman Street, Newcastle upon Tyne, NE6 2XX, pp. 69–86. Cambridge Scholars Publishing (2014)
32. Gross, M.: The Construction of Local Grammars. Finite-state language processing, p. 329, 2 (1997)
33. della Volpe, M., Siano, A., Vollero, A., Esposito, F.: Exploring curricular internships in Italy: towards entrepreneurial universities. Int. Bus. Res. **9**(9), 150–167 (2016). https://doi.org/10.5539/ibr.v9n9p150

Disambiguation for Arabic Question-Answering System

Sondes Dardour[✉], Héla Fehri, and Kais Haddar

MIRACL Laboratory, University of Sfax, Sfax, Tunisia
dardour.sondes@yahoo.com,
hela.fehri@yahoo.fr, kais.haddar@yahoo.fr

Abstract. Because of the increasing amounts of Arabic content on the Internet and the increasing demand for information, Arabic question answering (QA) systems are gaining great importance. Nevertheless, automatic answering of questions in natural language is one of natural language processing's most challenging tasks. In this paper, we address the issue of processing Arabic Question Answering in the medical domain where there are several specific challenges. The main challenge in dealing with medical field in Arabic language is the need to resolve ambiguity. This issue, though, was not thoroughly studied in related works. Therefore, our QA system requires disambiguation solution to select the correct meaning in order to return the correct answer. The goal of this work is to resolve Arabic-related ambiguities as well as medical-related ambiguities. To achieve this goal, we use dictionaries and transducers using NooJ platform to answer any factoid or complex medical question. Experimentations of the disambiguation task of our Arabic medical question answering system show interesting results.

Keywords: Disambiguation · Question Answering · Arabic language · Medical domain · Dictionary · Transducer · NooJ

1 Introduction

With the expanding growth of medical electronic documents, there is a particularly great and growing demand for Question-Answering (QA) systems, which can effectively and efficiently aid users in their medical information search. The aim of QA is to automatically extract a precise answer to a natural language question. Nevertheless, natural language is ambiguous.

Ambiguity is a critical challenge in any QA system due to the nature of idiosyncrasy of natural language question and the used corpus. Therefore, ambiguity occurs in QA because a word can be interpreted in multiple ways depending on the context in which it appears. However, not all ambiguities can be easily processed and some of them require a deep linguistic processing. In QA, ambiguity can cause confusion in interpretation of the answer or the user's question, and then affects negatively the performance of the QA system. Therefore, a QA system needs disambiguation solutions to improve its performance.

© Springer Nature Switzerland AG 2020
H. Fehri et al. (Eds.): NooJ 2019, CCIS 1153, pp. 101–111, 2020.
https://doi.org/10.1007/978-3-030-38833-1_9

To our knowledge, the suggested Arabic QA systems are so limited either in terms of the types of questions they are designed to answer or in terms of their performance. Furthermore, most of the attention in Arabic QA has been paid to answering factoid questions, in which the answer is a single word or a short phrase [1].

In this paper, we propose a new method to handle Arabic medical questions (factoid and complex questions). Moreover, our method overcomes the ambiguity, an issue that has not been appropriately addressed in existing Arabic QA systems.

Our paper deals with a brief overview of related works in Sect. 2. Our proposed method is presented in Sect. 3. Section 4 deals with the experimentation carried out to evaluate the efficiency of our disambiguation process. Finally, Sect. 5 draws the main contributions and proposes further perspectives.

2   Related Works

The problem of QA has been studied in the field of Information Retrieval (IR) since the mid-1990s [2]. However, unlike IR, the QA system returns most accurate answer to a natural language question instead of a large number of documents [3, 4].

As shown in Fig. 1, a typical QA system consists of three main modules [5]: question analysis, passage retrieval and answer extraction. Different QA systems may use different implementation for each module [6, 7].

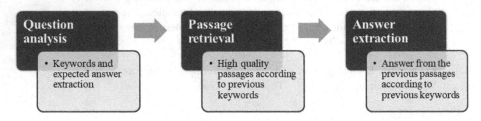

Fig. 1. General architecture of a QA system

Nowadays, QA systems do not always provide an exact answer. Ask.com [8] returns documents or sometimes exact answer, START [9] returns documents, a mixture of graphs, statistics or sometimes exact answer. Wolfram Alpha [10] also returns mixture of sources.

Building new QA systems for Arabic language have gained much interest in the community of Arabic Natural Language Processing (NLP). In what follows, we cite some of these systems.

QASAL [11, 12] tackled factoid questions (i.e., questions that have named entity answers) using NooJ local grammars. Experiments have been conducted and showed that for a test data of 100 questions the system obtained 94% as precision and 100% as recall. According to the small test-set size (100 questions), their experiments cannot be considered as reliable results in terms of comparison.

AQuASys [13] is an Arabic QA system which is composed of three modules: question analysis, sentences filtering and answer extraction. The authors segmented the question into interrogative noun, question's verb, and keywords. The reported performance obtained 66.25% precision, 97.5% recall and an F-measure of 78.89%.

Lemaza [14] is an attempt for building an Arabic QA which processes Why-questions. The system is composed of four main components: question analysis, document preprocessing, document/passage retrieval and answer extraction. The last component, answer extraction, employs Rhetorical Structure Theory to extract the exact answer.

The system of [15] and [16] are medical QA systems for Arabic language. These systems focus only on factoid questions. These two systems extract the focus and the topic of the question, and extract named entities. The system of [15] classifies the questions into person, location, viruses, diseases, treatment and organization.

From literature reviews, we can confirm that most Arabic QA systems guarantee factoid questions to be analyzed. Nevertheless, the issue of answering complicated questions has been resolved by few researches. Additionally, there are few works that have incorporated semantic analysis and handled the Arabic language medical field, making it essential to develop a new Arabic QA system.

3 Proposed Method

The challenges shown in the previous studies make clear the need for new method to deal with Arabic medical QA. In addition, the majority of Arabic QA systems are based on a superficial analysis of factoid questions (i.e. who, where, how much/many, when and what). The originality of our method lies in the disambiguation of factoid and complex questions (i.e. how to and why). In our proposal, questions and medical text are gathered and studied to define the disambiguation patterns. These patterns are transformed into transducers. Furthermore, questions will be processed using morphological grammar, syntactic grammars and dictionaries in order to get some useful keywords. These keywords allow the extraction of the correct answer.

In what follows, we will detail the construction of our corpus and the disambiguation process.

3.1 Corpus Study

We collected questions from several sources, namely, frequently asked questions (FAQ), discussion forums and some questions translated from Text REtrieval Conference (TREC). Currently, we gathered 350 questions which contain seven categories (see Table 1) and for each question we collected Arabic medical text on the internet.

According to our study, the collected questions showed us the existence of ambiguity. Indeed, if we solve this problem, our system will be more pertinent compared to existing Arabic QA systems.

Table 1. Collected questions

Question type	ما What	متى When	أين Where	من Who	كم How many/much	كيف How	لماذا Why
Number	85	53	42	38	45	39	48

3.2 Specific Arabic Difficulties Disambiguation

Specific Arabic difficulties consist in its complexity that needs special processing. One of these difficulties is the lack of short vowels (i.e. kasra, damma, fatha), which leads to more ambiguous situations than any other language (see Table 2). This ambiguity can be determined just by relevant data which is contextual feature.

Table 2. Disambiguation patterns for questions

	Example 1	Example 2
Question	متى يولد الدماغ الطاقة؟	متى يولد الجنين؟
Translation	When does the brain **generate** electricity?	When a baby is **born**?
Extracted rule	متى <V+Sense=« generate »> دماغ؟ <N> Answer type = « Time » <==	متى <V+Sense=« born »> جنين؟ Answer type = « Age » <==

As shown above, the lack of short vowels in the verb "يولد" make some ambiguities. In the example 1, the verb has the sense of "generate" and the sense of "born" in the example 2. To resolve this problem, the extracted rules are translated into transducer (see Fig. 2 for the example 1).

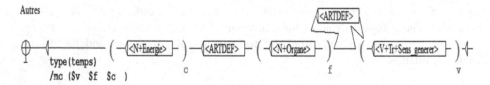

Fig. 2. Extract of the transducer for the question "When does the brain generate electricity?

As shown in Fig. 2, the ambiguous word is associated with semantic feature to identify the sense of the entry (sens_generer) because it is followed by an organ "دماغ" (brain).

Arabic language is exceedingly derivational and inflectional. Therefore, the morphology of an Arabic word is complex because a word token can replace a whole sentence in other languages. Let's take the example of the question "أيمكننا منع الجلطة؟" (*Can we prevent the clot?*). The expression "Can we" can be expressed in one Arabic word "أيمكننا" which includes the verb *can* "يمكن", the prefix "أ" and the pronoun *we* "نا". To resolve this problem, we build a morphological grammar (see Fig. 3).

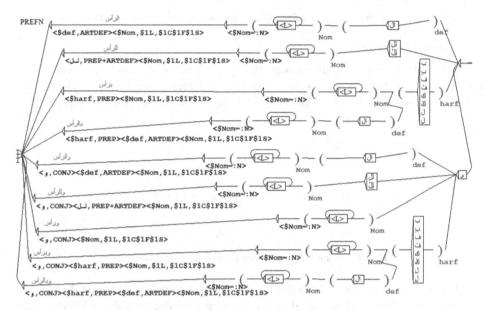

Fig. 3. Morphological grammar for "Prefix + Noun"

Let's note that the transducer of Fig. 3 resolves the problem of Prefix + Noun, for example "بالرأس" (*in the head*). We build also morphological grammars for Noun + Suffix, Prefix + Noun + Suffix and for verbs.

3.3   Specific Difficulties of Medical Domain Disambiguation

The previous studies emphasize that the Named Entity Recognition (NER) is important for all the QA system components. Nevertheless, medical question and medical text contain ambiguous medical entities. According to our corpus study, we observed that the more ambiguous terms are diseases names. For example, the term "التهاب المفاصل" (*arthritis*) means both a symptom and a disease. This issue can be explained through the question «ماهو التهاب المفاصل؟» (*What is arthritis?*); such system can extract the following answers:

(1)   التهاب المفاصل هو مرض التهابي مُزمِن يُمكِن أن يُؤَثِّر على ما هو أكثر من المفاصل...

(Arthritis is a chronic inflammatory disease that can affect more than joints...)

Definition of a disease

(2)   التهاب المفاصل هو عرض لأمراض متعددة ، بعضها شائع وبعضها أقل شيوعا...

(Arthritis is a symptom of multiple diseases, some common and some less common...)

Definition of a symptom

Indeed, to return the right answer, the system must understand the context. For example, in (2), the trigger "عرض" (*symptom*) indicates that it is a definition of the symptom "التهاب المفاصل" (*Arthritis*). Figure 4 shows the resolution of example 2.

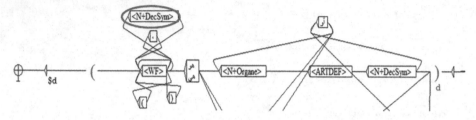

Fig. 4. Extract of transducer for definition of symptoms

The transducer in Fig. 4 illustrates the extraction of symptom definition through the trigger <N+DecSym>. However, if the symptom is preceded by a disease trigger then the named entity will be recognized as a disease such as in Fig. 5.

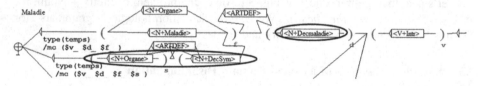

Fig. 5. Extract of transducer for definition of diseases

In open domain, the expected answer type is known from the interrogative pronoun. For example, in a When-question «متى اكتشفت امريكا؟» (*When was America discovered?*), the expected answer type is a time. Nevertheless, a When-question in medical domain can indicate a condition, an age, or a time. Indeed, we identified 158 syntactic patterns

Table 3. Ambiguity of the question "متى" (When)

Question	Translation	Expected answer
متى<Verb>رضيع| طفل | جنين؟	When<Verb>Fetus| Child |Infant?	Age
متى<Noun><Verb>طفل|جنين|رضيع؟	When<Verb><Noun>Child| Fetus| Infant?	Age
متى<Verb><Noun><Condition>?	When<Verb><Noun><Condition>?	Condition
متى<Verb><Trigger><Virus>?	When<Verb><Trigger><Virus>?	Time
متى<Verb><Disease>?	When<Verb><Disease>?	Time

that allow the disambiguation of questions. Table 3 gives an example for When-questions.

To resolve this problem, we build for each type of question (Table 1) a graph. Let's take the graph of When-question as an example (see Fig. 6).

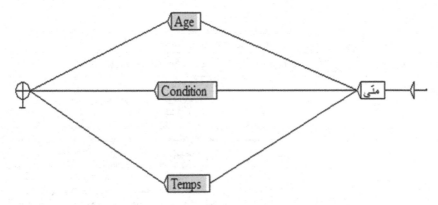

Fig. 6. Main transducer for When-questions

The transducer of Fig. 6 describes the different paths allowing the analysis of When-questions. The sub-graph "Age" describes the question where the expected answer type is Age. Figure 7 shows this sub-graph.

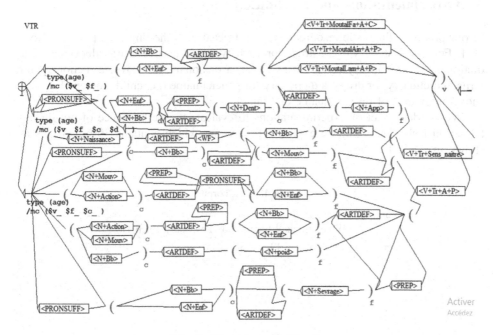

Fig. 7. The sub-graph "Age"

108   S. Dardour et al.

The identification of the expected answer type is related to the focus of the ques-
tion. For instance, the transducer of Fig. 7 can analyze a question like "متى يحبو الطفل؟"
(*When does the child crawl?*). According to the pattern "When<Verb>Fetus| Child |
Infant?", the focus is "طفل" (*child*), so the expected answer type is "Age" (Table 3).
Figure 8 gives the result of disambiguation of When-questions.

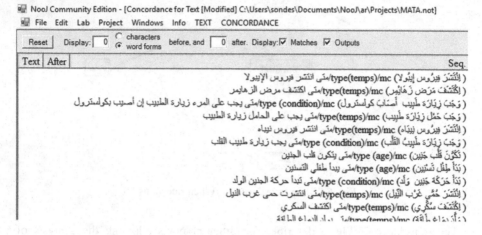

Fig. 8. The result of disambiguation of When-questions

4   Experimentation and Evaluation

In our proposal, linguistic resources are constructed with the linguistic platform NooJ
[17]. For our system, we construct for each type of question a transducer and five
dictionaries: a dictionary for diseases name, a dictionary for verbs, a dictionary for
virus, a dictionary for drugs, a dictionary for general name (i.e. child, doctor). Figure 9
shows an extract of diseases name dictionary.

We conduct a set of experimentations to evaluate the performance of our disambiguation task. Therefore, we exploit a test corpus which contains 399 questions as
shown in Table 4.

Table 4. Test corpus

| Question type | ما | متى | أين | من | كم | | كيف | لماذا |
	What	When	Where	Who	How many/much		How	Why
Number	95	65	49	38	45		49	58

الـتهاب الـحسᴎه,NᴛMaladieᴛGu

انـسداد الـصفـراويـة,N+Maladie+Gastro

الـتهاب الـعظم,N+Maladie+Sm

الـتهاب الـمعدة الـمزمن,N+Maladie+Gastro

الـتهاب الـبربخ,N+Maladie+Gu

الـتهاب الـقـولـون,N+Maladie+Gastro

اضطراب الـهلع,N+Maladie+Psy+Syno="نـوبات الـهلع"

نـوبات الـهلع,N+Maladie+Psy+Syno="اضطراب الـهلع"

الـتهاب الاحليـل,N+Maladie+Gu

الـتهاب الـلهاة,N+Maladie+Gastro

اجهاد الـعيـن,N+Maladie+Ophtalmologie

الـᴎᴛᴎ الᴎᴛᴎ,N+Maladie+Gynecologie

Fig. 9. Extract of diseases name dictionary

In our proposal, disambiguation task is applied to the question analysis module and to the answer extraction module. For instance, if the question contains some ambiguity such as "من المسؤول عن الحركة الذاتية للقلب؟" (*Who is responsible for the self-movement of the heart?*); the ambiguity of this question is that the user asks for an organ and not for a person (problem of Who-questions). After disambiguating the expected answer type which is organ using the transducer of Who-questions, the system can extract the correct answer. Figure 10 illustrates results of the disambiguation of some questions.

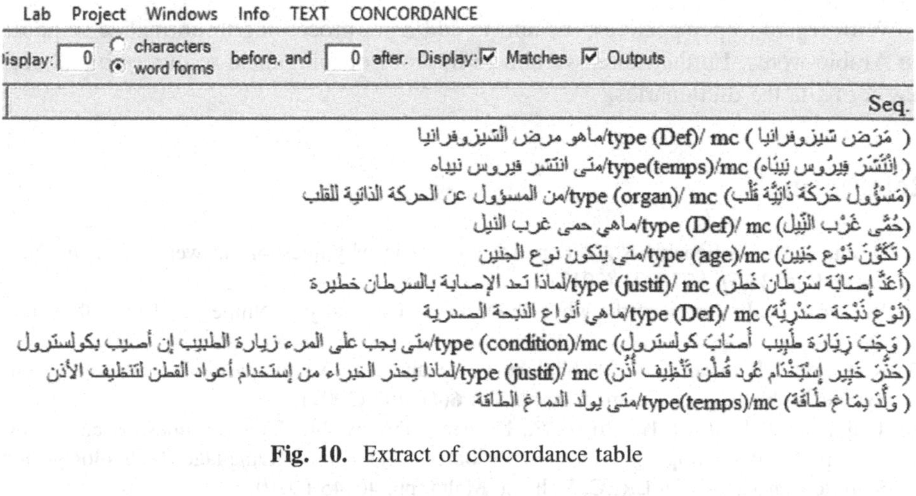

Lab   Project   Windows   Info   TEXT   CONCORDANCE

| display: | 0 | ○ characters ● word forms | before, and | 0 | after. Display:☑ Matches ☑ Outputs |

Seq.

(مَرَض شيزوفرانيا)type (Def)/ mc/ماهو مرض التيزوفرانيا

(إنتَشَرَ فيِرُوس نيباه)type(temps)/mc/متى انتشر فيروس نيباه

(مَسْؤُول حَرَكَة ذَاتِيَّة قَلْب)type (organ)/ mc/من المسؤول عن الحركة الذاتية للقلب

(حُمَّى غَرْب النِّيل)type (Def)/ mc/ماهي حمى غرب النيل

(تَكَّوُنَ نَوْع جَنِين)type (age)/mc/متى يتكون نوع الجنين

(أَعَدَّ إِصَابَة سَرْطَان خَطَر)type (justif)/ mc/لماذا تعد الإصابة بالسرطان خطيرة

(نَوْع نَبْحَة صَدْرِيَّة)type (Def)/ mc/ماهي أنواع النبحة الصدرية

(وَجَبَ زِيَارَة طَبِيب أَسْبَاب كُولِسْتِرُول)type (condition)/mc/متى يجب على المرء زيارة الطبيب إن أصيب بكولستِرول

(حَذَّرَ خَبِير إِسْتِخْدَام عُود قُطْن تَنْظِيف أُذُن)type (justif)/ mc/لماذا يحذر الخبراء من إستخدام أعواد القطن لتنظيف الأذن

(وَلَّدَ بِمَاغ طَاقَة)type(temps)/mc/متى يولد الدماغ الطاقة

Fig. 10. Extract of concordance table

We acquire the results illustrated in Table 5 after applying the evaluation to the test corpus using our linguistic resources.

Table 5 demonstrates that the disambiguation process enhances the F-Measure by 28%. It is then concluded that the results acquired will be improved by decreasing ambiguity, particularly when processing the medical domain in the Arabic language.

Table 5. Summarizing the measure values

Method	Before disambiguation	After disambiguation
Precision	0.66	0.93
Recall	0.58	0.87
F-Measure	0.61	0.89

Silence is often due to the problem in writing some Arabic letters such as the letter "ا" "A" which can also be written like "إ" ">" or "آ" "ا" or "ا" "<". For example, in some question, we can find the word "diseases" written like "امراض" or "أمراض". In fact, we need to rewrite the question by unifying all versions of a letter into one form to solve this issue. Furthermore, the silence is also due to dictionaries' coverage that must be improved and the complexity of some questions that requires special handling techniques.

5   Conclusion

In the present paper, we described our Arabic Question Answering systems achievements. The main goal of this work was to propose a new method for Arabic QA systems with a special focus on the ambiguity resolution. The disambiguation task is crucial due to Arabic language specification as well as medical domain specification. Therefore, we focused on disambiguation based on the NooJ language development platform using a set of linguistic resources. Our proposed method achieves satisfactory results.

With regard to perspectives, we aim to add a pre-processing to normalize some of the Arabic words. Furthermore, we aim to improve our linguistic resources by adding new terms in the dictionaries.

References

1. Azmi, A.M., Alshenaifi, N.A.: Lemaza: an Arabic why-question answering system. Nat. Lang. Eng. **23**(6), 877–903 (2017)
2. Verberne, S.: In search of the why. Ph.D. thesis, University of Nijmegen, The Netherlands (2010)
3. Kanaan, G., Hammouri, A., Al-Shalabi, R., Swalha, M.: A new question answering system for the Arabic language. Am. J. Appl. Sci. **6**(4), 797 (2009)
4. Trigui, O., Belguith, L.H., Rosso, P.: DefArabicQA: Arabic definition question answering system. In: Workshop on Language Resources and Human Language Technologies for Semitic Languages, 7th LREC, Valletta, Malta, pp. 40–45 (2010)
5. Lampert, A.. A quick introduction to question answering, December 2004
6. Benajiba, Y., Rosso, P., Gómez Soriano, J.M.: Adapting the JIRS passage retrieval system to the Arabic language. In: Gelbukh, A. (ed.) CICLing 2007. LNCS, vol. 4394, pp. 530–541. Springer, Heidelberg (2007). https://doi.org/10.1007/978-3-540-70939-8_47

7. Ezzeldin, A.M., Shaheen, M.: A survey of Arabic question answering: challenges, tasks, approaches, tools, and future trends. In: Proceedings of the 13th International Arab Conference on Information Technology (ACIT 2012), pp. 1–8 (2012)
8. Ask.com. https://www.ask.com/
9. Start question answering system. http://start.csail.mit.edu/
10. Wolfram Alpha. https://www.wolframalpha.com/
11. Brini, W., Ellouze, M., Trigui, O., Mesfar, S., Belguith, H.L., Rosso, P.: Factoid and definitional Arabic question answering system. Post-Proceedings NOOJ-2009, Tozeur, Tunisia, 8–10 June (2009)
12. Brini, W., Ellouze, M., Mesfar, S., Belguith, L.H.: An Arabic question-answering system for factoid questions. In: IEEE International Conference on Natural Language Processing and Knowledge Engineering, 2009. NLP-KE 2009, pp. 1–7 (2009)
13. Bekhti, S., Rehman, A., Al-Harbi, M., Saba, T.: AQuASys an Arabic question-answering system based on extensive question analysis and answer relevance scoring. Inf. Comput. Int. J. Acad. Res. 3(4), 45–54 (2011)
14. Azmi, A.M., Alshenaifi, N.A.: Lemaza: an Arabic why-question answering system. Nat. Lang. Eng. 23(6), 877–903 (2017)
15. Bessaies, E., Mesfar, S., Ben Ghzela, H.: Processing medical binary questions in standard Arabic using NooJ. In: Silberztein, M., Atigui, F., Kornyshova, E., Métais, E., Meziane, F. (eds.) NLDB 2018. LNCS, vol. 10859, pp. 193–204. Springer, Cham (2018). https://doi.org/10.1007/978-3-319-91947-8_19
16. Ennasri, I., Dardour, S., Fehri, H., Haddar, K.: Question-response system using the NooJ linguistic platform. In: Mbarki, S., Mourchid, M., Silberztein, M. (eds.) NooJ 2017. CCIS, vol. 811, pp. 190–199. Springer, Cham (2018). https://doi.org/10.1007/978-3-319-73420-0_16
17. Silberztein, M.: Using linguistic resources to evaluate the quality of annotated corpora. In: Proceedings of the First Workshop on Linguistic Resources for Natural Language Processing, pp. 2–11 (2018)

Recognition and Analysis of Opinion Questions in Standard Arabic

Essia Bessaies[✉], Slim Mesfar, and Henda Ben Ghezala

Riadi Laboratory, University of Manouba, Mannouba, Tunisia
{essia.bessaies,slim.mesfar}@riadi.rnu.tn,
henda.benghezala@ensi.rnu.tn

Abstract. Nowadays, most question-answering systems have been designed to answer factoid or binary questions (looking for short and precise answers such as dates, locations), however little research has been carried out to study complex questions.

In this paper, we present a method for analyzing medical opinion questions. The analysis of the question asked by the user by means of a pattern based analysis covered the syntactic as well as the morphological levels. These linguistic patterns allow us to annotate the question and the semantic features of the question by means of extracting the focus and topic of the question.

We start with the implementation of the identifying rules and the annotation of the various medical named entities. Our named entity recognizer tool (NER) is able to find references to people, places and organizations, diseases, viruses, as targets to extract the correct answer from the user. The NER is embedded in our question answering system. The task of QA is divided into four phases: question analysis, segmentation, and passage retrieval & answer extraction. Each phase plays a crucial role in the overall performance.

We use the NooJ platform which represents a valuable linguistic development environment. The first evaluations show that the actual results are encouraging and could be deployed for further question types.

Keywords: Information extraction · Medical questions · Arabic language · Local grammar · Named entities

1 Introduction

In recent years, the medical domain has a high volume of electronic documents. The exploitation of this large quantity of data makes the search of specific information complex and time consuming. This complexity is especially evident when we seek a short and precise answer to a human natural language question rather than a full list of documents and web pages. In this case, the user requirement could be a Question Answering (QA) system which represents a specialized area in the field of information retrieval.

The goal of a QA system is to provide inexperienced users with a flexible access to information allowing them to write a query in natural language and obtain not the documents which contain the answer, but its precise answer passage from input texts.

© Springer Nature Switzerland AG 2020
H. Fehri et al. (Eds.): NooJ 2019, CCIS 1153, pp. 112–122, 2020.
https://doi.org/10.1007/978-3-030-38833-1_10

Arabic QA systems could not match the (rapid) pace due to some inherent difficulties with the language itself as well as due to the lack of tools available to assist researchers. Therefore, (to bridge this gap), the current project attempts to design and develop the modules of an Arabic QA system.

For this purpose, the developed question answering system is based on a linguistic approach, using NooJ's linguistic [4] engine in order to formalize the automatic recognition rules and then apply them to a dynamic corpus composed of medical journalistic articles.

In addition, we present a method for analyzing medical questions (for opinion questions). The analysis of the question asked by the user by means of the syntactic and morphological analysis. The linguistic patterns (grammars) which allow us to extract the analysis of the question and its semantic features are able to extract the polarity and focus and the topic of the question.

In the next section, an overview of the state of the art describes related works to question answering system. Section 3 presents the generic architecture of the proposed QA system. In Sect. 4, we introduce our approach to recognition and analysis of opinion questions and extraction of right answer.

2 Related Works

As explained in the introduction, Question-Answering systems present a good solution for textual information retrieval and knowledge sharing and discovery. This explains the sheer number of Q-A systems which has been developed.

Research in building factoid QA systems has a long history. However, it is only recently that studies have started to focus also on the creation and development of QA systems for opinions.

To our knowledge, there are many research studies on opinion QA systems:

- The PolyU [7] system determines the sentiment orientation with two estimated language models for the positive versus negative categories.
- The QUANTA [2] system detects the opinion holder, the object and the polarity of the opinion using a semantic labeler based on PropBank3 and some manually defined patterns.
- The Alyssa system [5], classified the polarity of the question and of the extracted answer snippet, using a Support Vector Machines classifier trained on the MPQA corpus) [6].
- DAWQAS [8]: Dataset for Arabic Why Question Answering System. It consists of 3205 of why question-answer pairs that were first scraped from public Arabic websites, then texts were preprocessed and converted to feature vectors.
- There have been many attempts by Arab linguists to understand the use patterns and functions of DMs, but they still disagree on the basic issue of defining and classifying them [1]. The study in [1] examines the function of DMs in Arabic newspaper opinion articles at sentence and paragraph levels.

After this investigation, and in order to solve the problem of question answering system, the developed question answering system is based on a linguistic approach, using NooJ's linguistic engine to formalize the automatic recognition rules and then apply them to a dynamic corpus composed of Arabic medical journalistic articles.

3   The Generic Architecture of the Proposed QA System

From a general viewpoint, the design of a QA system (Fig. 1) must take into account four phases:

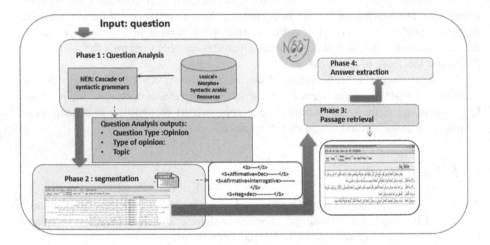

Fig. 1. Architecture of our Question Answering System

Phase 1: Question Analysis: This module performs a morphological analysis to determine the question class (Opinion question). A question class helps the system to classify the question type to provide a suitable answer. This module may also identify additional semantic features of the question like polarity or type of opinion or the type of opinion and the focus.

Phase 2: Segmentation: Will also identify the negation status of the sentence and the style of the sentence. This module is to develop the linguistic patterns for the segmentation of sentences. These patterns are helpful in segmentation and identifying the type of sentences.

Phase 3: Passage Retrieval: The third motivation behind the question classification task is to develop the linguistic patterns for the candidate answers. These patterns are helpful in matching, parsing and identifying the candidate answers.

Phase 4: The Answer Extraction: This module selects the most accurate answers among the phrases in a given corpus. The selection is based on the question analysis. The suggested answers are then given to the user as a response to his initial natural language query. We are working on the integration of similarity scores in order to better rank the retrieved passages.

4 Our Approach

4.1 Question Analysis

The system first takes the Arabic question which is preprocessed to extract the query that will be used in the Passage retrieval module and Text preprocessing segmentation. The question is also classified to get the type of the question (opinion question), and consequently the type of its expected answer, which will then be used in the Answer Extraction module.

Named Entity Recognition (NER)
The named entity recognizer (NER) is embedded in our question answering system in order to identify these answers and questions associated with the extracted named entities [3]. For this purpose, we have adapted a rule-based approach to recognize Arabic named entities and right answers, using different grammars and gazetteer.

We think that an integration of a Named Entity Recognition (NER) module will definitely boost system performance. It is also very important to point out that an NER is required as a tool for almost all the QA system components. Those NER systems allow extracting proper nouns as well as temporal and numeric expressions from raw text [6].

In our case, we used our own NER system especially formulated for the Arabic [4] medical domain. We have considered six proper names categories:

1. Organization: named corporate, governmental, or other organizational entity;
2. Location: name of politically or geographically defined location;
3. Person: named person or family;
4. Viruses: Names of medical viruses;
5. Disease: Names of diseases, illness, sickness;
6. Treatment: Names of Treatments

Then, in order to look for the best answer, the system gives the maximum amount of information (syntactic, semantic, distributional, etc.) from the given question, such as the expected answer, the type of question and the type of opinion question and topic of the question. This information will play an important role in the phase of extraction candidate answers.

- Type of question
- Extract the type of opinion question
- Topic of question

In this paper, we define six opinion question types as follows (Table 1):

Table 1. Opinion question types

Types	Definition	Examples
Majority definition	Asking which option, listed or not listed, is the majority.	Is Diabetes a Chronic Disease? = هل يعتبر مرض السكري من الأمراض المزمنة؟
Attitude Definition	Asking what the attitude of a holder to a specific target is	How does the patient feel about medical errors? = كيف يشعر المريض تجاه الأخطاء الطبية؟
Yes/No	Asking whether their statements are correct.	Stress causes weakness of the immune system? = هل الضغط النفسي يتسبب في ضعف المناعة ؟
Reason	Asking the reasons of an explicit or an implicit holder's attitude to a specific target.	Why Cancer Patients Think Chemotherapy Is Better? = لماذا يعتقد مرضي سرطان من الأفضل العلاج الكيميائي؟
Target	Asking whom the holder's attitude is toward.	Who is responsible for the spread of the AIDS virus? = من المسؤول على إنتشار فيروس السيدا؟
Holder	Asking who the expresser of the specific opinion	Who supports euthanasia?= من يدعم الموت الرحيم؟

The analysis of the question asked by the user by means of a pattern based analysis covered the syntactic as well as the morphological levels. These linguistic patterns allow us to annotate the question and the semantic features of the question to extract the type of opinion and focus of question: Apply the grammar of question analysis to annotate the question (Fig. 2).

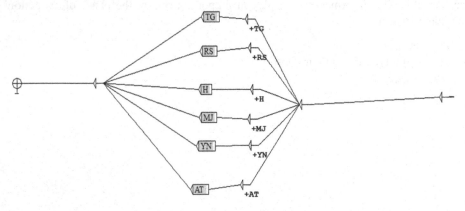

Fig. 2. Pattern of question analysis

The module of question analysis we also identify the type of opinion:

+RS = Reason
+TG = Target definition
+H = Holder
+MJ = Majority definition
+YN = Yes/No
+AT = Attitude Definition

The following example shows the detailed annotation of the identified parts of a question.

Example.

Who supports euthanasia?

من يدعم الموت الرحيم ؟

<ENAMEX+Medic>

من, Who is = innterrogative mark

يدعم, supports = Focus+H

الموت الرحيم, Euthanasia = Topic

4.2 Segmentation

Sentence segmentation is the problem of dividing a string of written language into its component sentences.

In this paper, we propose a rule-based approach to Arabic texts segmentation, where segments are sentences, our approach relies on an extensive analysis of a large set of lexical cues as well as punctuation marks. Our approach relies on morphological and syntactic information using several dictionaries and orthographic rectification grammar. To this end, we use NooJ linguistic resources [6] in order to perform surface morphological and syntactic analysis. Integration of segmentation tool for Arabic texts an enhanced version of [5].

The Sentence Style: +Declarative, +Imperative, +Interrogative OR + Exclamative.

This segmentation phase will, on the one hand, reduce the complexity of the analysis and, on the other hand, improve NooJ platform functionalities.

Also, we achieved our annotation phase by identifying different types of lexical ambiguities, and then an appropriate set of rules is proposed. These patterns are helpful in segmenting and identifying the type of sentences.

Example.

من يدعم الموت الرحيم ؟

تثير مسألة الموت الرحيم جدلا واسعا، ففي الوقت الذي أجازته بعض الدول الأوروبية لأصحاب الأمراض المستعصية التي لا يرجى شفاؤها للتخفيف من عذاباتهم، ترفض دول كبريطانيا والمنطقة العربية الموت الرحيم لمخالفته الشرع وأخلاق المجتمع السائدة، في حين يطالب الكثير من المرضى في الغرب باحترام الأطباء قراراتهم الشخصية، إذ سمح تمدد قيم الفردانية بتحول خيار الموت الرحيم أو الانتحار إلى قرار فردي، فالمريض يؤكد أنه مسؤول عن جسده وله حرية التصرف فيه.

Step 1: After the application of the grammars on this text we notice that the concordances are as follows. The segmentation tool will also identify: the type of sentence (Fig. 3).

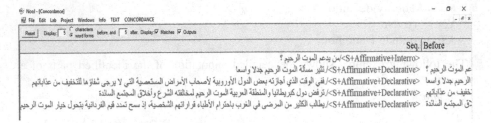

Fig. 3. Concordance of segmentation Tool

These patterns of segmentation are helpful in matching, parsing and identifying the candidate answers and type of sentence.

Step2: The annotation of the sentences by the recognition of the declarative sentences not the exclamatory and interrogative sentences (Fig. 4).

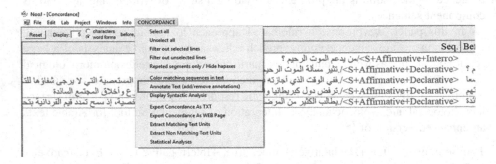

Fig. 4. Result of Annotation Text

With NooJ we can extract the annotated text in XML document with the regular expression:

‒   <S+affirmative+Interro>من يدعم الموت الرحيم؟

1. NooJ>Concordance>Annotate Text (add/remove annotation)
2. Text>Export annotated text as an XML document

After export text as an XML document we need too added tag annotation <S> (sentence). Added <S> (Fig. 5).

Fig. 5. Export text annotation

Exported text with XML tags

The segmentation process undertaken in this study will be described. Then the text segments will be discussed. On the macro-level, we introduce the units of analysis in this study, while on the micro-level, we examine the paragraph and the sentence as independent units of analysis (Fig. 6).

Fig. 6. Result annotation as an XML Text

4.3   Passage Retrieval

The third motivation behind the question classification task is to develop the linguistic patterns for the candidate answers. These patterns are helpful in matching, parsing and identifying the candidate answers.

Passage retrieval is typically used as the first step in current question answering systems. In particular, we show how a variety of prior language models trained on correct answer text allow us to incorporate into the retrieval step information that is often used in answer extraction (Fig. 7).

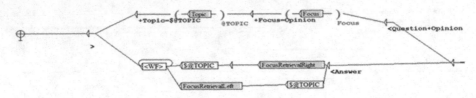

Fig. 7. Grammar of passage retrieval

Step3: After analyzing the opinion question and extracting the focus (type of opinion) and the question topic and segmenting the text in order to extract the candidate responses.

5 Experiments and Results

5.1 NER

Evaluation

To evaluate our NER local grammars, we analyses our corpus to extract manually all named entities. Then, we compare the results of our system with those obtained by manual extraction. The application of our local grammar gives the following result (Table 2):

Table 2. NER grammar experiments on our corpus

Precision	Recall	F-Measure
0,90	0,82	0,88

According to these results, we have obtained an acceptable identification of named entities. Our evaluation shows F-measure of 0.88. We note that the rate of silence in the corpus is low, which is represented by the recall value 0,88 because journalistic texts of our corpus are heterogeneous and extracted from different resources (Fig. 8).

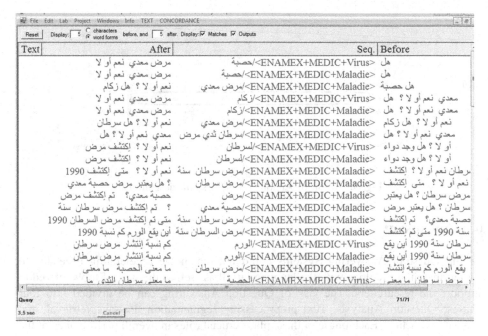

Fig. 8. Result of NER NooJ syntactic grammar

5.2 Recognition and Analysis of Opinion Questions

Evaluation

To evaluate our automatic annotation question local grammars, we also analyse our user's queries to extract manually the question analysis. Then, we compare the results of our system with those obtained by manual extraction. The application of our local grammar gives the following result (Table 3):

Table 3. Annotation question grammar experiments

Precision	Recall	F-Measure
0,75	0,72	0,73

According to these results, we have obtained an acceptable annotation of question. Our evaluation shows F-measure of 0.73. We note that the rate of silence in the corpus is low, which is represented by the recall value 0.72. This is due to the fact that this assessment is mainly based on the results of the NER module (Fig. 9).

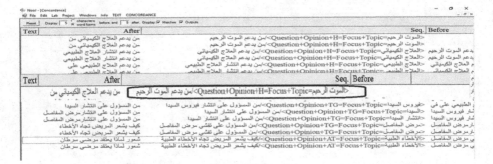

Fig. 9. Result of Annotation NooJ syntactic grammar

6   Conclusion

Arabic Question Answering Systems could not match the accelerating pace due to some inherent difficulties with the language itself as well as the lack of tools offered to support the researchers. The task of Question Answering can be divided into four phases; Question Analysis, Text preprocessing segmentation, Passage retrieval, and Answer extraction. Each phase of these plays crucial roles in overall performance of the Question Answering Systems.

References

1. Al Kohlani, F.A.: The function of discourse markers in Arabic newspaper opinion articles. Doctoral dissertation, Georgetown University (2010)
2. Li, F., et al.: THU QUANTA at TAC 2008 QA and RTE track. In: Proceedings of Human Language Technologies Conference/Conference on Empirical Methods in Natural Language Processing (HLT/EMNLP), Vancouver, BC, Canada (2008)
3. Mesfar, S.: Named entity recognition for Arabic using syntactic grammars. In: Kedad, Z., Lammari, N., Métais, E., Meziane, F., Rezgui, Y. (eds.) NLDB 2007. LNCS, vol. 4592, pp. 305–316. Springer, Heidelberg (2007). https://doi.org/10.1007/978-3-540-73351-5_27
4. Silberztein, M.: La formalisation des langues: l'approche de NooJ. ISTE, Londres (2015)
5. Shen, D., Leidner, J.L., Merkel, A., Klakow, D.: The Alyssa system at TREC QA 2007: do we need Blog06? In: Proceedings of the Sixteenth Text Retrieval Conference (TREC 2007), Gaithersburg, MD, USA (2007)
6. Wiebe, J., Wilson, T., Cardie, C.: Annotating expressions of opinions and emotions in language. Lang. Resour. Eval. 39, 165–210 (2005)
7. Li, W., Ouyang, Y., Hu, Y., Wei, F.: PolyU at TAC 2008. In: Proceedings of Human Language Technologies Conference/Conference on Empirical methods in Natural Language Processing (HLT/EMNLP), Vancouver, BC, Canada (2008)
8. Walaa, I., Homsi, M.: DAWQAS: a dataset for Arabic why question answering system. In: The 4th International Conference on Arabic Computational Linguistics (ACLing 2018), Dubai, United Arab Emirates, 17–19 November 2018 (2018)

A NooJ Tunisian Dialect Translator

Roua Torjmen[1]([✉]), Nadia Ghezaiel Hammouda[2], and Kais Haddar[3]

[1] Faculty of Economic Sciences and Management of Sfax, Miracl Laboratory,
University of Sfax, Sfax, Tunisia
rouatorjmen@gmail.com
[2] Miracl Laboratory, Institute of Computer Sciences and Communications
of Hammam Sousse, Sousse, Tunisia
ghezaielnadia.ing@gmail.com
[3] Faculty of Sciences of Sfax, Miracl Laboratory,
University of Sfax, Sfax, Tunisia
kais.haddar@yahoo.fr

Abstract. The elaboration of a translator system from Arabic dialect to modern standard Arabic becomes an important task in Natural Language Processing applications in the last years. In this context, we are interested in building a translator from Tunisian dialect to modern standard Arabic. In fact, Tunisian dialect is a variant of Arabic as much as it differs from modern standard Arabic. Besides, it is difficult to understand for non-Tunisian people. Intending to elaborate our translator, we study many Tunisian dialect corpora to identify and investigate different phenomena such as Tunisian dialect word morphology and also Tunisian Dialect sentences. The proposed translation method is based on a bilingual dictionary extracted from the study corpus and an elaborated set of local grammars. In addition, local grammars are transformed into finite state transducers while using new technologies of NooJ linguistic platform. To test and evaluate the designed translator, we apply it on a Tunisian dialect test corpus containing more than 18,000 words. The obtained results are ambitious.

Keywords: Word-to-word translation · Bilingual dictionary · Finite transducer · Tunisian dialect · MSA

1 Introduction

The Tunisian Dialect translator is a beneficial task in the domain of Natural Language Processing (NLP). Indeed, it facilitates the diffusion of Tunisian Dialect (TD) to the Arab world. Moreover, thanks to Modern Standard Arabic (MSA) translators to other languages, translating TD to another language will be easy. Besides, our translation system helps in several fields such as the subtitling of Tunisian Dialect artistic works (films, series and novels) and the communication with dialogue systems (Automated Teller Machine ATM).

Unfortunately, TD is not taught in Tunisian schools. This fact causes the absence of standard spelling. Furthermore, the origin of TD's words is a mixture of several languages such as Arabic, French, Ottoman, Italian, Amazigh and Maltese. Besides, popular vocabulary is constantly evolving because of rap songs, the increasing use of

© Springer Nature Switzerland AG 2020
H. Fehri et al. (Eds.): NooJ 2019, CCIS 1153, pp. 123–134, 2020.
https://doi.org/10.1007/978-3-030-38833-1_11

social networks and new technologies. During the construction of our translation system, we have encountered many problems. Among them, the target language, compared to TD, has different word inflections as well as the change of the word order.

In this context, our principal objective is to build a translator from TD to MSA. To achieve our goal, we need to carry out several steps. The first one is to provide a deep linguistic study for TD sentences and TD word morphology. Then, we have to construct a bilingual dictionary from TD to MSA. Afterward, we have to establish a set of finite state transducers that offers a word-to-word translation using new technologies such as grouping technique, variable usage and testing. Finally, we have to implement them in NooJ linguistic platform [7].

The paper is structured in six sections. In the second section, we present previous works dealing with the translation of Arabic Dialect (AD) to MSA and other studies conducted with finite state transducers. In the third section, we perform a linguistic study on the translation of TD verbal and nominal phrases to MSA. In the fourth section, we propose a method for our TD translator. In the fifth section, we experiment and evaluate our translator on the TD test corpus. Finally, this paper is completed by a conclusion and some perspectives.

2   Related Work

The number of translation system work from TD to MSA and TD morphological analyzer is parsimonious because it essentially concerns the speech recognition.

Mentioning the translation work, we quote the work of [2]. The authors have provided a translation system between TD and MSA verbal forms. The work relied on deep morphological representations of roots and patterns. This system offers translation in both directions. The result of the recall is 0.84 from TD to MSA and 0.8 on the opposite side.

The authors [3] have presented a translation system named PADIC (Parallel Arabic DIalect Corpus) including MSA and AD such as Maghrebi dialects (Tunisian and Algerian) and Levantine dialects (Syrian and Palestinian). To analyze the impact of the language model on machine translation, the authors have varied the smoothing techniques and have interpolated them with a larger one. Focusing on TD and MSA and using the BLUE metric, the obtained results are around 25 from TD to MSA and 20 on the opposite side.

In [4], the authors were interested in TD's translation to MSA for collected social media texts. For this context, the authors have presented a word-based translator. So, they have created a bilingual lexicon. In addition, they have adopted a set of grammatical mapping rules and have performed a disambiguation step that relies on MSA language modeling to select the best translation phrases. The obtained results with the BLUE metric on a set of 50 TD sentences are 14.32.

The authors [9, 10] have constructed a morphological analyzer. They have started by creating a self-constructed dictionary extracted from a TD corpus and then they have built a set of morphological local grammars that are transformed into finite state transducers and implemented in the NooJ linguistic platform.

Turning now to the Moroccan dialect (MD) works, the authors [8] have presented a machine translation system from MD to MSA based on the rule-based approach and language model. They have used Alkhalil morphological analyzer ad they have added Moroccan dialect affixes. The obtained results are not indicated.

The author [5] has presented a machine translation system from AD (middle-east, Tunisian, Moroccan and Libyan dialects) to English based on the hybrid approach. The author has used MSA as a pivot language.

The authors [1] have created a system for translating the Sanaani dialect to MSA founded on a rule-based approach. Using metric accuracy, their system obtains 0.77 when it was tested on a Sanaani corpus of 9386 words.

TD's works do not have significant coverage, especially with words of non-Arabic origin. Also, rule systems are not well developed. The work on TD translation to MSA does not give good results because the rules of the tool are not well developed and the dictionary coverage is not large.

3   Linguistic Study

Our linguistic study brings a new vision that promotes the contribution of local grammars based on finite state transducers. In this section, our goal is to identify the TD verbal and nominal phrases that have an agglutination phenomenon or the change of the word order. We also look forward to studying their translation into MSA. In the following subsections, we detail this specificity of TD verbal and nominal phrases.

3.1   Verbal Phrase

Comparing to MSA, we notice the absence of the third person plural in the feminine and the dual in both genders. We notice also that there is no difference between the second person singular feminine and masculine.

The TD verb has many forms of agglutination different from those of the MSA. We cite, for example, the interrogative adverb and the verb which are concatenated in TD. However, they are separated in MSA. The verbal phrase "شكتبت" 'ichktibt' (what did you write) is translated to MSA as "ماذا كتبت" 'maadhaa katabta'. There are other agglutination forms like MSA. We cite, for example, the verb and the direct object are concatenated in TD and MSA. The verbal phrase "كتبتلو" 'ktibtlou' (you write to him) is translated to MSA as "كتبت له" 'katabta lahu'.

In the past, present and imperative tense, we translate the TD verb by taking into account the characteristics of the verb in MSA. Furthermore, TD future verb is a present verb preceded by the TD adverb "باش" 'baach' (will). But in MSA, the TD adverb is replaced by "س" 'sa' and the MSA verb becomes agglutinated.

In the present tense with negation, the TD verb can have two different forms. The first one is a conjugated verb in the present tense preceded by the adverb "لا" 'laa'. The second one is a conjugated verb in the present tense preceded by the adverb "ما" 'maa' and followed by the adverb "ش" 'ch'. Its translation to MSA is a conjugated verb in the present tense preceded by the adverb "لا" 'laa'. Besides, in the accusative present tense, the TD verb is composed of the adverb "ما" 'maa' followed by a personal pronoun and the adverb "ش" 'ch'. Its translation to MSA is a conjugated verb in the present tense preceded by the adverb "لن" 'lan'. Moreover, in the apocopate present tense, the TD verb is conjugated in past tense preceded by the adverb "ما" 'maa' and followed by the adverb "ش" 'ch'. Its translation to MSA is a conjugated verb in the present tense preceded by the adverb "لم" 'lam'.

In the following example, Table 1 illustrates these conjugation cases through the regular verb "كتب" 'ktib' (To write) in the first person singular.

Table 1. Example of regular verb conjugation in first person singular

	TD	MSA	English
Past tense	"كتبت" 'ktibt'	"كتبت" 'katabtu'	I wrote
Present tense	"نكتب" 'niktib'	"أكتب" 'aktubu'	I write
Present tense with negation	"مانكتبش" 'maniktibch' or "لا نكتب" 'laa niktib'	"لا أكتب" 'laa 'atubu'	I do not write
Accusative present tense	"مانيش باش نكتب" 'maniich baach niktib'	"لا أكتب" 'laa 'atubu'	I will not write
Apocopate present tense	"ماكتبتش" 'maaktibtich'	"لم أكتب" 'lam 'aktub'	I did not write
Future tense	"باش نكتب" 'baach niktib'	"ساكتب" 'sa'aktibu'	I will write

Like MSA, regular and irregular verbs do not share the same conjugation. For this reason, we classify TD verbs under different classes according to the characteristics of each verb.

3.2 Nominal Phrase

The TD nominal phrase has many forms of agglutination different from those of the MSA. We cite, for example, the demonstrative pronoun and the definite noun are concatenated in TD. However, they are separated in MSA. The nominal phrase "هالطفل" 'haltful' (this boy) is translated to MSA as "هذا الطفل" 'hadhaa altuflu'. There are other agglutination forms like MSA. We cite, for example, the noun and the noun suffix are concatenated in TD and MSA. The nominal phrase "طفلها" 'tfulhaa' (her son) is translated to MSA as "طفلها" 'tufluhaa'.

Moreover, the TD genitive nominal phrase has many forms of agglutination different from those of the MSA. The preposition and the definite noun are concatenated in TD. However, they are separated in MSA. In the following example, Table 2 illustrates the different agglutination form between TD and MSA.

Table 2. Example of regular verb conjugation in first person singular

TD	MSA	English
"مالمدرسة" 'milmadrssah'	"من المدرسة" 'min almadrassati'	From school
"فالمدرسة" 'filmadrssah'	"في المدرسة" 'fii almadrassati'	In school
"عالمدرسة" 'almadrssah'	"على المدرسة" 'alaa almadrassati'	On school
"للمدرسة" 'lilmadrssah'	"الى المدرسة" 'ilaa almadrassati'	To school

However, the TD genitive nominal phrase can have the same forms of agglutination as MSA. The preposition and the definite noun can be concatenated in TD and MSA. For example, the genitive nominal phrase "بالمدرسة" 'bilmadrssah' (in school) is translated to MSA as "بالمدرسة" 'bi'almadrassati'.

Furthermore, we notice also the order of words in the nominal phrase can change between TD and MSA. For example, the demonstrative pronoun exists after the definite noun in TD. However, it becomes before in MSA. The nominal phrase "الطفل هاذا" 'altful haathaa' (this boy) is translated to MSA as "هذا الطفل" 'hadhaa altuflu'.

We also notice that the word count of a nominal phrase is not stable and can change from TD to MSA. For example, the "موتور" 'muutuur' (a motorcycle) is translated to MSA as "دراجة نارية" 'darraajatun naariyatun'.

The nominal phrase has different transformations at the level of translation from TD to MSA. These transformations must be respected during the construction of our TD translation system.

This linguistic study will help us construct our bilingual dictionary from TD to MSA, and elaborate different rules as well as translate verbal and nominal phrases and obtain a good quality translation.

4 Proposed Method

Our proposed method is based on the rule-based approach and contains two main steps. The first one is the creation of a bilingual dictionary. Besides, the second step is the development of finite state transducers that offer the word-to-word translation with readjustment rules from TD to MSA.

4.1 Bilingual Dictionary

The bilingual dictionary that we have created contains a set of entries with appropriate grammatical categories and also with the possibility of having inflectional and derivational paradigms [6]. In addition, we have provided the translation of the TD entries thanks to the command "+AR=" followed by the translated word in MSA. The illustrated fragment in Fig. 1 is an example of the bilingual dictionary entries, especially for TD verbs.

بْكُى,V+TVDefective+FLX=VERBE1+AR="بكى"
زُ اِ زْ,V+TVHollow+FLX=VERBE2+AR="زاِر"
وْثِقْ,V+VTAssimilated+FLX=VERBE1+AR="وثق"

Fig. 1. Entries example of dictionary

As presented in Fig. 1, we associate with each irregular TD verb the nature of its weakness. These tags V+TVDefective, V+TVHollow and V+VTAssimilated respectively represent the defective verb, the hollow verb and the assimilated verb.

We present an extract of a transducer illustrated in Fig. 2 which allows the conjugation of the TD defective verb. As we see, this transducer provides all different inflection forms. Besides, we use the grouping technique that places words with common characteristics in the same node. For example, it allows the recognition of two different writing forms of the second person plural.

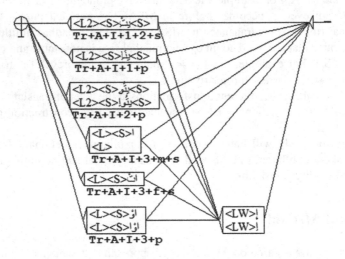

Fig. 2. Inflectional transducer for TD defective verb

Hitherto, our designed bilingual dictionary from TD to MSA contains 4417 entries and generates around 174000 forms thanks to the established derivational and inflectional grammars.

4.2 Morphological Grammars

To process the agglutination phenomenon, we establish ten morphological grammars based on a set of finite state transducers. Figure 3 presents an extract of the morphological grammar dealing with the treatment of agglutination of TD noun.

In this transducer, the noun is stored in the variable named N indicating that the loop (<L>) means a sequence of letters. All the noun suffixes are stored in the variable named Pron. Thus, the content of the two variables N and Pron are verified by a search in the dictionary.

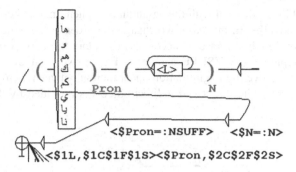

Fig. 3. Extract of morphological transducer for agglutinate noun

The output defines the category ($1C), the inflectional feature ($1F) and the semantic and syntactic feature ($1S) for the first lemma ($1L). In the same way, it defines the content of Pron. In addition, the output displays the characteristics of variable contents successively by following the order of the tracking at the variable test level.

4.3   Local Translation Grammars

The constructed local grammar is a set of finite state transducers. Thereby, it contains 13 graphs. This grammar offers a word-to-word translation from TD to MSA for verbal and nominal phrases. We add several readjustment rules to improve the word-to-word translation. These rules are essentially related to word order and agglutination.

Figure 4 presents the main graph. This graph consists of two sub-graphs which are the verbal phrase named Verbal phrase and the nominal phrase named Nominal phrase. In this transducer, the union is used.

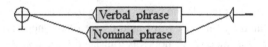

Fig. 4. Main graph

The sub-graph of the verbal phrase transducer, illustrated in Fig. 5, includes all the conjugation tenses. Indeed, the sub-graph named Verb Apo translates TD verbs in the apocopate present tense and the sub-graph named Verb translates TD verbs in other tenses. In this transducer, concatenation is used.

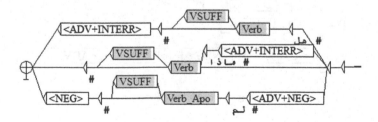

Fig. 5. Verbal phrase transducer

As shown in Fig. 5, we deal with the agglutination phenomenon between TD verbs and interrogative adverbs. In this case, we change the order of the words in the output relative to the initial verbal phrase, if necessary, to obtain the correct translation.

In the sub-graph named VSUFF shown in Fig. 6, we treat direct and indirect objects. Besides, we solve the agglutination phenomenon between them and TD verbs. The separation between the direct and indirect objects is provided by the code "#".

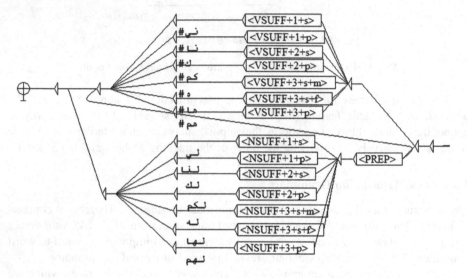

Fig. 6. Direct and indirect object transducer

In Fig. 7, we translate TD verbs in past, present, future and imperative to MSA with all persons. Moreover, we provide the corresponding tools to each tense. Sometimes, a single node is translated by another word as the case of the negative adverb "لا" 'laa' and sometimes one of the successive nodes is translated by a single word as the case of the word tool "لن" 'lan'.

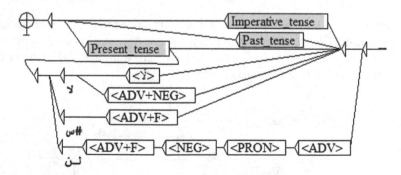

Fig. 7. Verb transducer

The sub-graph of nominal phrase grammar shown in Fig. 8 includes two types of nominal phrases. Indeed, the sub-graph named Ordinary nominal phrase deals with the normal nominal phrase and the other sub-graph named Genitive nominal phrase deals with a genitive one.

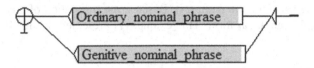

Fig. 8. Nominal phrase transducer

In Fig. 9, we present an extract of a genitive nominal phrase that solves the agglutination problem identified in Table 2 and we provide the correct translation in MSA thanks to the precision of the nature of each preposition such as FII, MIN and ALA.

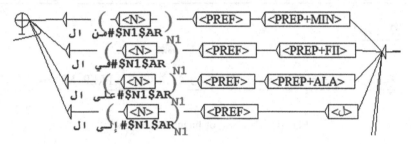

Fig. 9. Transducer extract of genitive nominal phrase

In conclusion, we have developed up to now a derivational and inflectional grammar containing 25 finite state transducers, 10 morphological grammars dealing with agglutination processing and finally a local grammar containing 13 finite state transducers processing the translation from TD to MSA.

5   Experimentation and Evaluation

As indicated previously, the bilingual dictionary from TD to MSA and the set of finite state transducers are implemented in NooJ linguistic platform. The file barcha2.nod is considered as the extensional version of our dictionary existing in file barcha2.dic. In fact, our corpus is collected from social networks and Tunisian novels. We divide 1/3 of the corpus for the study and 2/3 of the corpus for the test and evaluation. In addition, our test corpus contains 18134 words.

To experiment our translator, we first need to prepare the lexical resources to use which are the bilingual dictionary and the 10 morphological grammars that deal with agglutination phenomena for all grammatical categories.

The linguistic analysis of the test corpus took only 33 s. For example, after the linguistic analysis of the following TD sentence: "خرّجوهم مالمدرسة" 'kharrajuuhum milmadrssah' (get them out of school), we obtain that the word "خرّجو" 'kharrajuu' (get out) is recognized as a verb (V) conjugated to the third person in the past or conjugated to the second person in imperative time. The lemma "هم" 'hum' (them) is recognized as a direct object (VSUFF). Moreover, the recognized lemma "م" 'm' (of) is a proposition, the recognized lemma "ال" 'il' (the) is a prefix and finally the word "المدرسة" 'madrssah' (school) as a singular feminine noun (N). Besides, the translation of recognized words is also provided in canonical form. This example is presented in Fig. 10.

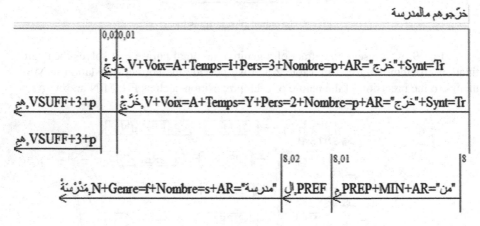

Fig. 10. Example of linguistic analysis

In Fig. 11, we present an extract of results after applying the local transition grammar named "Verbal and nominal phrases.nog" on our test corpus. The obtained result is given in the NooJ concordance table.

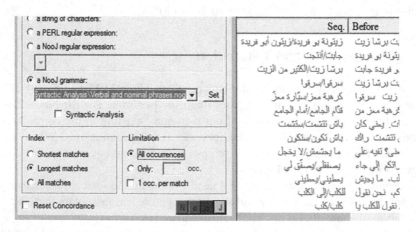

Fig. 11. Concordance table of translation

On the concordance table, we find different verbal phrases such as verb in future tense such as "باش تكون" 'baach tkuun' "will be" translated to "ستكون" 'satakuun', past tense "جابت" 'jaabit' (has produced) translated to "أنتجت" 'antajat'. We also find the agglutinate verb with a direct object like "يعطيني" 'ya'atiinii' (give me) translated to "يعطيني" 'yu'atiinii' and with an indirect object like "يصفقلي" 'ysaffaklii' (applauds me) translated to "يصفق لي" 'yussafiku lii'.

Regarding the nominal phrase, we find the annexation compound such as "كرهبة معز" 'karhbit mu'iz' (Moez's car) translated to "سيّارة معز" 'sayyarat mu'iz' and "برشاً زيت" 'barchaa ziit' "a lot of oil" translated to "الكثير من الزيت" 'alkathiir min alzayti'. We also find genitive nominal phrase like "قدام الجامع" 'kuddaam aljaami'a' (in front of the mosque) translated to "أمام الجامع" 'amaama aljaami'i' and agglutinate genitive nominal phrase like "للكلب" 'lil kalb' (to the dog) translated to "إلى الكلب" 'ilaa alkalbi'.

In Table 3, we present the number of verbal and nominal phrases in our test corpus and their number of recognized phrase.

Table 3. Obtained result of phrase

	Verbal phrase	Nominal phrase
Corpus	4123	4732
Recognized	3782	3815

Considering the recall as a metric, we obtain 0.91 for the verbal phrase and 0.8 for the nominal phrase. The obtained results show that our translator processes and translates verbal phrases better than nominal phrases.

We notice that our bilingual dictionary treats words of different origins. Besides, our local translation grammars translate phrases that contain agglutination. Moreover, they detect the different compounds of nominal phrases such as annexation and adjectival compounds.

In fact, unrecognized TD phrases are caused by missing rules or typographical errors in TD test corpus. In addition, we notice that the noise is present in the obtained results due to a lack of disambiguation rules.

The obtained results are ambitious for the translation of TD phrases to MSA and can be improved by increasing the coverage of our dictionary and by treating other TD phrase forms.

6 Conclusion and Perspectives

In the present paper, we have developed a translator from TD to MSA in NooJ linguistic platform based on a deep linguistic study. This translator translates different nominal and verbal phrases. Also, it is based on a bilingual dictionary extracted from TD corpus and some local grammars. Thereby, the local grammars are specified by a set of finite state transducers and by adopting the NooJ's new technologies. Thus, the evaluation is performed on a set of sentences belonging to a TD corpus. The obtained results are ambitious and show that our translator can translate efficiently sentences having different TD nominal and verbal phrases despite the different origins of TD words and the agglutination phenomenon.

With respect to perspectives, we will expand the coverage of our designed bilingual dictionary from TD to MSA. Furthermore, we will create disambiguation rules of words and will treat other different complex TD nominal phrases such as the relative compound. Moreover, we seek to translate TD sentences.

References

1. Al-Gaphari, G.H., Al-Yadoumi, M.: A method to convert Sana'ani accent to Modern Standard Arabic. Int. J. Inf. Sci. Manag. (IJISM) **8**(1), 39–49 (2012)
2. Hamdi, A., Boujelbane, R., Habash, N., Nasr, A.: The effects of factorizing root and pattern mapping in bidirectional Tunisian-standard Arabic machine translation (2013)
3. Meftouh, K., Harrat, S., Jamoussi, S., Abbas, M., Smaili, K.: Machine translation experiments on PADIC: a parallel Arabic dialect corpus. In: The 29th Pacific Asia Conference on Language, Information and Computation, Shanghai, China, October 2015 pp. 26–34 (2015)
4. Sadat, F., Mallek, F., Boudabous, M., Sellami, R., Farzindar, A.: Collaboratively constructed linguistic resources for language variants and their exploitation in NLP application–the case of Tunisian Arabic and the social media. In: Proceedings of the Workshop on Lexical and Grammatical Resources for Language Processing, Coling 2014, Dublin, Ireland, pp. 102–110 (2014)
5. Sawaf, H.: Arabic dialect handling in hybrid machine translation. In: Proceedings of the Conference of the Association for Machine Translation in the Americas (AMTA), Denver, Colorado (2010)
6. Silberztein, M.: NooJs dictionaries. In: Proceedings of LTC, Poland, 21–23 April 2005, vol. 5, pp. 291–295 (2005)
7. Silberztein, M.: The Formalisation of Natural Languages: The NooJ Approach, 346 p. Wiley, Hoboken (2016)
8. Tachicart, R., Bouzoubaa, K.: A hybrid approach to translate Moroccan Arabic dialect. In: Proceedings of the 9th International Conference on Intelligent Systems: Theories and Applications (SITA-14), pp. 1–5. IEEE (2014)
9. Torjmen, R., Haddar, K.: Construction of morphological grammars for the Tunisian dialect. In: Mauro Mirto, I., Monteleone, M., Silberztein, M. (eds.) NooJ 2018. CCIS, vol. 987, pp. 62–74. Springer, Cham (2019). https://doi.org/10.1007/978-3-030-10868-7_6
10. Torjmen, R., Haddar, K.: Morphological aanalyzer for the Tunisian dialect. In: Sojka, P., Horák, A., Kopeček, I., Pala, K. (eds.) TSD 2018. LNCS (LNAI), vol. 11107, pp. 180–187. Springer, Cham (2018). https://doi.org/10.1007/978-3-030-00794-2_19

Automatic Text Generation: How to Write the Plot of a Novel with NooJ

Mario Monteleone[(⊠)]

Dipartimento di Scienze Politiche e della Comunicazione,
Università degli Studi di Salerno, Fisciano, Italy
mmonteleone@unisa.it

Abstract. Automatic Text Generation (ATG) is a Natural Language Processing (NLP) task that aims at writing acceptable and grammatical written text exploiting machine-representation systems, such as for instance knowledge bases, taxonomies and ontologies. In this sense, it is possible to state that an ATG system works like a translator that converts data into a natural-language written representation. The methods to produce the final texts may differ from those used by compilers, due to the inherent expressivity of natural languages.

ATG is not a recent discipline, even if commercial ATG technology has only recently become widely available. Today, many software environments cope with ATG, as Text Spinner, DKB Lettere, or textOmatic*Composer, just to mention a few.

Keywords: Automatic Text Generation · NooJ · NooJ paraphrases · Lexicon-Grammar · Semantic predicates · Text Linguistics · Formal Linguistics · Formal Semantics

1 ATG and NLP

As a discipline strictly connected to NLP, ATG should be based strongly on morph-syntax formalization and semantic predicate use [1]. However, in some cases it seems possible to avoid these steps. A simple example of ATG not involving the use of morph-syntactic and semantic rules may be the generation of texts using only simple alphabetic letters. This method can prove itself useful when the text to generate is somehow generic in terms of semantics and fix in terms of syntax. For instance, it can be used to generate a letter to a consumer stating that a credit card spending limit has been reached, or also to generate receipts from an ATM machine, or Social Media notifications.

However, in theory and practice the automatic generation of more complex texts can only be based on a complete system of Natural Language Formalization (NLF), such as/for instance Maurice Gross' Lexicon-Grammar [1–4]. Therefore, in order to build an ATG procedure for novel plots, in this paper we will use both Lexicon-Grammar theoretical and practical framework and Max Silberztein's NooJ NLP Environment [5, 6], and the two of them are well known to be in a strict connection. Going from Gross' definition of semantic predicates [1] to the NooJ paraphrase generation routine [5, 6], our aim will be to write automatically the basic plot of a novel.

© Springer Nature Switzerland AG 2020
H. Fehri et al. (Eds.): NooJ 2019, CCIS 1153, pp. 135–146, 2020.
https://doi.org/10.1007/978-3-030-38833-1_12

While achieving our aim, we will take into due account that the novel is a kind of writing that is difficult to define formally [7], and that the automatic writing of a novel plot is probably one of the most complex challenges an ATG routine can choose to tackle.

Finally, in carrying out our research, we will also make extensive references to Text Linguistics (TL) and its theoretical and practical contact points with Formal Linguistics (FL).

2 Text Linguistics

TL is a theoretical approach resulting from the analysis of enunciation linguistic structures [8], aiming at the study of text structure and speech analysis. TL consists of a set of notions and methods of analysis dedicated to the way the text is organized. The object of TL analysis is text structure rather than the isolated sentences by which a text is formed. This means that a text is seen as a system, i.e. a set of elements that constitute a whole range of functions.

Actually, texts may be divided into two main text categories:

– Performative texts (textbooks, essays, software or technical-scientific manuals…), in which the authors seek objectively to describe factual and/or procedural aspects of reality, with a necessary chronologically linear exposure of contents.
– Narrative texts (novels, poems, plays, newspaper articles…) in which the authors "tell a story" not necessarily linked to factual reality aspects, except those needed by the development of the story itself. In these texts, the chronologically linear exposure of contents is not compulsory.

According to [9], textuality has seven basic criteria:

1. **Cohesion**, i.e. the set of (also but not always morphosyntactic) mechanisms that a text uses to ensure the connection between its parts at the superficial level. Means of text cohesion are: Ellipses, Anaphoric/Cataphoric Pronouns, Recurrence, Conjunctions, Disjunctions, Counterjunctions, Subordinations, and Deictics;
2. **Coherence**, which concerns the semantic structure of a text and the logical and psychological structure of the concepts expressed. Means of text coherence are Continuity and Consistency of Meaning.
3. **Intentionality**, which refers to the (descriptive, narrative) intention of those who produce a coherent and cohesive text.
4. **Acceptability**, which concerns the recipient of a text. This means that a coherent text is produced with a certain intentionality, and it is to be accepted by the recipient with reference to the specific context of a given social and cultural background. Acceptance of the recipient includes both the tolerance of certain disruptions in communication and the search for cohesion and coherence, even when they are apparently lacking (as, for instance, in James Joyce's *Stephen Daedalus* and *Ulysses*, with their well-known stream of consciousness technique).
5. **Informativeness**, which refers to the degree of predictability or probability about the occurrence of certain elements or information specified inside a text. In this

case, the enunciative exchange is made possible by the fact that the writer and the recipient have in common a well-defined knowledge base, obtained from previous parts of the text or by references to extra-linguistic experience. The writer will assume that the recipient can easily reconstruct the subject he is describing, even though it has not been formulated explicitly.

6. **Situationality**, which concerns the relevance and adequacy of a text in a given communication situation (i.e. all both linguistic and social circumstances in which the linguistic act is produced).

7. **Intertextuality**, that links the text to other texts with which it has significant connections (interdependencies between the production and reception of the text; communication knowledge of other texts, as for J. R. R. Tolkien's *The Lord of the Rings* in relation to all his other novels on the *Saga of Middle-earth*).

3   General Linguistics and Text Linguistics

For TL, the interest in the textual level is born with reference to connection relationships placed at the higher level than the sentence. At any rate, it is worth stressing that there are morphosyntactic relationships that operate beyond the limits of a single sentence (therefore at a textual level), such as the agreement between a substituent and its antecedent, or the relationships between verb tenses in a narrative. The following text gives an example of this type of relationships:

(A)   *Marco needed a new car. Paolo really wanted to buy one. Since he had changed job, his economic availability was rather limited. He was happy to accompany his friend to the Alfa Romeo dealership. The chosen car was a gray 146.*

At the same time, there exist thematic and logical relations between the sentences of a text, which are indicated by conjunctions and connectives. Therefore, if we look at the following text:

(B)   *The story of Napoleon is the story of a great conqueror. Once upon a time, there was a little girl named Elena.*

We can state that (B) is only a sequence of statements, while (A) is a text. In fact, in (A) we observe the pronominal recall in the second sentence (*to buy one*, complete pronoun) referring to an element of the preceding sentence (*car*). Also, we may observe:

– The use of a consecutio temporum[1];
– The repetition *needed a new car/wanted to buy one*, which creates cohesion;
– The presence of different types of connections;

---

[1] The term comes from the Latin grammar, and indicates the norms that regulate the concordance of the tenses in the text sentences linked to the main proposition by a relationship of contemporaneity, anteriority or posteriority.

- The choice of the article, which does not rely on grammatical facts, but on extra-linguistic ones (one writes of *a car* because it is a new element, not given, whereas *the car* refers to an already known element);
- The order of the constituents, i.e. the fact that the sequence *new car* is introduced by an indefinite article, due to the fact that from a pragmatic point of view, it transmits new information.

Actually, we must note that General and Structural Linguistics (GSL) do not seem equipped to study text structures and their interconnections in the way previously exemplified. GLS copes with natural language as with a system of systems, that is, as a defined number of elements, the identity of which is given by contrastive relations with other elements, i.e. by their occurrence, co-occurrence restriction selection, and distribution. On the contrary, writing a text means to combine set of elements in non-interrupted sequences, without the intent of identifying contrastive relationships. Therefore, we may state that if the purpose of GSL is to examine structures, then the goal of TL is to examine the selections of structures produced in order to construct higher-level linguistic units (which is: a text, and not a sequence of sentences). Apparently, a grammar of the utterance based on Morphosyntax may not account for these higher-level linguistic unit constructions. In fact, together with Formal Semantics (FS), Morphosyntax must primarily validate the acceptability and grammaticality of sentences, not their relations of coherence, cohesion, intentionality, acceptability, informativeness, situationality and intertextuality.

4   The Basic Structure of a Novel

In order to write a novel, we must primarily and mainly define:

1. A specific topic, developing the well-known questions: *What happened? When? Where? Who did it and with whom? Why?*.
2. The *Fabula*, which is the logical and chronological order of the set of events to narrate.
3. The *Plot*, i.e. a term of narratology used by the Russian formalists (in Russian: фабула) which refers to the organization of the events narrated as structured by the author(s). It defines the order in which the events progress. When the plot follows the logical and chronological order, the *fabula* and the plot coincide;
4. Within the novel, the placing of the climax(es), i.e. the culminating and turning point(s) of the events.
5. How to structure and use:
   a. Twists, i.e. those unforeseen events, for the reader/spectator and sometimes for certain characters, occurring during any kind of story.
   b. Analepsis or flashback, which create an interruption of the chronological sequence of events by recalling events or scenes of earlier occurrence.
   c. Prolepsis, which is the representation/assumption of a future act, or its development, as if it were presently existing or accomplished.

With regard to the correspondingly important development of the Characters of a novel, in [7] we may find a main standard typology, which include roles such as *The Protagonist*, *The Antagonist*, *The Object* (desired or feared), *The Destinator* or *Playmaker* (manipulating the destiny/fate of the object), *The Recipient*, and *The Helper*. Ideally, a good novel will balance well-defined characters (whom the reader will focus on or even identify with) and a plot skillfully developed (with an adequate number of twists, analepsis and prolepsis). Therefore, for each character, it will be necessary to establish a *physiognomy* (age, physical appearance, conformation); the *social characteristics* (name, nationality, social status, cultural level, economic situation, lifestyle, life habits, dressing style); the *ideological characteristics* (conception of the world, political vision, religious faith, existential values); and the *psychological characteristics* (personality, behavior, moral values, strengths and weaknesses, hopes, goals, fears).

In the following paragraph, we will see how and to which degree all these features may be formalized to become tags of a NooJ electronic dictionary.

5 How to Write the Plot of a Novel with NooJ: Electronic Dictionaries and Tag Sets

In order to write automatically a novel plot with NooJ, the first step to take is to create a customized electronic dictionary, transforming into tags all the features described in our previous paragraph, and applying these tags to the dictionary entries. Besides, it will be necessary to associate the new tags to the already existing Lexicon-Grammar semantic properties, as NHum, NAnim, and others (as showed in Fig. 1). A further association will be necessary to classical semantic/logical Roles, as for instance: *agent* (AG), *patient* (PA), *instrument* (INS), *date* (DA), *place* (PL), *direction* (DIR), *goal* (GL), *cause* (CA), *procedure* (PR) and others, depending on the plot to develop, and on syntactic-semantic profiles of the verbs to use.

Furthermore, storytelling roles will also have their specific tags. Some examples are *The Protagonist* (PAGN), *The Antagonist* (AAGN), *The Object* (OBJT), *The Destinator or Playmaker* (PLMK), *The Recipient* (RECP), *The Helper* (HLPR), and so on. We may also have possible subsets of tags, with reference to specific characters' features. For instance: *The Bad* (BD); *The Betrayed Husband* (BTRH); *The Betrayed Lover* (BTRL); *The Betrayed Wife* (BTRW); *The Cheater* (CHTR); *The Fool* (FL); *The Gambler* (GMLR); *The Good* (GD); *The Killer* (KLR); *The Mad Man* (MdMn); *The Liar* (LIR); *The Lolita* (LLTA); *The Lover* (LVR); *The Lunatic* (LNTC); *The Serial Killer* (SKLR); *The Spree Killer* (SPKLR); and *The Traitor* (TRT).

The second step to take on Lexicon-Grammar basis will be choosing the semantic-predicate and/or verb-expressions sets needed to write our plot. We will also choose specific support-verb constructions, compound verbs, frozen verbs, idioms, and so on, taking into due account their syntactic and formal behaviors. Combining these syntactic aspects with the tags created for our characters will help us in outlining a set of possible actions the same characters might take, depending on the events we want to deal with

Abb	noun of a clothing article
AlimE	noun of an edible substance
AlimP	noun of a potable substance
ALoc	locative adverb
AMod	modal adverb
Anim	animal noun or animate non-human being noun
AQuant	quantity adverb
~~Ast~~	~~abstract noun~~
Atmo	noun of an atmospheric event
ATmp	time adverb
Coll	collective human noun
~~Conc~~	~~concrete noun~~
DDef	defined (pre)determiner
Des	obsolete term
DIndef	indefinite (pre)determiner
DNum	numerical (pre)determiner
EComOr	oral element of communication
EComScr	written element of communication
Farm	noun of a drugs or medication
Fig	figurative noun (also as a part of idiomatic sentences)
Gramm	noun of a grammatical, morphological, syntactic element
HDisc	noun referring to investigative/contemplative humanistic disciplines
Hum	human noun
Lin	noun of a tongue, a dialect, a jargon
Loc	locative noun, noun of a place
Lud	game/sport noun
Mal	illness/disease noun
Mass	mass noun
Mis	unit of measure noun
Mon	currency noun
Mus	musical instrument noun
Num	numeric noun
PC	body-part noun
Psic	noun of sentimental, psychic or psychological state
Qual	noun expressing a quality
QuantD	Conventionally-defined quantifier noun
QuantI	undefined quantifier noun
SDisc	noun referring to investigative scientific disciplines
SostG	noun of a gaseous state substance
SostL	noun of a liquid-state substance
SostS	noun of solid-state substance
Strum	mechanical tool noun
Tmp	noun of a period of time/event with defined or undefined duration
Veg	noun of plants, vegetables, flowers

Fig. 1. Set of semantic tags used in Italian electronic dictionaries.

or imagine. For instance, a character tagged as FL (*the Fool*) will be equipped with, or better denoted and connoted by the following morphosyntactic set of support/ compound verb constructions and idioms:

– *be a fool, act like a fool, look like a fool, play fool, pretend to be a fool, be fooled by, think like a fool, speak like a fool, be robbed like a fool, take someone for granted,* and so on.

The third step to take will be the building of the FSAs/FSTs that will allow us to produce the NooJ paraphrases for our plot. We will build these automata describing a specific simple sentence (i.e. a nuclear declarative sentence) set, accounting for the syntactic profile of its predicates. With NooJ, this will allow us to produce an elevate number of acceptable and grammatical nuclear sentences, that subsequently will be used to develop our plot.

The fourth and final step to take will be to ontologize all the procedure previously described. For this purpose, we could create a Knowledge Management System (KMS) in which the previous three steps described will be interactively operational to structure novel plots. We may imagine this KMS as a searchable and dynamic database in which, for example, we will be able to check if our idea of plot has already been treated or coped with, in whole or in part, and with what linguistic forms. Therefore, this KMS will be also functional to sketch interactively a plot and have it completed automatically, taking also inspiration from the already existing plots to create one's own, or to write for instance sequels and/or prequels.

6   Validation of the Procedure

To validate our procedure, we created a Declarative Sentence Grammar (see Fig. 2) loosely inspired by E. A. Poe's *A Descent into the Maelström* (Italian version *Una discesa nel Maelström*), freely downloaded from [10]. As for the Italian Lexicon-Grammar Classes, as established by [11], we chose two verb sets, i.e. (Figs. 3, 4, 5, 6 and 7):

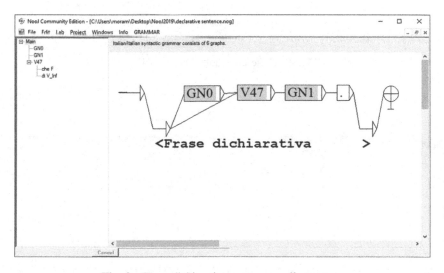

Fig. 2. Frase dichiarativa.nog – overall structure

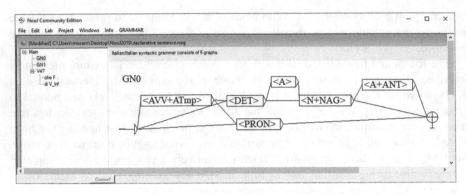

Fig. 3. Frase dichiarativa.nog – GN0

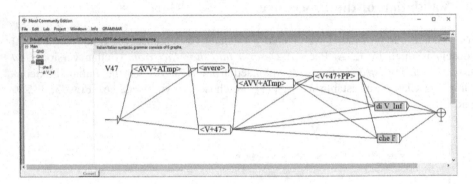

Fig. 4. Frase dichiarativa.nog – V47

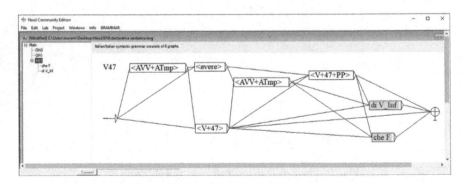

Fig. 5. Frase dichiarativa.nog – che F

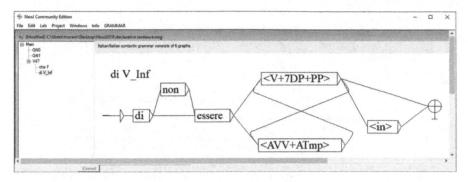

Fig. 6. Frase dichiarativa.nog – di V_Inf

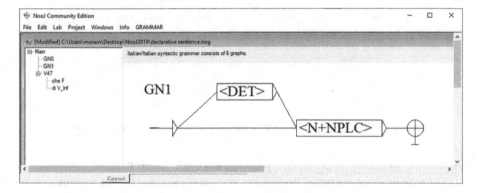

Fig. 7. Frase dichiarativa.nog – GN1

- 7DP = *Il marinaio cade nel Maelström* (The sailor falls into the Maelström);
- 47 = *Il marinaio racconta (di essere+che è) caduto nel Maelström* (The sailor says he fell into the Maelström).

As for our Italian electronic dictionary (frasi dichiarative-flx.dic, see Fig. 8), we added tags for the following grammatical and syntactical categories:

- adverbs of time (AVV+Atmp);
- adjectives of nationality (A+ANT);
- personal pronouns (PRON);
- verbs of the class 47;
- verbs of the class 7DP;
- possible N0s of the class 47 (tagged as "Agent", N+NAG);
- possible N1s of 7DP class (tagged as "Place", N+NPLC);
- the Negation Adverb *non*.

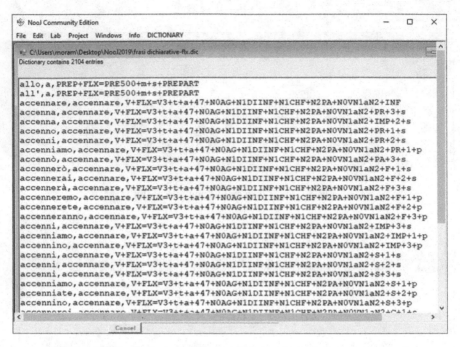

Fig. 8. An excerpt from the electronic dictionary frasi dichiarative-flx.dic

After the linguistic analysis of [10], we used the NooJ Routine *Grammar ->
Generation* to produce the set of declarative sentences provided by our grammar, using
the option "ending it after 5 s". This procedure resulted in more than 3500 valid
declarative sentences, as showed also by the debug of our grammar (see Figs. 9 and
10):

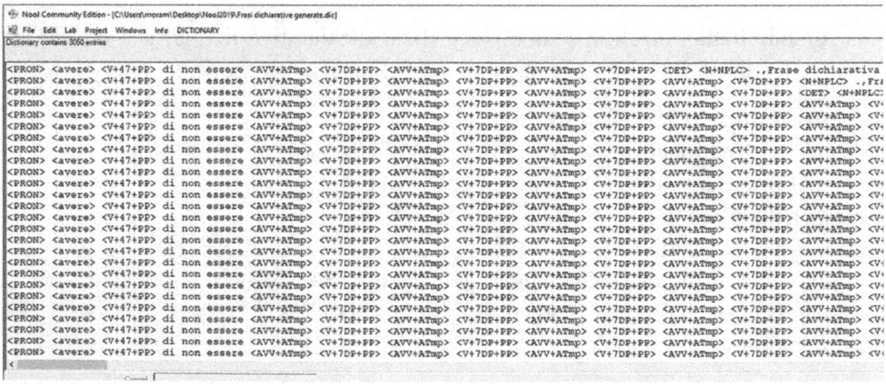

Fig. 9. An excerpt from the electronic dictionary frasi dichiarative generate.dic

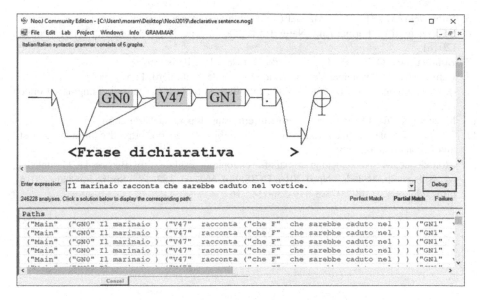

Fig. 10. Debug of the grammar frase dichiarativa.nog

7 Conclusions

The procedure here validated can be largely improved, enriched and as already stated, embedded inside a KMS. After revising the sentences generated, it would be useful to formalize other types of semantic predicates, always in line with the contents of the story to narrate. Another improvement would be the expansion of the right-context of the grammar "declarative sentence.nog", accounting for discourse paratactic and/or hypotactic relationships like in *Il marinaio racconta che sarebbe caduto nel vortice se non si fosse aggrappato alla botte* (The sailor says he would fall into the vortex **had he not clung to the barrel**). Additionally, inside the grammar we could account for all the transformations acceptable for the active declarative sentence set (passives, split sentences, endophora [12] and so on). Finally, it would be useful to link up specific transformations, in order to build even a raw version of the desired novel, possibly splitting up the grammars and cascading the different parts.

References

1. Gross, M.: Les bases empiriques de la notion de prédicat sémantique. Langages **63**, 7–52 (1981)
2. Gross, M.: Grammaire transformationnelle du français: Tome 1. Syntaxe du verbe. Larousse, Paris (1968)
3. Gross, M.: Méthodes en syntaxe: régime des constructions complétives. Hermann, Paris (1975)
4. Gross, M.: Grammaire transformationnelle du français: Tome 2. Syntaxe du nom. Cantilène, Paris (1996)

5. Silberztein, M.: The NooJ Manual (2018). http://www.nooj-association.org
6. Silberztein, M.: Formalizing Natural Languages: The NooJ Approach. Wiley, London (2016)
7. Bourneuf, R., Oullet, R.: L'Univers du Roman. PUF, Paris (1972)
8. Benveniste, E.: Problèmes de linguistique générale. Gallimard, Paris (1966)
9. de Beaugrande, R.-A., Dressler, W.U.: Introduction to Text Linguistics. Longman, London (1981)
10. https://digilander.libero.it/lordsofterror/inferno/singoli/poe/maelstrom.htm
11. Elia, A.: Tavole Lessico-Grammaticali dei verbi dell'italiano. http://dsc.unisa.it/composti/tavole/combo/tavole.asp
12. Monteleone, M.: NooJ local grammars for endophora resolution. In: Barone, L., Monteleone, M., Silberztein, M. (eds.) NooJ 2016. CCIS, vol. 667, pp. 182–195. Springer, Cham (2016). https://doi.org/10.1007/978-3-319-55002-2_16

NooJ for the Digital Humanities

Arabic Learning Application to Enhance the Educational Process in Moroccan Mid-High Stage Using NooJ Platform

Ilham Blanchete[✉], Mohammed Mourchid, Samir Mbarki,
and Abdelaziz Mouloudi

MIC Research Team, MISC Laboratory, IbnTofail University, Kenitra, Morocco
ilham.blanchete@gmail.com, mourchidm@hotmail.com,
mbarkisamir@hotmail.com, mouloudi_aziz@hotmail.com

Abstract. The article presents a learning web application, which contributes to enhancing the educational process of the Arabic language, especially in Moroccan Mid-High (schools). We use NooJ linguistic platform [1] to analyze the given syllabus. NooJ's linguistic engine with its Text Annotation Structure (TAS) returns an annotation file after doing the linguistic analysis. The application stands on this returned annotation file to recognize and represent both nouns and adjectives that occur in the lesson.

We assume that Learners in preparatory stage must be able to distinguish between nouns, verbs and other grammatical categories, but they are not able to extract more sophisticated linguistic features, e.g. the pattern of a noun that has a duplicated root. The difficulty lies in the changes that occur in this kind of words, also in the rule/rules that were used to generate a certain Broken Plural Forms (henceforth BPF) from a singular noun/adjective. The application is meant to recognize and represent these sophisticated linguistic features and provide them to the learner.

The representation process provides the learner with the linguistic features of any noun or adjective that occurred in the lesson, e.g. the application would be able to return root, singular pattern, gender, grammatical category, Broken Plural pattern/patterns and other morphological, phonological and semantic features of a certain noun or adjective. The application can also examine rule/rules that were used to generate BPFs from its singular ones.

The lesson is divided into two main sections; the theoretical part where the learner is able to extract the linguistic features of any noun or adjective. The practical section aims to make the learner capable of recognizing these linguistic features and representing them in any text. In this first version we provide only one lesson, which is the Arabic Broken Plural lesson.

Keywords: Arabic learning system · Arabic nouns · Arabic adjectives · Arabic Broken Plural · Inflections · Derivations · Lexical grammars · Arabic morphology · NooJ platform · Linguistic features · Singular form

© Springer Nature Switzerland AG 2020
H. Fehri et al. (Eds.): NooJ 2019, CCIS 1153, pp. 149–160, 2020.
https://doi.org/10.1007/978-3-030-38833-1_13

1   Introduction

"Natural Language Processing NLP can be effectively applied in the educational process, which helps in promoting the language learning and enhancing students' academic performance" [2]. For this reason, we have used a linguistic approach to build full Arabic resources. Each resource consists of a dictionary that is based on root and pattern approach, and grammars that give the inflectional and the derivational forms of dictionary's entry. More details are provided in next section. The linguistic approaches can be applied in the educational settings to ensure that students can develop a better understanding of the educational material and curriculum [2].

As we mentioned above, beginner students can easily distinguish between nouns, verbs and other grammatical categories; the difficulty lies in the extraction of the linguistic properties of these words. For instance, the most important linguistic features of any Arabic word are the root and pattern [3]. It is not easy to extract the root especially from words on which the morph-phonological changes were made. For example, the verb [to sell-BaAEa-بَاعَ] has the root (B Y Eع ي ب-).As we can see the letter (Yي-) is the second letter of the root, even if it does not appear in the verb, which is the result of an interlock between its root and pattern (B Y E-ع ي ب)and (FaEaLa-فَعَلَ). After applying a morph-phonological changes on the interlock process the letter (y-ي) disappears and it is substituted with the letter (A-ا). Thus the result is the verb[to sell-BaAEa-بَاعَ] and not [BaYaEa-بَيَعَ]. It is a somewhat difficult for students in the Mid-High stage to examine all changes that have occurred on the root and the pattern of any Arabic word.

We face the same difficulty to extract the pattern from a given Arabic noun. For instance, the noun (letters - MaA'LiK-مَآلِك) has the root (H L K-ك ل ه) and the pattern (MaFaAEiL-مَفَاعِل). As we can see here the letter (A'-آ) appears in the noun even if it is not in the root letter. Changes have been made on the outcome of the interlock process. It is not easy for a beginner student to understand all these changes and examine the rules that have been made on the root and pattern to get the final lemma. These changes happen if the root contains vowels [(W-و), (A-ا) and (Y-ي)] or hamza (H-ا) letter.

Students can extract roots and patterns from words that have a 'sound' root. Generally, sound roots do not need changes after the interlock process. The verb (to write-KaTaBa-كَتَبَ) or the noun (writer-KaATiB-كَاتِب) has the root (K T B ب ت ك) and the pattern (FaEaLa-فَعَل) and (FaAEiL-فَاعِل). No changes have been made, but it is slightly difficult to ask them how we can generate BPF/BPFs from its singular or to ask them for rule/rules that were followed to get the BPF/BPFs from its singular form, even if the root is sound.

Our application facilitates the learning process and develops the learner autonomy. We provide all linguistic features of any word in the lesson. It is worth mentioning that we did not store the BPF's generation rules in the application, the application tests the linguistic features of the singular form, and examines the used rule/rules. The idea is about to move from a static Arabic book to a dynamic one, which facilitates the syllabus changes.

This paper is organized as follows. First, section two enumerates previous applications that have been developed to serve in several domains. Second, the focus of the third section will be on the used linguistic resources. Third, our contribution will be detailed in section four. Forth, the implementation of our web application will be presented in section five. Finally, a conclusion and perspectives will be presented in section six.

2   Previous Works

Many research studies have been conducted using NooJ platform in several domains such as education, translation, health, politics and other fields. Here are the most recent ones.

2.1   Health: A Decision-Support Tool of Medical Plants Using NooJ Platform

A Decision-Support Tool allows the identification of the recommended medical plant name according to the patient's symptoms [4]. The tool uses NooJ's local grammar to make a decision. It follows two steps: collecting criteria from the patient and deciding process to return the desired plant.

2.2   Politics: Generating Alerts from Automatically-Extracted Tweets in Standard Arabic

As a first step, Chenny and Mesfar [5] built a NooJ corpus by extracting data from twitter using specific tool called Twitter API. The corpus contains 27419 tweets that were extracted from different twitter web media. The application uses NooJ's local grammar to extract events from the extracted corpus, then it classes these events into domains. An alert will be generated and trigged when an abnormal score is noticed in a given domain.

2.3   Educational Domain: Using Serious Games to Correct French Dictations: Proposal for a New Unity3D/NooJ Connector

This important work gives a serious game that connects the NooJ platform with a game platform to produce an automatic correction of a French dictation exercise [6]. The game enhances the skills of writing and dictation of French. As a first step, Bououd and Fafi have developed a linguistic resource using NooJ platform. The linguistic resource consists of a dictionary, morphological and syntactical grammar. This resource tests the player entry and proposes solutions to the player. NooJ analyzes the player entry, detects the misspelled words and sends an indexed file to the game platform to correct and give the right solution.

3 Language Resources

The most important thing during building any language recourse is to ensure that it reflects the structure of this language. For this reason, all our Arabic resources were built using root and pattern approach. We have built-in previous stages two full Arabic resources, as Fig. 1 shows. The first one is a fully Arabic verb model based on root and pattern approach [3] that contains all Arabic verbs models with their inflectional and derivational forms.

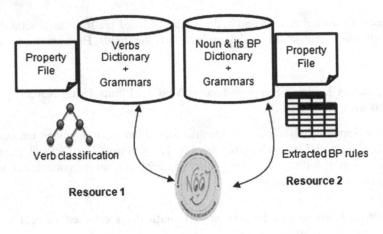

Fig. 1. Arabic linguistic resources

And the second one is a full Arabic nouns and adjectives model also based on root and pattern approach [4], which contains all singular forms linked to their BPF/BPFs.

In this article we are going to use the full nouns and adjectives resource, which contains three files:

- The dictionary, which contains nouns and adjectives linked to their morphological, phonological and semantic features, they are linked also to their inflectional forms and their BP forms. Currently we are still developing this dictionary. A part that contains the first seven Arabic letters is finished. Whereas the rest is still in progress.
- Grammars that contain all inflection forms of any dictionary entry. Grammars that generate the BPF/BPFs.
- Property file, which plays the same rule as variables declaration play in any programming language.

A noun/adjective is declared in the dictionary with all their linguistic features, as Table 1 shows how we represent the noun [book-KiTaAB-كِتَاب] in the dictionary as follows:

Table 1. A dictionary entry.

The category	Explanation
N	The grammatical category is a noun
M	Gender is masculine
CCC	All root's letters are consonants
FiEaAL-فعال	The pattern
K T B- ك ت ب	The root
Obj	Semantic case, the entry is an object
FLX	Its inflectional paradigm, this paradigm contains all inflectional forms of the entry
DRV	Its derivational paradigm

We are going to use pre-implemented linguistic resources. The first resource is a Verb classification that presents all Arabic verbs models, which means that any Arabic verb must belong to one and only one of the classification models. A model contains verbs that inflect on the same manner. The second resource is the nouns and adjectives model with the BP generation rules. The rules are sort of linguistic conditions, each singular's linguistic features must achieve one/several linguistic conditions to be able to own BPF/BPFs, in another way a singular form has a BPF/BPFs if its linguistic features achieve one of our extracted rules.

In this article, we use the second to develop our web application, as the second step, we will use the first one. This resource has been exploited to develop a web application, which aims to enhance the educational process. The next section explains how the application helps learners to gain time and returns the linguistic details of any word, which occurs in the lesson.

As we see in Fig. 2, NooJ uses the provided resource to analyze a given text; it also returns the annotations, which contains the linguistic details about the given text. NooJ also returns the annotations as an XML file we considered this file as the main input in our application. Many ideas could be achieved using the XML annotations, because it tells you about the position, linguistic features and the number of any verbs, nouns, adjectives, pronouns, or other words occurred in the text, in other word the annotation file reflects how you represent Arabic words in your resource. NooJ's annotations are stored in the Text Annotation Structure TAS. "An annotation is a pair (position, information) that states that a certain sequence of the text has certain properties" [1].

4   Our Contribution

NooJ platform is ready to do a linguistic analysis of any text in any language if the right resource is available. The first step is to analyze a given syllabus using NooJ platform, as the Fig. 2 shows, then, NooJ returns the annotations file, which is readable by both of the linguists and the developers. Linguists and developers use the standard

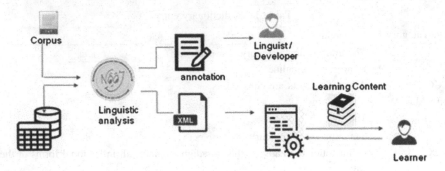

Fig. 2. Arabic resources

annotations to test their resource if it is well implemented or not, developers can also ask NooJ to return the annotation file as an XML file.

Unlike developers, linguists always get satisfied when they read NooJ's standard annotations, but developers get more satisfaction when they get both of the standard annotation and the XML annotation file. Our application uses the XML file, which contains all linguistic features of any word occurring in the lesson and produces exercises to help the learner to know the linguistic detail about the Arabic word even if this word has sophisticated features. In the next sections we give more details about the application tasks. We have developed the web application using HTML5, CSS, Bootstrap, Angular v6. In the next section, we are going to detail the structure of the annotation files.

4.1   The Standard Annotation

In Fig. 3 we give an example of several nouns with their BPF. If you put the cursor on the first noun you will get the following annotation:

- Lemma = [Witness-SHaAHiD-شَاهِد].
- Grammatical category = Noun.
- Gender = masculine.
- Root = [SH H D- ش ه د].
- Root Information = CCC (Consanant).
- Semantic Domain = Human.
- Pattern = [FaAEiL-فَاعِل].
- Number = singular.
- Diacritic =[u-DaMaH-ُ].

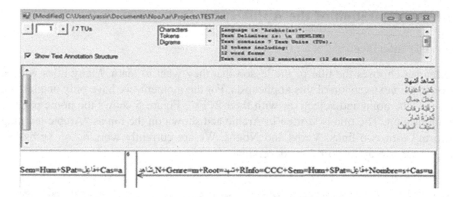

Fig. 3. NooJ standard annotation.

TAS returns annotations as it is declared in the resource. Grammars and dictionaries can be used to get specific annotations. For example, in our resource, we have defined the singular form with its linguistic features in the dictionary, while we have generated the BPF with its pattern in the grammars, after making the linguistic analysis, NooJ's linguistic engine with TAS return the annotated file. As we have mentioned previously linguists are satisfied with this annotation file, they get all linguistic features of their corpus, while developers use NooJ's annotation file as the entry of their application. For this reason, NooJ also provides the annotation file as an XML file, as we are going to clarify in the next section.

4.2   The XML Annotation

As previously mentioned, NooJ also returns annotations as an XML file to standardize the output and make it readable and compatible with other programming languages. Figure 4 shows the structure of this file more detailed than the previous one. In this structure, NooJ specifies the used inflectional and the derivational paradigm for each analyzed word; it also gives the original grammatical category of the BPF. This file is considered as the input for our web application.

Fig. 4. XML annotation file.

5   Implementation of the Application

5.1   The Interface

The learner chooses the title of the lesson that they want to learn. Many titles will be added in the next version of this application. For the moment, we have only one lesson, which is "the noun and adjectives with their BPFs". Figure 5 shows the home page of the application. The title is written in Arabic and shown on the top as "Arabic learning platform" with two links: Verbs and Nouns. We are currently working on verbs lessons, so we can add it to the next versions.

Fig. 5. Home page of the application.

After choosing the noun link a content table gives several lessons. As Fig. 6 shows, our resources represent the nouns and adjectives with their BPFs. The learner must click on the BP link, other links will be provided in the next version of the application.

Fig. 6. Subtitles provided by the application.

The learner gets a learning content from the application, each learning content is divided into two sections, the lesson and the exercise/exercises, as illustrated in Fig. 7. After reading the lesson carefully, the learner must be able to apply for an exercise and answer the given questions. The main question is to examine the most important linguistic features of the nouns and adjectives like the root, pattern or the BPF/BPFs for certain nouns or adjectives. After answering the questions the learner can display the morphological, phonological and semantic features of any noun or adjective with one click on the button "analysis".

Fig. 7. A learning content

5.2 The Exercise

Each exercise contains several sentences. As discussed before, the learner must be able to extract singular and BPFs in a given sentence. They must be able also to examine the linguistic features of nouns and adjectives that occurred in the sentence. E.g. extracting the root of the nouns [school-maDoRaSaa-مَدْرَسَة], which is [D R S- س د ر] , they must be able also to extract the pattern, which is [maFoEaLaa-مَفْعَلَة] and he/she has to know that the root is sound, and the gender is feminine. The learners know that the plural form of this noun is [shools-maDaARiS-مَدَارِس] that takes the pattern [maFaAEiL-مَفَاعِل] but they don't know which rule has been used to generate this BP form and they do not know if there are other BP forms for this singular noun or not. The application examines the used generation rule/rules for any BPF and shows up the used rule/rules to the learner. It is necessary to mention that we stocked the generation rules neither in NooJ level nor in the application level, which means the rules that generate the BPF are not stocked. The application examines the used rule by analyzing the singular form's linguistic features. There are many ideas to develop the exercise form. For instance, a gap-filling task. We can suggest more than BPFs that share the same meaning with different patterns, and ask the learner to fill in the gaps with the correct BPF. To suggest this example, the learner must read the lesson of Arabic patterns and the lesson of BP generation rules, which is considered as an advanced level in Arabic language. To extract BP generation rules we have carried out a deep linguistic study [4]. The result was about 128 BP generation rule, each rule can form an advanced lesson, which can be taught in higher levels.

As previously described, the exercise consists of several sentences as Fig. 8 shows. Learners have to perform several tasks. First, they extract all the singulars and the BP forms with their linguistic features from these sentences. Second, they examine their roots, singular and plural patterns, the root kind if it is sound or duplicated or any other root kind, then, the gender of the noun/adjective and other linguistic features. The translation of the sentences is shown in Fig. 8:

- We went with **teachers** to pick the **fruits**.
- Five **injured** behind this **accident**.
- North African **countries** gathered to negotiate.

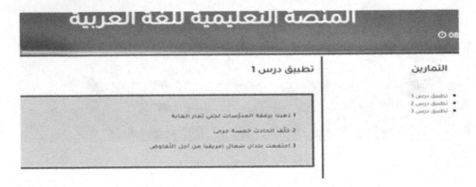

Fig. 8. BP exercise

To get the correct answer, the learner has to put the cursor on the desired noun, this action induces the application to fetch the linguistic features from the XML annotation file. Figure 9 shows the result of putting the cursor on the desired word [Fruits-THiMaAR-إثَمَار]. The result appears inside the white box.

The box includes the following linguistic information:

- Lemma = Fruits.
- Category = noun.
- Gender = feminine.
- Root = TH-M-R.
- Singular pattern = [FaAEoLaAA-].
- BPPattern = [FaEaAL-فعَال].
- Semantic Domain = Food +Plant.
- Root Information = CCC, all its root letters are consonants.
- Number = broken plural.

Fig. 9. Linguistic features of a selected noun

- Cas = no diacritic is specified.
- The used rule: If **the singular pattern** is [FaAEoLaAA or FaEoL/not duplicated] And[N] and [its third root letter is sound] Then[**BPPattern is FaEaAL**].

The most important phase in the application is when it gives the learner the generation rules that were used to generate the BPF/BPFs from the singular form. As previously stated, BP generation rules are not stored in our resources, we examine the used rule by verifying the linguistic features of the singular form.

6   Conclusion and Perspectives

In this paper we have developed a web application that helps learners to learn the Arabic language. We have used a full Arabic nouns and adjectives resource based on root and pattern approach. We have also used this resource in NooJ platform, which gives a detailed annotation file after making a linguistic analysis on the given syllabus. We have used these annotations in our application to retrieve the morphological, phonological and semantic features of any noun/adjective occurring in the lesson text. The application also examines the rule/rules that were applied to generate the BPF from its singular one. Behind this process a deep linguistic study was made, which yielded 182 generation rules. Each rule consists of testing the singular's form of linguistic features to get the BP form/BP forms. Rather than storing these rules in a database or in the resource, the application tests the linguistic features of the singular form to know which rule has been used to generate the BP form.

The perspectives emerging from this work are to complete the web application by finishing the verb chapter especially that we have its resource, and it is ready to be used. We are going to add more lessons for the noun chapter, such as the lesson of the extracted rules that generate the BPF from its singular form but in advanced-level classes of the Arabic language learning.

Using command-line noojapply [6] to avoid the pre-analysis step that we have done to the syllabus, and using other analyzers like the morphological and the syntactic one, we can add more advanced exercises to the lessons.

References

1. Silberztein, M.: Nooj Manual. www.nooj-association.org
2. Alhawiti, K.M.: Natural language processing and its use in education. IJACSA Int. J. Adv. Comput. Sci. Appl. 5(12), 72 (2014)
3. Blanchete, I., Mourchid, M., Mbarki, S., Mouloudi, A.: Formalizing Arabic inflectional and derivational verbs based on root and pattern approach using NooJ platform. In: Mbarki, S., Mourchid, M., Silberztein, M. (eds.) NooJ 2017. CCIS, vol. 811, pp. 52–65. Springer, Cham (2018). https://doi.org/10.1007/978-3-319-73420-0_5
4. Seideh, M.A.F., Fehri, H., Haddar, K.: Recognition and extraction of latin names of plants for matching common plant named entities. In: Barone, L., Monteleone, M., Silberztein, M. (eds.) NooJ 2016. CCIS, vol. 667, pp. 132–144. Springer, Cham (2016). https://doi.org/10.1007/978-3-319-55002-2_12
5. Chenny, H., Mesfar, S.: Generating alerts from automatically-extracted tweets in standard Arabic. In: Barone, L., Monteleone, M., Silberztein, M. (eds.) NooJ 2016. CCIS, vol. 667, pp. 145–154. Springer, Cham (2016). https://doi.org/10.1007/978-3-319-55002-2_13
6. Bououd, I., Fafi, R.: Using serious games to correct french dictations: proposal for a new Unity3D/NooJ connector. In: Proceedings of the Linguistic Resources for Automatic Natural Language Generation-LiRA@ NLG 2017, pp. 49–52 (2017).https://www.aclweb.org/anthology/W17-3808.10.18653/v1/W173808

Causal Discourse Connectors in the Teaching of Spanish as a Foreign Language (SLF) for Portuguese Learners Using NooJ

Andrea Rodrigo[1(✉)], Silvia Reyes[1(✉)], Cristina Mota[2(✉)],
and Anabela Barreiro[2(✉)]

[1] Facultad de Humanidades y Artes, Universidad Nacional de Rosario, Rosario,
Argentina
andreafrodrigo@yahoo.com.ar, sisureyes@gmail.com
[2] INESC-ID Lisbon, Lisbon, Portugal
cmota@ist.utl.pt, anabela.barreiro@inesc-id.pt

Abstract. Our paper focuses on the teaching of causal discourse connectors to learners of Spanish as a foreign language (SFL) whose mother tongue is Portuguese. It relies on the project about the pedagogical application of NooJ carried out by the IES_UNR research group since 2015, which mainly follows [11] and [12], and which makes use of [13]. The contrastive analysis in Portuguese is based on [14]. To develop discourse strategies for text comprehension and production, we implemented tags related to discursiveness and causality. Discourse connectors or markers may be understood as "constituents that exceed the limit of units such as the word, the phrase or the sentence" [7]. As cause and consequence concur, they involve the use of causal discourse connectors such as *porque, ya que, gracias a,* in Spanish, and *porque, já que, graças a,* in Portuguese (because, since, thanks to). We created dictionaries and grammars including two new features: Connector [C] (to name discourse connectors), and causal [+caus] (to identify causal discourse connectors). These features can be more effective for learners of Spanish, especially the one related to causality, since they refer to more general semantic knowledge.

Keywords: NLP · NooJ · Pedagogy · Causal discourse connectors · SFL

1 Introduction

1.1 The Research Subject Matter

This paper relies on a research project carried out by the IES_UNR research group since 2015, which is composed of academics and researchers of two Argentine educational institutions: the Instituto de Enseñanza Superior IES N° 28 "Olga Cossettini" and the Universidad Nacional de Rosario (Centro de Estudios sobre Tecnología

H. Fehri et al. (Eds.): NooJ 2019, CCIS 1153, pp. 161–172, 2020.
https://doi.org/10.1007/978-3-030-38833-1_14

Educativa y Herramientas Informáticas, Facultad de Humanidades y Artes).[1] This project is based on the assumption that it is possible to teach languages using computer tools for natural language processing. And we again make use of the NooJ Platform, since it provides different modules for various languages. Previous papers about adjectives by [8] and about adverbs by [9] account for our research.

On the other hand, language proficiency increases within diversity, which leads us to consider multilingualism as a horizon towards which it is necessary to lead language teaching. Moreover, the NooJ platform provides us with a common basis to create dictionaries and grammars. By focusing on natural language processing, it is possible to set comparisons and arrive to linguistic hypotheses common to various languages. In this respect, we draw on some observations made by [2], who based on scientific evidence points out how the learning of languages after L1 acquisition facilitates the acquisition process depending on experience widening and linguistic creativity. The research question is about how existing linguistic knowledge influences foreign language learners. This enables us to preliminarily conclude that it is important to include linguistic variety in language classes as a way to induce metalinguistic reflection. From this approach, reflection is understood as a learning generator.

1.2   The Learners

Within the field of teaching Spanish as a foreign language –thought of in a broad sense–, defining the population of learners is undoubtedly a key element. Thus [10] focused on learners of Spanish whose mother tongue is Italian by analysing the category adjective with the purpose of developing strategies to increase its use. In this paper we turn our attention to another population: learners of Spanish whose mother tongue is Portuguese. This choice is motivated by a fundamental reason: in the linguistic map of Latin America, Spanish is predominant in the area and therefore relevant for learners whose mother tongue is Portuguese, specifically in Brazil. However, it is not our intention to consider the peculiarities of Brazilian Portuguese in contrast to European Portuguese, or Rioplatense Spanish as opposed to European Spanish. We will only try to outline general considerations that may be useful in all cases.

Returning to [2], and to continue with the details of our research framework, we introduce the notion of linguistic distance. To our knowledge, it is important to bring up this notion since we partially deal with the comparison of languages. From this parameter, which may be defined as the distance the linguist perceives between languages, and not necessarily the one perceived by the speaker, it is possible to assert that Spanish and Portuguese are closely related languages, since both derive from Latin. But the proximity between these languages does not always mean that learners will find fewer difficulties, and it sometimes becomes an obstacle from a semantic viewpoint, when the resemblance between words makes learners think they are alike from a morphological viewpoint, or when a different gender is assigned to the same word.

---

[1] In this paper, two members of our research group, Ángela Salvarezza e Iván Oliva, have participated in searching digital newspapers in Portuguese to look for news about DNA recognition of buried soldiers in Malvinas.

Additionally, we can allude briefly here to *portuñol* (Spanish spelling) or *portunhol* (Portuguese spelling),[2] which is the fruit of the mixture of Portuguese and Spanish, typical of South America, although we will not deal with it here.

1.3   The Purpose of Our Paper

Up to now and within the Spanish Module Argentina available in NooJ, we have been working with grammatical categories such as Noun, Adjective, Adverb and Verb, to cite some of the most important ones. However, the use of these categories brought us some inconveniences:

- Sometimes there seems to be no general consensus about how grammatical categories are considered by different languages, especially adjectives or adverbs.
- Learners of Spanish do not always have propositional knowledge about their mother tongue or about other languages.

To find a way out, we began to design tags related to discursiveness in a more general sense. From this perspective, some contributions of [6], who defines the notion of discourse marker, are very useful. Moreover, [7] paraphrases [5] in simple terms: "connectors have the task of relating semantically and pragmatically two discursive elements, that is, sequences of constituents that exceed the limit of units such as words, phrases or sentences".

Within this framework, we choose a starting point that will allow us to show the relevance of this approach. Thus, we particularly focus our attention on causality as a more universal concept, since not a very specific grammatical knowledge is necessarily required to understand what the cause-consequence relation means, and the knowledge about the world gives an idea of what it is about. This notion involves the use of discourse connectors such *as porque, ya que, gracias a*, in Spanish (*porque, já que, graças a*, in Portuguese, "because, since, thanks to"). We will try to consider here affirmative as well as interrogative sentences (of the question-answer type).

1.4   The Corpus

Every teaching-learning instance involves a specific standpoint. We understand that language teaching cannot be detached from the socio-historical and cultural context. For this reason, and thinking about the Argentine history of the last decades, there is a significant unpleasant event that marked a before and an after turning point. We are especially referring to the *Guerra de Malvinas* (for the British, the Falklands War), when Argentina and Britain embarked upon an armed conflict during seventy four days in 1982. The war occurred during the last stage of the military dictatorship that had begun in 1976 and that promised the Argentine people the recovery of the islands' territory. The war occurred in a very dark moment of the Argentine history, which was marked by the enforced disappearance of persons during the military regime, and by

---

[2] We will not deal here with *portuñol* or *portunhol*, for it is not easy to define: for some it is a dialect, for others a stage of acquisition. You may consult [4], who offers a more linguistic approach, or [3], who refers to a more literary approach, to mention only a few works.

the *madres de Plaza de Mayo* (mothers of the Plaza de Mayo) demanding the appearance of their missing sons and daughters or *desaparecidos*. Argentina went through a period of several controversial facts during the war. But many years later, in December 2017, a painful although comforting event happened, when the bodies of fallen soldiers buried without names in Malvinas were finally identified, and their relatives could finally travel to Malvinas to visit the tombs, thanks to an agreement between Argentina and the United Kingdom, and the intervention of the International Red Cross.

In a synchronic cut, we selected some journalistic publications (Appendix 1) in Spanish that took this news, and collected a corpus of 33,700 characters and 6,794 tokens. The corpus contains expressions referring to causality, for example: *Gracias al ADN, un complejo acuerdo entre Argentina y el Reino Unido y el trabajo de la Cruz Roja Internacional, 90 tumbas del cementerio de Darwin tienen nuevo nombre.* "Thanks to DNA, a complex agreement between Argentina and the United Kingdom, and the work of the International Red Cross, 90 tombs of Darwin cemetery have new names". A similar sentence will be analysed in Sect. 4 using NooJ.

At the same time, as some publications (Appendix 2) in Portuguese also wrote about this event, we collected a corpus of 18,769 characters and, likewise, we extracted expressions referring to causality to be analysed with NooJ.

2 Working with NooJ in Spanish

2.1 The "properties.def" File

First, it is necessary to introduce a new tag into the property definition file by incorporating a new category to name discourse connectors: Connector [C]. In this case, we simply added the category to the existing ones (Noun, Adjective, Verb, etc.) since it is not possible to work with two properties' definition files simultaneously. Then, within the category connector [C], the tag [+caus] is added, in order to name the class of causal discourse connectors.

2.2 The Dictionary

New entries are introduced into the dictionary, which include some of the most usual causal discourse connectors in Spanish[3] (Fig. 1):

Applying Locate. After applying Locate to search causal discourse connectors, several occurrences were found, such as *por eso* (for that reason), *porque* (because), *gracias al* (thanks to) and *ya que* (since). Next, the search of *gracias al* and *ya que* is displayed (Fig. 2):

---

[3] Only generalities that apply to Spanish thought of in a broader sense, but not particularly to the Rioplatense variety, are considered.

```
# NooJ V5
# Dictionary
#
# Language is: sp
#
# Alphabetical order is not required.
#
# Use inflectional & derivational paradigms' description files (.nof), e.g.:
# Special Command: #use paradigms.nof
#
# Special Features: +NW (non-word) +FXC (frozen expression component) +UNAMB (unambiguous lexical entry)
#                   +FLX= (inflectional paradigm) +DRV= (derivational paradigm)
#
# Special Characters: '\' '"' ' ' ',' '+' '-' '#'
#
porque,C+caus
gracias a,C+caus
gracias al,C+caus
ya que,C+caus
a causa de,C+caus
por eso,C+caus
pues,C+caus
puesto que,C+caus
dado que,C+caus
por el hecho de que,C+caus
en virtud de,C+caus
```

Fig. 1. Dictionary of causal discourse connectors in Spanish

sus seres queridos 'fue posible	gracias al	diálogo con Gran Bretaña', ya
al diálogo con Gran Bretaña',	ya que	señaló que 'en el conflicto
sólo conocido por Dios". Ahora,	gracias al	ADN, un complejo acuerdo entre

Fig. 2. Locate *"gracias al"* and *"ya que"* in the Spanish text

3   Working with NooJ in Portuguese

3.1   The "properties.def" File

Causal discourse connectors in Portuguese are very similar to the ones used in Spanish. By applying to Portuguese the same methodology used for Spanish in order to keep unified criteria, we added the category Connector [C] to the existing ones (Noun, Adjective, Verb, etc.), and within this category, the tag [+caus] that identifies causal discourse connectors was entered.

By selecting the same event from a synchronic point of view, the need to recognize the bodies of fallen Argentine soldiers in Malvinas, we collected journalistic publications written in Portuguese and created a corpus of 18,769 characters.

3.2   The Dictionary

The most usual causal connectors in Portuguese are introduced into the dictionary (Fig. 3):

Applying Locate. The search of causal discourse connectors gave the following occurrences: *porque* (because), *por causa do* (because of), *devido a* (due to), *por conta disso* (on account of this) and *graças a* (thanks to). Next, the search of *porque* is displayed (Fig. 4):

```
# NooJ V5
# Dictionary
#
# Language is: pt
#
# Alphabetical order is not required.
#
# Use inflectional & derivational paradigms' description files (.nof), e.g.:
# Special Command: #use paradigms.nof
#
# Special Features: +NW (non-word) +FXC (frozen expression component) +UNAMB (unambiguous lexical entry)
#                   +FLX= (inflectional paradigm) +DRV= (derivational paradigm)
#
# Special Characters: '\' '"' ' ' ',' '+' '-' '#'

porque,C+caus
por causa do,C+caus
devido ao,C+caus
por conta disso,C+caus
graças a,C+caus
```

Fig. 3. Dictionary of causal discourse connectors in Portuguese

File Edit Lab Project Windows Info TEXT CONCORDANCE			
Reset Display: ⬚ ⬚ ○ characters ● word forms before, and ⬚ 5 after. Display:☑ Matches ☐ Outputs			
Text	Before	Seq.	After
ser difícil visitá-lo e	porque	ainda não se identificou a
tarefa, que é bastante complexa,	porque	as condições meteorológicas não são

Fig. 4. Locate "*porque*" in the Portuguese text

By applying Locate in the Portuguese module, the presence of similar expressions using causal discourse connectors is noticed. This represents an enormous advantage for Portuguese learners wishing to learn Spanish as a foreign language, since the expression of causality adopts similar forms. The format provided by the NooJ platform simplifies the comparison between languages.

4   The Grammar

At this point, a sentence in Spanish is selected and then a sentence in Portuguese with the same structure is shown. For this purpose, we chose a very representative sentence:

Fue posible gracias al diálogo con Gran Bretaña. "(It) was possible thanks to the dialogue with Great Britain".

This sentence is extremely relevant from a semantic viewpoint, since it constitutes a sample of how an agreement between countries is the best way to achieve peaceful international relations, and this is the main theme on which this corpus is organised.

The Portuguese equivalent for the sentence is:

Foi possível graças ao diálogo com a Grã-Bretanha.

When comparing both structures, a remarkably distinctive feature in both languages is worth mentioning: the presence of a Pro-Drop ("pronoun dropping") subject, that is, a null (pronoun) subject easily retrievable from verbal agreement morphology in finite clauses. Spanish and Portuguese, as Pro-Drop or null subject languages, share this "pronoun dropping" feature that differentiates them from other languages, for example English or French, for which this phonetically empty or implicit subject is not possible.

To account for the Pro-Drop subject and a causal discourse connector in the predicate, the following grammar is created (Fig. 5):

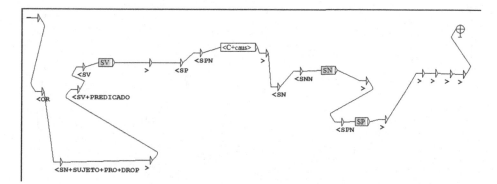

Fig. 5. Main grammar in Spanish with a Pro-Drop subject and a causal discourse connector

In the above main grammar, embedded graphs are presented, which also have other embedded graphs inside them. For example, the verb phrase (SV) *fue possible* "(It) was possible", which includes a nucleus verb phrase (SVN) *fue* "was" and a nucleus adjective phrase (SADJN) *possible* "possible", is inside a verb phrase + predicate (SV +PREDICADO). By applying Show Structure, the structure of the grammar is dis played as follows: - Main [SNN - SPN (SNN) – SV (SADJN) (SVN)], where there are embedded graphs containing other embedded graphs inside them.

With respect to the other embedded graphs, the nucleus noun phrase (SNN) and the nucleus prepositional phrase (SPN), we will briefly refer to the SPN, since it also has embedded graphs inside it. In fact, the preposition *con*, nucleus of the SPN, is followed by the proper noun *Gran Bretaña*, nucleus of SNN.

4.1   The Null (PRO+DROP) Subject in the Grammar of Spanish

It was not easy to introduce the empty category <E> inside the set of nodes in order to account for an elided subject that has no phonological expression. However, we were able to do so by resorting to features[4] (PRO + DROP).

Thus, the following analysis is obtained by resorting to Locate > Grammar and then Outputs:

---

[4] Please note that for this grammar we took as a reference the work of [1] about the nucleus verb phrase in French. Greater phrases such as verb phrase <SV> or prepositional phrase <SP> are determined, which contain nucleus phrases inside such as a nucleus adjective phrase <SADJN> or a nucleus noun phrase <SNN>.

<OR<SN + SUJETO + PRO + DROP > < SV + PREDICADO < SV< SVN> < SADJN >>
<SP< SPN>< SN < SNN > < SPN < SNN>>>>>>

And then, by applying Show Debug to the grammar, it can be noted that the structure is admitted for the newly created grammar (Fig. 6).

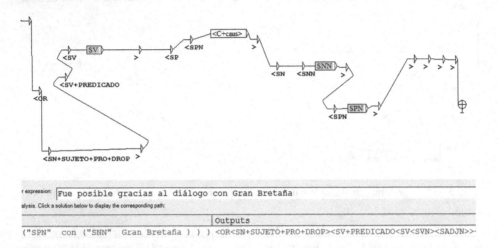

Fig. 6. Applying Show Debug to the grammar in order to express the null (PRO + DROP) subject in the sentence containing a causal discourse connector (Perfect Match)

It is important to highlight the presence of the SNN (Nucleus Noun Phrase) embedded inside the SPN (Nucleus Prepositional Phrase), with double embedding in order to mark the structural difference between the SNN *<diálogo>* with respect to the SNN *<Gran Bretaña>*, the first inside a SN (Noun Phrase) and the second inside a SPN (Fig. 7).

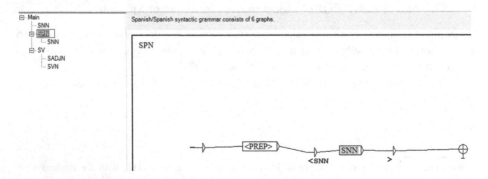

Fig. 7. Show structure makes visible the difference between the two SNN (the one inside the SN and the one inside the SPN)

Moreover, after applying Display Syntactic Analysis, the syntactic structure is shown (Fig. 8):

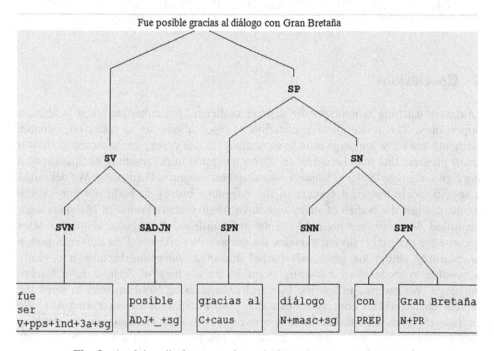

Fig. 8. Applying display syntactic analysis to the sentence in Spanish

In Portuguese, we work with a similar structure and apply Show Debug to the grammar of Portuguese (Fig. 9).

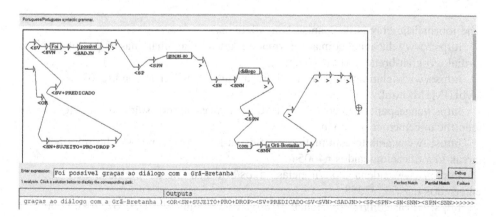

Fig. 9. Applying Show debug to the grammar of Portuguese

Finally, the following analysis is obtained by resorting to Locate > Grammar and then Outputs:

$$< OR< SN + SUJEITO + PRO + DROP> < SV + PREDICADO < SV< SVN>$$
$$< SADJN>> < SP < SPN > < SN< SNN> < SPN < SNN>>>>>>$$

5   Conclusions

Language teaching is undoubtedly a great challenge, but consequently it is also an opportunity. The pedagogical application of NooJ allows us to count on valuable elements that show language in its systematicity. In this paper, we attempted to show a small progress that may be useful for those interested in the teaching of Spanish as a Foreign Language (SFL) to learners whose mother tongue is Portuguese. We delimited a specific socio-historical context in the Argentine history to build our corpus: the moment when the bodies of many unknown fallen soldiers buried in Malvinas were identified. Many journalistic publications in Spanish and Portuguese about this news became the material collected to create the corpora. We addressed the universal notion of causality within the great universe of discourse connectors because it is really accessible to students as a starting point in the teaching of Spanish as a foreign language. We resorted to specific tags and features using NooJ in order to show the typical characteristics concerning causality both in Spanish and in Portuguese. We exclusively focused on the similarities between Spanish and Portuguese when thinking about common dictionaries and grammars. We especially presented a grammar capable of expressing an elided (+PRO+DROP) subject in Spanish and Portuguese that is not formally reported in English or French, which are considered non pro-drop languages.

Appendix 1

The journalistic corpus in Spanish is available at:

https://www.lacapital.com.ar/informacion-gral/el-viaje-malvinas-es-posiblegracias-al-dialogo-gran-bretana-n1578465.html.

https://www.clarin.com/revista-enie/ideas/tumbas-malvinas-nombre_0_BybUJM1Mf.html.

https://cnnespanol.cnn.com/2017/12/01/malvinas-cuerpos-soldados-muertos-identifican-cementerio-darwin/.

https://www.ambito.com/malvinas-ya-estan-listos-los-primeros-ocho-informes-tareas-identificacion-caidos-n4005408.

https://www.cadena3.com/noticias/juntos/britanico-que-dio-dignidad-los-enterrados-darwin_32398.

https://elpais.com/internacional/2018/03/26/argentina/1522078167_708033.html.

Appendix 2

The journalistic corpus in Portuguese is available at:

https://www1.folha.uol.com.br/mundo/2017/03/1865666-vitimas-enterradas-nas-ilhas-malvinas-sao-tema-pendente-da-guerra.shtml.

https://br.sputniknews.com/americas/201708089058652-Argentina-Gra-Bretanha-Malvinas-conflito-identificacao-ajuda-humanitaria/.

https://www.bemparana.com.br/noticia/mundialmente-conhecidos-forenses-da-argentina-param-de-atuar-por-corte-de-verba#.XLo8KTBKjIU.

https://sylviacolombo.blogfolha.uol.com.br/2018/03/24/soldados-caidos-nas-malvinas-finalmente-recebem-sepulturas-com-nome-completo/.

https://www.clarin.com/clarin-em-portugues/destaque/dor-sepultar-um-parente-36-anos-depois_0_By2S2ALcf.html.

References

1. Bès, G.G.: La phrase verbal noyau en français. In: Recherches sur le français parlé, vol. 15, pp 273–358. Université de Provence (1999)
2. Fessi, I.: Influencias interlingüísticas: desarrollos recientes transferencias en adquisición de tiempo y aspecto en español 3. In: Marcoele, Revista de Didáctica ELE Número, vol. 19 (2014). ISSN 1885-2211
3. Bonfim, C.: Portuñol salvaje: arte licuafronteras y tensiones contemporáneas. In: Kipus, Revista Andina de Letras, 31/ I semestre, Quito, pp. 69–86 (2012). http://repositorio.uasb.edu.ec/bitstream/10644/3470/1/07 DO-Bonfim pdf
4. Lipski, J.M.: Too close for comfort? The genesis of "Portuñol/Portunhol". The Pennsylvania State University. In: Face, T.L., Klee, C.A. (eds.) Selected Proceedings of the 8th Hispanic Linguistics Symposium, Somerville, MA, pp. 1–22 (2006). Cascadilla Proceedings Project. http://www.lingref.com/cpp/hls/8/paper1251.pdf
5. Martín Zorraquino, M.A., Portolés Lázaro, J.: Los marcadores del discurso. In: Bosque, I., Demonte, V. (eds.) Gramática descriptiva de la lengua española, pp. 4051–4213. Espasa-Calpe, Madrid (1999)
6. Portolés, J.: Marcadores del discurso, Ariel, Barcelona (2001)
7. Ramírez, S.Q.: Identificación de los conectores discursivos de más alta frecuencia en notas periodísticas deportivas. RLA Revista de lingüística teórica y aplicada, **53**(2), 47–71 (2015). https://scielo.conicyt.cl/pdf/rla/v53n2/art_03.pdf
8. Rodrigo, A., Reyes, S., Bonino, R.: Some aspects concerning the automatic treatment of adjectives and adverbs in spanish: a pedagogical application of the NooJ platform. In: Mbarki, S., Mourchid, M., Silberztein, M. (eds.) NooJ 2017. CCIS, vol. 811, pp. 130–140. Springer, Cham (2018). https://doi.org/10.1007/978-3-319-73420-0_11
9. Rodrigo, A., Reyes, S., Alonso, P.: Some considerations regarding the adverb in Spanish and its automatic treatment: a pedagogical application of the NooJ platform. In: MM, I., Monteleone, M., Silberztein, M. (eds.) NooJ 2018. CCIS, vol. 987, pp. 95–100. Springer, Cham (2019). https://doi.org/10.1007/978-3-030-10868-7_9. ISBN 3030108686, 9783030108687
10. Rodrigo, A., Monteleone, M., Reyes, S.: A pedagogical application of NooJ in language teaching: the adjective in Spanish and Italian. In: COLING 2018, Santa Fe, New-Mexico, USA, 20–26 August 2018. http://aclweb.org/anthology/W18-3807

11. Silberztein, M.: La Formalization des Langues, l'approche de NooJ. ISTE Editions, London (2015)
12. Silberztein, M.: Formalizing Natural Languages: The NooJ Approach. ISTE-Wiley, London (2016)
13. Spanish Module. http://www.noojassociation.org/index.php?option=com_k2&view=item&id=6:spanish-module-argentina&Itemid=611
14. Portuguese Module. http://www.nooj-association.org/index.php?option=com_k2&view=item&id=27:portuguese-module&Itemid=611

Construction of Educational Games with NooJ

Héla Fehri$^{(\boxtimes)}$ and Ines Ben Messaoud

Laboratory Mir@cl, University of Sfax, Sfax, Tunisia
hela.fehri@yahoo.fr, ines.benmessaoud@fsegs.rnu.tn

Abstract. Combining learning and entertainment is an interesting concept involving the game. The latter does not require any specific effort; it allows learning while having fun. Thanks to the game, the user is not under any pressure and progresses at his own pace. Using the game in teaching has several advantages. In fact, it represents a source of motivation and pleasure for the players. In addition, it is an opportunity to practise certain skills (language, reflection, actions). Moreover, it develops the consideration of rules and mutual respect. In this paper, we propose two educational games named: *ProMoNooJ* and *AlphaNooJ*.

Keywords: Educational game · Dictionary · Transducer · NooJ · Learning · Knowledge learners

1 Introduction

Games based learning embeds education as well as entertainment. The objective of this concept is to immerse children in educational activities while playing. Indeed, children learn better, when they are not under pressure and even more when their learning is channeled into a funny game [1]. In perpetual evolution, this approach diversifies as much as possible by integrating each time an educational content.

The educational games are precisely designed for the education context [2, 3]. They allow the child to build essential skills in reading, writing, and more. They help children practise the skills they need to succeed, while making learning a positive experience they are excited to continue. Furthermore, they give the chance to refresh memories and sharpen skills (language, reflection, actions).

The aim of this paper is to propose two educational games developed with NooJ platform [4, 5]. These games improve players' skills by permitting them learning and discovering new words in different languages. The first game is named *ProMoNooJ*. It consists in classifying a set of words according to their category in a field chosen by the player. For example, in the field of medicine, the player must classify the given words in different categories such symptoms, organs or diseases. The second game *Alpha-NooJ* is presented as a competition between two players. Each player must propose a word from a set of given letters. Whoever builds the longest word wins. Note that this game contains several levels and the winner is the player who obtains the highest score.

The implementation of these games is based on dictionaries in different languages (e.g., _sdic.nod, _dm.nod, verbesarabes.nod) and transducers. These games are easy to play and do not require computer skills using Java interface.

© Springer Nature Switzerland AG 2020
H. Fehri et al. (Eds.): NooJ 2019, CCIS 1153, pp. 173–184, 2020.
https://doi.org/10.1007/978-3-030-38833-1_15

The remaining of this paper is structured as follows. Section 2 presents the two proposed educational games. Section 3 deals with the experimentation carried out to evaluate the games efficiency. Finally, the paper ends with a conclusion and some perspectives.

2 Proposed Educational Games

An educational game implements educational theory. More precisely, it is a kind of game created with the purpose of teaching a particular set of concepts, either formally or informally. The teaching can be in or out of the classroom and for apprentices of any age [6].

In this context, and with this topic at hand, we introduce our two proposed educational games namely: *ProMoNooJ* and *AlphaNooJ*.

2.1 ProMoNooJ Educational Game

ProMoNooJ is a multilingual game. It consists of developing and evaluating leaner's knowledge in several fields. In our work, we are interested in the areas: Geography, Sport, Health and Zoology. We assess the knowledge of the apprentice twice. That is why the game has two levels: *easy* and *difficult*. The first level requires the learner to classify a set of words according to a set of categories. Whereas, the second level (i.e., difficult level) is characterized by a more redefined classification.

The proposed approach for the educational game ProMoNooJ is composed of three phases called (a) *Identification of Resources,* (b) *Building of Resources* and (c) *Playing Steps.* Figure 1 depicts this approach.

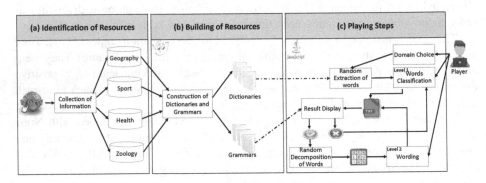

Fig. 1. ProMoNooJ proposed game

Identification of Resources

The *Identification of Resources* (Fig. 1a) phase is based on a collection of information from Internet. It determines the necessary information for each dictionary. It identifies the required resources for words classification. Indeed, it details the particularities of each domain, breaking it down into categories in order to define the entries and the relative features for each entry. We note that each domain is divided into two levels (easy and difficult) according to the classification theme.

Building of Resources

The second phase *Building of Resources* (Fig. 1b) constructs dictionaries and grammars for each domain from information collected in the first phase (i.e., Identification of resources). It uses the linguistic platform NooJ.

The construction of dictionaries formalizes a specialized one. It reformulates the properties of this dictionary in a well-defined domain in order to be processed by the automatic analysis programs: NooJ. First, it selects the words belonging to the same dictionary. These words are added manually to create specific dictionaries for each domain. The creation of a dictionary begins with the choice of the language. In our game, we treat the three languages: French, English and Arabic. These dictionaries deal with the same areas. Figure 2 shows an example of a dictionary associated to the geography field. Each lexical entry, in NooJ, consists of a set of data: *Lemma, Label* and *Optional list of syntactical-semantic information*. The *Lemma* is the basic form of the word. The *Label* indicates the grammatical category of a word, for instance, *N* means that the word added to the dictionary is a name. The optional list of syntactical-semantic information presents the category of the word. It allows refining the entry by giving more details avoiding ambiguity [7].

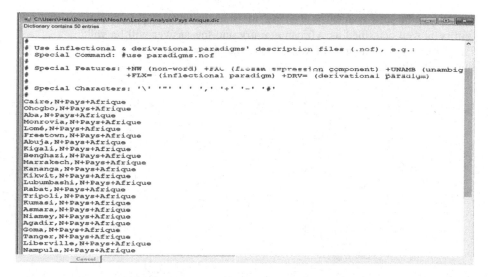

Fig. 2. Extract from the geography dictionary

The dictionary represented in Fig. 2 gives the list of countries and more precisely those of Africa. Thus, for example, we can filter the countries that are African from those that exist. We can also distinguish African countries from European countries.

The construction of grammars (i.e., transducers) consists of formalizing rules for each domain. It implements the data collected from the Identification of Resources phase using the transducer formalism. It is used to check the player's answers and correct them. Figure 3 is an example of a proposed grammar for the geography domain. It is used to recognize if the country is in Africa.

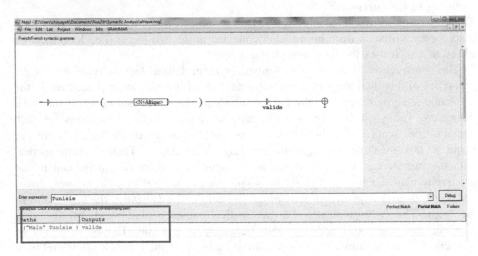

Fig. 3. Transducer for the recognition of African countries

If the introduced country is Tunisia, the transducer of Fig. 3 determines that this country is well classified as African country and the answer will be valid.

Figure 4 is an example of transducer that is used to display the correction for country classification.

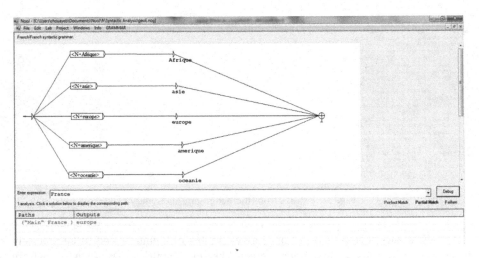

Fig. 4. Transducer for the recognition of the location of France

Playing Steps

Once the dictionaries and the grammars are built, using NooJ, there is a set of six steps to be followed (Fig. 1c).

First, the player chooses the domain (Geography, Sport, Health or Zoology). Second, the *Random Extraction of Words* step is realized. It extracts words haphazardly from a particular dictionary belonging to the chosen field. After that, the *Words Classification* step allows the player to organize the extracted words in the previous step. This step presents the first level of the *ProMoNooJ* Game: Easy level. The answer is stored in a text file as input to dictionaries and grammars. Then, the *Result Display* step specifies if the player answer is correct. There are two possible situations, either an incorrect or a correct answer. If the answer is wrong, the player can reclassify the incorrectly classified words. Otherwise, the player goes automatically to the second level: Difficult level. As an example of this level, a new random word extraction is performed. An example of a difficult level is that the words will be broken down into letters. From these letters the player must formulate the answer and classify it according to the new theme of the domain. Finally, the player verifies his answer.

2.2 AlphaNooJ Educational Game

The second game *AlphaNooJ* requires two players. It can be played through many rounds. Its main objective is to expand players' knowledge by defining new words starting from a set of letters. In fact, it proposes a set of letters to the apprentice (i.e., player). The learner tries to build a correct word and at the same time the longest in a definite time. This game is developed with two solutions: solution based on a random draw and solution based on a server.

Figure 5 describes the proposed approach for the first solution of the educational game *AlphaNooJ*. Firstly, the two players roll the dice (i.e., Random Draw first step) in order to define the player that will start the game. Secondly, a number of letters are displayed randomly and the stopwatch starts (i.e., the second step Displaying of Letters). Obviously, the player with the highest number starts the game. He initiates the discovery and enters a word with the suggested letters before the end of the chronometer time. Likewise, the other player defines a word from the advocated letters (i.e., Word Entry third step). Finally, the Calculation of Scores step computes the score of each player according to the validity and the length of the word (i.e., the number of letters in the word). This step uses NooJ linguistic platform. More particularly, it employs a _dm dictionary [8] and a grammar to determine if the introduced word is correct or not.

The second solution is based on server. Therefore, we do not need to do a random draw. The two players introduce words at the same time. Players can play multiple times. Let us note that this solution uses the same resources. Figure 6 describes the proposed approach for the second solution of the educational game *AlphaNooJ*.

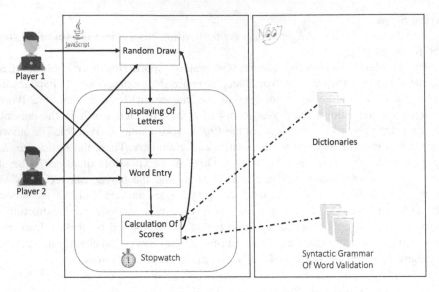

Fig. 5. AlphaNooJ proposed game: first solution

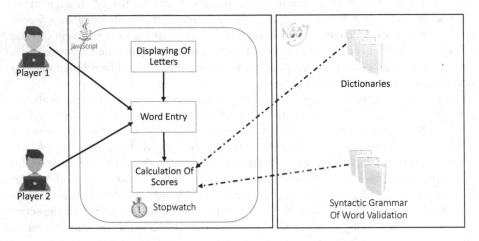

Fig. 6. AlphaNooJ proposed game: second solution

_dm NooJ Dictionary

The French dictionary "_dm.dic" (Fig. 7) contains the different French entries (i.e., verbs, Adjectives, Nouns) with their semantic and syntactical features.

This dictionary includes:

- 67983 entries.
- A derivation model to recognize the derived forms of the input.
- An inflectional model to recognize the inflected forms of the entry.

Fig. 7. Extract from the dictionary _dm

- Seven verbal modes are taken into account in this dictionary: four personal modes that combine: indicative, conditional, subjunctive and imperative and three impersonal modes that do not conjugate infinitive, participle and gerundive.

Syntactic Grammar of Word Validation

To develop AlphaNooJ game, only one grammar is built. This grammar verifies whether the word introduced by a player is valid or not. Figure 6 represents this grammar.

In the grammar of the Fig. 8:

- <DIC> indicates that the word belongs to the French dictionary.
- <!DIC> indicates that the word is not in the French dictionary.
- "valide" represents an annotation that will be displayed when the word is valid.
- "non valide" represents an annotation that will be displayed when the word is invalid.

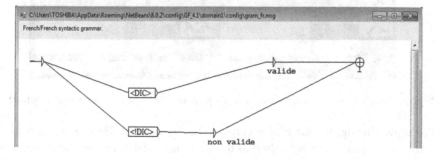

Fig. 8. Syntactic grammar of word validation

3 Experimentations

To validate our two proposed approaches, we have implemented two software tools called *ProMoNooJ* Educational game and *AlphaNooJ* Educational game.

3.1 ProMoNooJ Experimentation

ProMoNooJ is designed for the evaluation of student's knowledge in the four domains: Geography, Sport, Health and Zoology. To do this, we created a set of 81 dictionaries (Domain Geography: 30 dictionaries, Domain Sport: 18 dictionaries, Domain Health: 18 dictionaries and Domain Zoology: 15 dictionaries) and 81 transducers.

At the beginning, the learner chooses Arabic, French or English language. Then, he picks an evaluation field. He evaluates his knowledge in two levels. The first level is simple. It consists in a simple classification of words. Figure 9 depicts an example of the first level in ProMoNooJ game.

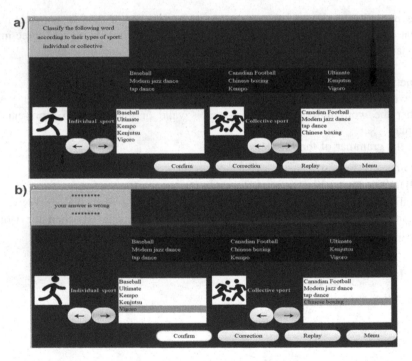

Fig. 9. Simple classification of words: easy level of *ProMoNooJ* (Color figure online)

As shown in Fig. 9a, the player chooses the Sports field. He tries to classify the randomly displayed words according to the requested categories: Individual sport and Collective sport. He verifies his answer by using the bottom "Confirm". Figure 9b shows the result of the first level. It presents the incorrect answers with a different color: purple color.

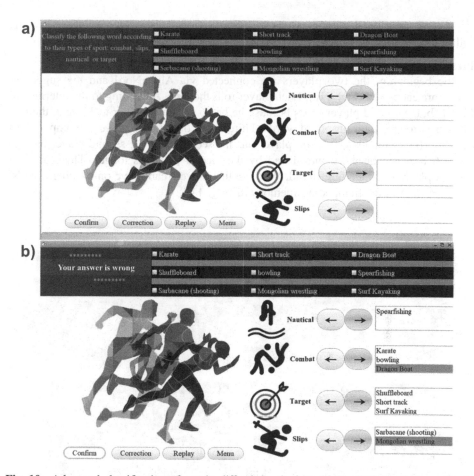

Fig. 10. Advanced classification of words: difficult level of *ProMoNooJ* (Color figure online)

Provided that all the responses in the first level are correct, the learner goes automatically to a more difficult level. In this level, the player moves to a more refined classification in the same domain. Figure 10a describes an advanced classification of a set of words in sports field. The player classifies the words in the four categories: Nautical, Combat, Target and slips.

By confirming his answer, the interface of Fig. 10b is displayed to show the incorrect answers in purple color. The player can correct by clicking on the "correction" button.

3.2 AlphaNooJ Experimentation

AlphaNooJ enlarges students' information. It allows specifying words from a set of predefined letters. It uses NooJ platform. Especially, it employs _dm dictionary and a transducer to check the validity of the introduced words.

As we mentioned earlier, *AlphaNooJ* is developed using two solutions. In the following section, we describe the experimentation of each solution.

First Solution

At the beginning, the two players are connected via AlphaNooJ and the suggested letters are encrypted (Fig. 11a). Each player rolls the dice. According to the interface of Fig. 11b, the second player starts because he had 6 which is higher to 1. Next, the two players introduce their proposed words. Third, the score of each player is computed. In our case (i.e., Fig. 11c), the first player has the score 0 and the second player has the score 6 because the word introduced by the second player is longer. Therefore, the second player wins the first round. We note that players can move on to other rounds. In addition, all the attempts are memorized (Fig. 11d).

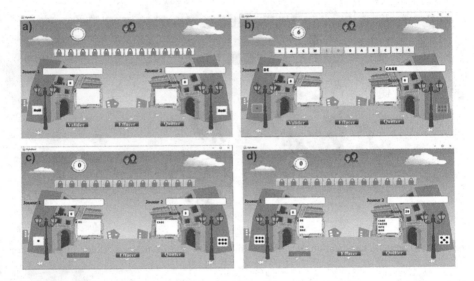

Fig. 11. Steps interface of *AlphaNooJ* : fist solution

Second Solution

The second solution requires authentication (Fig. 12a). Each player should enter the login and a password. When the first player is connected, his name is then displayed in the dedicated interface (Fig. 12b). When the second player is connected, the game begins. Thus, the twelve letters are displayed in a random manner and the stopwatch is started for the two players in question (Fig. 12c).

When there is not much time to type the word, the color of the stopwatch becomes red (Fig. 12c). When the player clicks on "Valider" button, the score is displayed and the proposed word is saved in a table of two columns: one for the word and the other for its validity (Fig. 12d).

At the end of the game, a congratulatory video is displayed to the winner and a chess message is displayed to the loser.

Fig. 12. Steps interface of *AlphaNooJ* : second solution (Color figure online)

4 Conclusion and Future Work

In this paper, we have proposed two educational games. The development of these games is based on a linguistic approach using dictionaries and transducers. These resources are built in the NooJ platform and the implementation is done using Java. The connection between NetBeans and NooJ is done with noojapply. Based on the experimentation, we managed to develop serious games with simple NooJ resources. Thus, we ensure openness between two areas: NLP and serious games.

In the future, we plan to make AlphaNooJ games multilingual by adding resources related to English and Arabic. Furthermore, we plan to integrate other domains to the ProMoNooJ game.

References

1. Iten, N., Petko, D.: Learning with serious games: is fun playing the game a predictor of learning success? Br. J. Educ. Technol. **47**(1), 151–163 (2016)
2. Ge, X., Ifenthaler, D.: Designing engaging educational games and assessing engagement in game-based learning. In: Zheng, R., Gardner, M. (eds.) Handbook of Research on Serious Games for Educational Applications, pp. 253–270. IGI Global, Hershey (2017). https://doi.org/10.4018/978-1-5225-0513-6.ch012
3. Concilio, I.D., Braga, P.H.: Game concepts in learning and teaching process. In: Krassmann, A., Amaral, É., Nunes, F., Voss, G., Zunguze, M. (eds.) Handbook of Research on Immersive Digital Games in Educational Environments, pp. 1–34. IGI Global, Hershey (2019). https://doi.org/10.4018/978-1-5225-5790-6.ch001
4. Silberztein, M.: The NooJ manual. www.nooj-association.org (213 pages) (2003)

5. Silberztein, M.: La formalisation des langues: l'approche NooJ. Collection Sciences Cognitive et Management des Connaissances. Edition ISTE, London (2015)
6. Evans, M.: I'd Rather be playing calculus: adapting entertainment game structures to educational games. In: Felicia, P. (ed.) Handbook of Research on Improving Learning and Motivation through Educational Games: Multidisciplinary Approaches, pp. 153–175 (2011)
7. Fehri, H., Haddar, K., Ben Hamadou, A.: Automatic recognition and semantic analysis of Arabic named entities. In: Vàradi, T., Kuti, J., Silberztein, M. (eds.) Applications of Finite-State Language Processing: Selected Papers from the 2008 International NooJ Conference, pp 56–68. Cambridge Scholars Publishing (2008). ISBN (10): 1-4438-2573-5, ISBN (13): 978-1-4438-2573-3
8. Trouilleux, F.: A new French dictionary for NooJ: le DM. In: Automatic Processing of Various Levels of Linguistic Phenomena: Selected Papers from the NooJ 2011 International Conference, pp. 16–28. Cambridge Scholars Publishing (2012). 1-4438- 3711-3 (2011)

Detecting Hate Speech Online:
A Case of Croatian

Kristina Kocijan[1](✉) (iD), Lucija Košković[2], and Petra Bajac[2]

[1] Department of Information and Communication Sciences,
University of Zagreb, Zagreb, Croatia
krkocijan@ffzg.hr
[2] Department of Linguistics, Faculty of Humanities and Social Sciences,
University of Zagreb, Zagreb, Croatia
{lkoskovi,pbajac}@ffzg.hr

Abstract. This project proposes a NooJ algorithm with the task to find and categorize various slurs, insults and ultimately, hate speech in Croatian. The results also provide a more detailed insight into inappropriate language in Croatian. We strongly emphasize the ethical considerations of (mis) identifying hate speech and as a result, an unethical and undeserved censorship of inappropriate, but free speech. Thus, we tried to make a clear distinction between insults and hate speech.

The test corpus consists of written online comments and remarks posted on five Croatian Facebook news pages during one week period. Given the differences between the standard Croatian grammar and syntax, and what is actually being used in informal on-line communication, the false negatives present the biggest difficulty since some variations (substandard usages of cases, spelling errors, colloquialisms) are impossible to predict, and therefore, extremely hard to implement into the algorithm.

Keywords: Hate speech · Insults · Pattern detection · Information extraction · Syntactic grammars · Croatian · NooJ

1 Introduction

With the growing power of social media and the internet, especially now days, given the global political situation and its controversies, the need to detect and identify hate speech is of crucial importance. Web sites have already implemented various systems for such purposes, not only to locate hate speech in different languages, but also to block it to provide a more civilized and safe cyberspace for its users.

People are often guided by the thought of having the right to their own opinion, of having the right to say what is on their mind, regardless of the content and heaviness of the spoken. However, there is a thin (fine line) line between freedom of speech, and hate speech or insults. As Serrano (2016, as cited in [1]) states, multiple violations of others' rights often occur as a consequence. Nevertheless, Jakubowicz et al. [2] argue how those freedoms have enhanced the impact of hate, which comes to the fore with the growing power of the Internet and social media.

© Springer Nature Switzerland AG 2020
H. Fehri et al. (Eds.): NooJ 2019, CCIS 1153, pp. 185–197, 2020.
https://doi.org/10.1007/978-3-030-38833-1_16

Since the moment it emerged, social media has not been used only for updates, news or maintaining private conversations, but also as an outlet for public commentary and discussions on diverse topics [1]. Isolation and potential anonymity of Web users protects them from accountability [3], which partially explains why it is so easy to write a "hate comment". Bearing in mind that language is one of the mechanisms through which violence spreads and that shapes ways people perceive or understand events, it is important to acknowledge the danger of violent escalations when "one discourse gains the upper hand and stifles alternative voices" [4].

There are various hate speech definitions. Silva et al. state that hate speech can be defined as an offense motivated, "in whole or in part, by the offender's bias against an aspect of a group of people" [5]. As Gagliardone et al. accentuate [6], it relies on tensions, which it seeks to reproduce and amplify, dividing and uniting at the same time, creating "us" and "them". It goes beyond targeting people based on their characteristics (hate speech vs. insults). Its intention is to degrade, intimidate or incite violence or prejudice against a person or group on various grounds. Specifically, hate speech in Croatia is defined by the legislation as an act that spreads, incites, promotes and encourages racial, ethnic, gender, political and religious, language or sexual hatred [7]. On the other hand, insult can be defined as an unallowed/inadmissible oral or written statement, gesture or any other behavior expressing a negative value judgment on a person, and thereby offending their honor, reputation or dignity [8]. Insults are most often achieved by verbal humiliation.

The main focus of this paper is to describe the algorithm designed to detect hate speech and insults in the Croatian Web space. The structure of the paper aims to give a brief theoretical overview on algorithms for detection of insults and hate speech in general in Sect. 2, followed by the description of Croatian dictionary entries prepared for this project in Sect. 3, the overview of the morphological and syntax grammars in Sects. 4 and 5 respectfully, and the discussion of our results on the prepared corpus in Sect. 6. The paper concludes with an outline of future work.

2 Theoretical Overview and Related Work

The growing power of social media has a serious untamed consequence – the greater representation of hate speech and insults. Over the past years, there have been numerous studies reporting on computational methods to detect hate speech and insults online. In spite the fact that the majority of social media Terms of Services documentation explicitly or implicitly prohibits hate speech [6], these sites have proved to be a rich pool for different research projects on hate speech, like Twitter and Wisper [5], or Twitter alone [1, 9, 10]. Malmasi and Zampieri [9] give a short five-year overview of such projects ranging from applying sentiment analysis to detect bullying in tweets, using binary classification for detecting non-hate speech vs. hate speech, to investigating hate speech in non-english texts like Arabic, Chinese, Slovene or German. Another detailed overview is presented in Al-Hassan and Al-Dossari [11] including work carried out from 2011 to 2018 on insults, cyberbullying, radicalization, hate speech (religious, racial, general) in English, cyberbullying in Turkish, general hate speech in Italian, Indonesian and German, insults, violent content, adult content, cyberbullying, terrorism and religious hate speech in Arabic. Their summary includes the data on authors, corpus source, ML approach, algorithm type and standard measures (Precision, Recall, F1-Score).

Mitrović et al. [12] also report that, in the last decade, different methods and models have been proposed which tend to identify hate speech and insults on the Internet. The same group of authors suggests the model for the identification of offensive language in tweets, using the model C-Bigra, which combines a Convolutional Neural Network (CNN) with a bidirectional Recurrent Neural Network (RNN) and word2vec in order to note semantic similarities between words. Authors state that bidirectional Recurrent Neural Network (RNN), instead of a unidirectional Long Short-Term Memory (LSTM) recurrent neural network, allows capturing of past and future information about the input sequence and exploits better performance of GRU networks on smaller data sets. It is through this unidirectional approach (LSTM), and in relation with the same topic, that Bansal et al. [10] made their work. Malmasi and Zampieri [9] have used the machine learning algorithm, a linear Support Vector Machine (SVM) classifier, with the three groups of features to detect hate speech and insults on 14, 509 English tweets, reporting the 78% accuracy for their 4-gram model. On the other hand, Monteleone [13] warns about potential imprecision and wrong assessment of statistical algorithms. In his work on Italian texts, he gives a greater importance to the on-line hate speech detection based on the formalization of the morphosyntactic rules of a given language, with a minimal margin of error. He also provides a summary of methodological and functional differences between statistical and rule-based approach. The reference to the understanding of the algorithm used in the former, i.e. lack of the understanding in the prior approach, seems of the greatest importance between the two, especially when dealing with the projects that include automatic hate speech recognition. However, to this date, there has not been a standard evaluation set with which different methods could be compared. In spite of the several NLP methods proposed, their features have never been combined or evaluated against each other [14]. Closest to the goals of this paper was work done on the FRENK Project [15] which combines research studies from the fields of NLP, sociolinguistics, sociology and law in order to develop resources, methods and tools for the understanding, identification and classification of various forms of socially unacceptable discourses in Slovenian.

In Croatia, the research on detecting hate speech is still in its infancy. Thus far, researches in Croatia have only gone so far as analyzing the theoretical [16, 17], psychoanalitical [18], anthropological [19] and legislative [20, 21] side of hate speech and insults. To be more precise, they are mostly concerned with the freedom of speech, and its boundaries as stated in Article 16 of the Constitution of the Republic of Croatia. With this paper, we will try to make the next logical step, i.e. use the power of NLP to detect and mark hate speech and insults in Croatian on-line texts.

3   Preparing the Dictionary Entries

In order to make the syntactic grammars cleaner and easier to construct and maintain, we decided to add some semantic features to our dictionary entries. This was done for verbs, nouns and adjectives, since they are the carriers of pejorative meanings found in syntactic constructions in the test corpus. We are talking about the words that are meant to offend, scorn or ridicule another person or a group. Often, it is realized as a diminutive or augmentative noun, but also as irony[1]. A tag *+pejor* is added to 46 verbs (out of 4 889), 362 nouns (out of 27 636 nouns in total) and 62 adjectives (out of 14 503).

As we have progressed in our research, we found some additional patterns that we could use in the grammar, if semantic tags were added directly through the dictionary entries. To be more precise, we have noticed that the choice of verbs in hate speech constructions are related with a behavior suggesting violence (*klati* – to slaughter, *poubijati* – to kill, *objesiti* – to hang), so we decided to use a tag *+violence* to describe them within the dictionary. We detected 26 of such verbs used repeatedly throughout the test corpus.

Furthermore, we have observed that Croatian insults tend to revolve around family members, mostly females, but also around animals. Thus, we have reused the semantic tags for nouns denoting family members <N+obt> as defined in [22], and added a new dictionary tag for animals <N+animal>. These additional semantic tags allowed us much cleaner grammatical notations (see Sect. 5).

4 Morphological Grammar

Before we can start recognizing syntactic constructions, we need to make sure that each element of that construction is recognized. However, this is not always the case when the corpus is built from the on-line texts where we found spelling errors to be quite common. We detected several reasons for this that can be viewed from the orthographic or lexicographic perspective. No matter the perspective, the algorithm cannot recognize these variations unless we instruct it what to do when it encounters the unknown word. This is true for all of the following examples.

The first one is pure spelling error i.e. *lapsus calami* caused most likely by the speed of writing or a psychological state of a writer while the second type of error is due to a lower level of literacy. The third one has to do with 5 diacritics [č, ć, đ, š, ž] which in online communication are often replaced with [c, c, d, s, z] respectfully, usually due to technological restrictions of the keyboards being used to type the text (e.g. from the mobile phones). The fourth type of error is incorrect usage of '*ije*' and '*je*'. All of these errors fall into unintentional type of errors that in more cases than not, can be recognized by a specially designed algorithm.

However, there are also intentional spelling variations [e.g. repetitions of a vowel] and puns (e.g. *CRO-magnon*) where the variation is used for a humorous and emphatic effect – impossible to predict and very difficult to describe. On the lexicographic level, we had to manage regionalisms and slangs as well as many other uncommon words, neologisms and nonce words, born from creative language use, that were originaly missing from the NooJ dictionary of standard Croatian. In addition to afore listed problems, we have also encountered a morphological problem connected with irregular

---

[1] At this time, we did not deal with detecting irony in the text.

usage of vocative case, i.e. nominative form is mainly used where the vocative should appear (e.g. *okotu partizanski*), or some rather unpredictable (incorrect) version is used.

At this time, we were able to solve the issues of missing diacritics and missing *ije/je*, as well as the repetition of vowels (Fig. 1). The algorithm checks if a word exists in a dictionary after undergoing specified changes on the orthographic level. If such a word is found in a dictionary, the word recognized by the transducer is marked as if it was originally found in the dictionary, i.e. it inherits all its syntactic and flective features. Since all three phenomena are possible on the same word, they were dealt with inside the same morphological grammar.

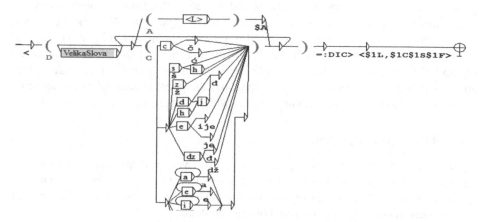

Fig. 1. Excerpt of the morphological grammar for recognizing missing diacritics, repetition of vowels and missing *ije/je*

The steps the algorithm makes can be demonstrated via following few examples:

- *politicka* [replaces c with č -> checks if '*politička*' is in the dictionary -> marks the input word with all the properties of word '*politička*']
- *jaaaadan* [replaces *aaaa* with *a*-> checks if '*jadan*' is in the dictionary -> marks the input word with all the properties of word '*jadan*']
- *bedne* [replaces *e* with *ije* -> checks if '*bijedne*' is in the dictionary -> marks the input word with all the properties of word '*bijedne*']
- *cetnickaaaa* [replaces 1st c with č & replaces 2nd c with č & replaces *aaaa* with *a*-> checks if '*četnička*' is in the dictionary -> marks the input word with all the properties of word '*četnička*'].

If the word is not found in the main dictionary, it remains in the unknown set of words. If this word is relevant for detecting an insult or hate speech, it will affect the result for these syntagmas i.e. the syntagmas will not be recognized which will in turn lower the recall.

5   Syntax Grammar

We think it is important to make a clear distinction (as clear as it can be) between mere "inappropriate language" with words and phrases such as "*stupid whore*", and that which obviously has broader and direr implications and could without a doubt be categorized as hate speech, such as "*death to all westerners*" With that in mind, our algorithm will consist of two major categories, insults and hate speech. We feel this need for caution on such a slippery slope and our goal is to carefully categorize and mark these differences, using Article 127 of the Croatian Criminal Law as a reference.

The design of syntactic grammar fallows a two-way branch i.e. it has two main graphs: one for hate speech constructions and the second for insults. Consequently, all the results for the first graph are marked with <HS> tags, and <INS> for the second graph. This allowed us to measure the performance of our algorithm in finding each of the syntagmas separately as will be shown in Sect. 6.2. At this time, we avoided making the distinction within these two branches more granular but, with further analysis of our data, we expect to find categories like race, gender, ethnicity, religion, sexual orientation, class or disability, in line with findings in similar research [5, 13].

5.1   Hate Speech Algorithm

At the preliminary stage of this project, while we were just learning about our test corpus, we listed the examples in the graph one by one, trying to detect some patterns. As soon as we identified a way of merging two nodes into one, they would be replaced with a more general description that both nodes share.

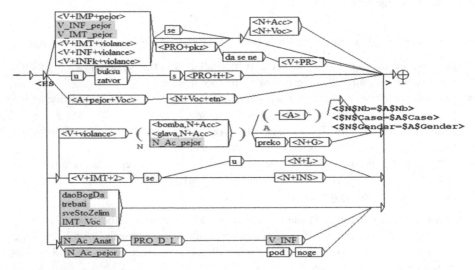

Fig. 2. Local grammar that recognizes Croatian hate speech syntagmas (Color figure online)

An example of such description is **<N+Acc>** with a meaning that any noun in accusative case can be found at that position. Similarly, notation **<N+Acc+pejor>** means that any noun in accusative case that also carries semantic tag +*pejor* can be found at the specified position (Fig. 2). The detected patterns build paths of a graph that consists of descriptive nodes and link nodes. The descriptive type of nodes give an exact word(s) (e.g. *zatvor*) or a more general description of a word expected at that position (e.g. <N+L>), while the link (yellow) nodes act as a door to another graph (e.g. :V_INF_pejor, :N_Ac_pejor, :daoBogDa) with descriptive nodes and/or more link nodes. We will proceed with the description of two link nodes from Fig. 2 (:*daoBogDa* and :*trebati*) with an excerpt from the concordance list.

If we take a look inside the link node ':*daoBogDa*' (Fig. 3) we see that it holds some descriptive nodes but also two additional link nodes (:*PRO_D_L* and : *V_IMT_pejor*) second of which is used at 3 different positions inside this sub-graph, as well as in several other sub-graphs across this entire grammar. Syntagmas that the sub-graph:*daoBogDa* recognizes, must start with the saying 'dao Bog da' (God permit). However, there are nine realizations of this saying in our corpus. Although not all are in standard Croatian (marked with asterisk), we decided to take them into the account, nevertheless: *neka | dabogda | dabog da* | dao Bog da | dao bog* da | da Bog dao | da bog* dao | da Bog dao da | da bog* dao da.*

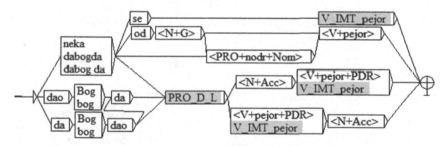

Fig. 3. Algorithm for recognizing constructions starting with '*dao Bog da...*' [God allowed...]

Some of the examples recognized by the grammar (Fig. 3) are:

a. ***Da Bog dao*** *mu dusu iscupali*   [**God permit**, they rip his soul out.]
b. ***dabogda*** *od gladi svi pocrkali*   [**God permit**, they all starve to death.].

The link node:*trebati* takes us into another sub-graph which recognizes hate speech syntagmas that use the verb should (*trebati*) somewhere along the path. We can say that these syntagmas carry a slightly stronger connotation than the previous one. However, at this time, we did not mark these nuances in the annotation tag. Some of the examples recognized by this part of the algorithm are:

c. *sve ih **treba** spaliti na lomaci*   [They **should** all be burned at the stake.]
d. *zivog ga zapalit **treba***   [He **should** be burned alive.]

5.2   Insults Branch

In the insults sub-graph (Fig. 4), we are mostly looking for the NP's where either a noun or an adjective carries a pejorative semantic tag as explained in Sect. 3. What is important is that all the adjectives and nouns included in the NP match in case, gender and number. This proved to be tricky since not all the examples we found are using the proper gender forms of adjectives. The following are some examples of insults from the test corpus:

e. *obično govno neodgojeno*   [Basic disrespectful shit]
f. *sotonistička-masonska bagra*   [Satanic-masonic scum]
g. *krivousto govno*   [Tilt-mouth shit]

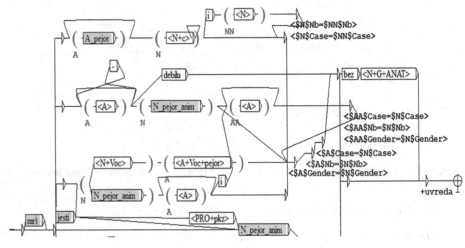

Fig. 4. An excerpt from the algorithm describing insults

It is not uncommon to find profanities next to an insult phrase in Croatian daily discourse, as well as in literature. The same is true for our test corpus. They mostly deal with some sex-related activities or organs and include closer family members and animals. For this reason, we have included a subgraph that recognizes and annotates such expressions, as well. This section of the algorithm recognizes syntagmas like the ones that follow:

h. *marš ti brale **u pm***   [Get lost, friend, **in your mc (*mother's cunt*)**]

i. ***je… vam mater lopovsku***   [I **f.ck** your thieving mother]

We were surprised to learn how common the usage of postposition is in NP constructions, which is rather atypical for the Croatian language. Some of the examples include:

j. *bagro **šugava***   [**Scabby** scum]

k. *kozo **jedna nepodojena***   [You unmilked goat]

l. *đubrad **policijska***   [Police scum]

m. *obično smeće **debilno nakaradno***   [Basic moron qrotesque trash].

6 Results

6.1 Test Corpus

We have manually built a corpus of 9 345 words by collecting comments under the posts on five Croatian Facebook news pages during a week between 18.03.2019 and 24.03.2019. We have opted for Facebook posts since this social media was voted[2] the most popular in Croatia during the given period. Our decision was further supported by the statement that Facebook "*has become the breeding ground for the promotion of the harshest types of expression of hatred*" [16].

The reason behind the selected news pages that include *'24sata.hr'*, *'Dnevnik.hr'*, *'Net.hr'*, *'Tportal.hr'*, and *'Vecernji.hr'* is that these five pages had the greatest number of views during the selected time period[3] which indicated that we should find the greatest number of posts on them. All of the comments containing an insult or a case of hate speech were put in a single file and no data was kept to differentiate which portal it came from originally. There were several occurrences of full names in the corpus, which we have decided to delete due to the recent GDPR regulations.

It must be noted that the insults and hate speech found in our test corpus are very culture and time specific. The history and the geopolitical situation in Croatia give pejorative meanings to certain phrases which are not intrinsically insults and which, in some other era or some other context, would be considered a compliment (e.g. *partizančino*). For these reasons, it is important to accentuate that the proposed algorithm may perform differently on texts from different time period or different geopolitical area and would need to undergo specific changes in order to accomodate the differences. We would expect that these modifications would be lesser for languages from the dialectal and cultural continuum i.e. Bosnian and Serbian.

---

[2] StatCounter Global Stats: Social Media Stats Croatia, http://gs.statcounter.com/social-media-stats/all/croatia/#weekly-201912-201912-bar.

[3] Rating of Croatian portals - https://rating.gemius.com/.

6.2   NooJ Grammar Results

Although results on precision are quite close for both branches resulting in an overall precision of 90%, when it comes to recall the algorithm on insults outperforms the one detecting hate speech by 36% (Fig. 5).

INSULTS	HATE SPEECH	OVERALL
▪ RECALL: 84%	▪ RECALL: 48%	▪ RECALL: 66%
▪ PRECISION: 91%	▪ PRECISION: 89%	▪ PRECISION: 90%
▪ F-MEASURE: 88%	▪ F-MEASURE: 63%	▪ F-MEASURE: 76%

Fig. 5. Algorithm performance

6.3   Problems

The main problems we encountered and that influenced the performance of the algorithm, are categorized into the following eight domains:

Spelling errors - one of the most unpredictable issues we faced in trying to improve the recall of our algorithm. Such errors make it impossible for NooJ [23] to recognize the words necessary to perform the classification. The most common type of such errors are typos, impossible to predict like in the following example where the verb 'to lock up' is written as '*pozazvarat*' instead of '*pozatvarat*'.

> a.   *treba vas sve drogerase gejeve **pozazvarat** isprebijat*
> [all of you gay narcos should be **locked up** and beaten].

Also common is the omitance of final 'h'. For example, according to the standard Croatian, the adverb 'immediately'is written as '*odmah*' i.e. with an 'h' at the end. However, we have found numerous examples, of this and other words as well, with the final 'h' missing:

> b.   *to treba **odma** strijeljat*   [*that* should be shot **immediately**].

No capitalization - online community prefers using lowercase letters. Orthographical rules for capitalization in Croatian are often ignored which, in turn, makes word recognition more difficult.

Merged words - there are times when two words (rarely, more than two) are written as one. This is both an issue of dialectal variation and illiteracy levels. For example, the negation of the Croatian verb should be written apart from the verb [*ne znam, ne čujem*], but some people fuse it together, given that it is one phonological unit in spoken language [*neznam, nečujem*]. This creates a problem for NooJ which recognizes this as one unknown unit.

Self-censorship - letters replaced with symbols * or. or, (n repetitions) – like in the example [*takvima treba je*** mater*]. People sometimes censor their own inappropriate language by using symbols to "hide" parts of the insulting phrase. This also makes it hard to recognize with an existing algorithm and needs further attention.

Foreign words or dialectal variations - use of foreign words and dialectal variation - [*pes vusrani – pas usrani*] are quite common. While dialects are considered to be a linguistic treasure, these variations are mostly not covered in dictionaries and other linguistic resources. Some of the examples include high level of dialectal variation including non-standard lexemes (*plejati, benzinem, vuzgati*), prepositions fused with their complements (*zbenzinem*) and different instrumental case ending (*benzinem*):

> c.   treba vas **plejati zbenzinem** i **vuzgati**
> [you should be **doused** in **gasoline** and **set on fire**].

Slang - quite common in everyday communication, including the on-line communication as well. Since we do not have dictionary of slang prepared in the NooJ environment, we were not able to recognize such occurrences, like in the following example:

> d. *treba ga **skuriti***   [He should be **burned**.]

Missing verbs and hate speech - we worked under the assumption that we needed a verb with a violent meaning to create hate speech, but with the language creativity and general freedom offered by the Croatian language, sometimes the verb is missing and/or implied like in the following example.

> q. *Metak u čelo.*   [Bullet to the forehead].

Pragmatics - words that usually do not carry negative or violent meanings, change their polarity if written inside the quotation marks. We have not dealt with problems on this level and such uses are left unrecognized by the algorithm. We can see this in the following example with the verb "to cleanse" (*očistiti*) that does not in itself hold a violent meaning. But, when put under quotation marks, it receives a very dire connotation. These types of pragmatic nuances still need to be dealt with in the algorithm.

> r. *tu policiju treba "**očistiti**"*   [The police should be "**cleansed**".]

7   Conclusion and Future Work

Algorithms for hate speech detection fall under the category of ethical algorithms, which pose ethical questions of censorship and freedom of speech. This is at the same time very delicate, but extremely important subject in today's online society. We cannot emphasize enough the importance of carefully drawing the line between insults and hate speech, since they are on opposite sides and while the first is just rude, the other one is a crime that more often than not goes unchallenged.

One should also be vary of culture and context, where, in a society riddled with insults which have become basically a part of everyday speech, there is a gradient on the severity an insult has, as opposed to a "polite" culture where even a minor insult by Croatian standards may be very inappropriate. Deeper analysis of our results still remains to be done. We hope it will be fruitful in finding new patterns that may help us specify the type of hate speech, and the type and intensity of an insult.

Our first aim is to improve the recall, generally with regards to describe uncommon words, borrowed words, especially the most common ones from English, German and Serbian, and to overcome the challenge of spelling errors and language creativity. Also, given the fact that Croatian has many dialects, we will aim to cover not only the standard, but to include the variations spoken by the people, too. Although beautiful and linguistically very interesting segment of language in itself, is the very language creativity that has proven to be quite a nuisance when building rule-based algorithms and will probably continue to be a problem that will elude the algorithm. We may never be able to complete improving the algorithm since there will always be new and creative ways to insult someone, but that should never be used as an excuse to do better.

References

1. Barrios, M.M., Estarita, L.M.V., Gil, L.M.: When online commentary turns into violence: the role of Twitter in slander against journalists in Colombia. Confl. Commun. 18(1), 1–16 (2019)
2. Jakubowicz, A., et al.: Cyber Racism and Community Resilience. Springer, Cham (2017). https://doi.org/10.1007/978-3-319-64388-5
3. Jakubowicz, A.: Cyber racism. In: More or Less: Democracy and New Media (2012). http://www.futureleaders.com.au/book_chapters/pdf/More-or-Less/Andrew_Jakubowicz.pdf. Accessed 10 May 2019
4. Buyse, A.: Words of violence: fear speech, or how violent conflict escalation relates to the freedom of expression. Hum. Rights Q. 36, 779–797 (2014). The Johns Hopkins University Press
5. Silva, L.A., Mondal, M., Correa, D., Benevenuto, F., Weber, I.: Analyzing the targets of hate in online social media. In: ICWSM, pp. 687–690 (2016)
6. Gagliardone, I., Gal, D., Alves, T., Martinez, G.: Countering Online Hate Speech. UNESCO, Paris (2015). ISBN 978-92-3-100105-5
7. Pendeš, A., Pekas, M., Juršetić, A., Krajnović, T., Jagnić Nenadić, G., Dojčinović, I., Nikšić, D.: ELSA Croatia. Final report on online hate speech, Legal Research Group on Online Hate Speech, pp. 94–111. The European Law Students' Association (2014)
8. Hrvatska enciklopedija: Uvreda. (Insult) In Hrvatska enciklopedija, mrežno izdanje. Leksikografski zavod Miroslav Krleža (2019). http://www.enciklopedija.hr/natuknica.aspx?id=63546

9. Malmasi, S., Zampieri, M.: Detecting hate speech in social media. In: Proceedings of the International Conference Recent Advances in Natural Language Processing, RANLP 2017, pp. 467–472. INCOMA Ltd. (2017). https://doi.org/10.26615/978-954-452-049-6_062
10. Bansal, H., Nagel, D., Soloveva, A.: HAD-Tübingen at SemEval-2019 Task 6: deep learning analysis of offensive language on Twitter: identification and categorization. In: Proceedings of the 13th International Workshop on Semantic Evaluation, pp. 622–627. Association for Computational Linguistics (2019). https://doi.org/10.18653/v1/s19-2111
11. Al-Hassan, A., Al-Dossari, H.: Detection of hate speech in social networks: a survey on multilingual corpus. In: Computer Science & Information Technology, pp. 83–100 (2019). https://doi.org/10.5121/csit.2019.90208
12. Mitrović, J., Birkeneder, B., Granitzer, M.: nlpUP at SemEval-2019 Task 6: a deep neural language model for offensive language detection. In: Proceedings of the 13th International Workshop on Semantic Evaluation, pp. 722–726. Association for Computational Linguistics (2019). https://doi.org/10.18653/v1/s19-2127
13. Monteleone, M.: NooJ Grammars and ethical algorithms: tackling on-line hate speech. In: Mauro Mirto, I., Monteleone, M., Silberztein, M. (eds.) NooJ 2018. CCIS, vol. 987, pp. 180–191. Springer, Cham (2019). https://doi.org/10.1007/978-3-030-10868-7_16
14. Nobata, C., Tetreault, J., Thomas, A., Mehdad, Y., Chang, Y.: Abusive language detection in online user content. In: Proceedings of the 25th International Conference on World Wide Web, pp. 145–153. International World Wide Web Conferences Steering Committee (2016)
15. Fišer, D., Erjavec, T., Ljubešić, N.: Legal framework, dataset and annotation schema for socially unacceptable online discourse practices in Slovene. In: Proceedings of the First Workshop on Abusive Language Online, pp. 46–51 (2017)
16. Vilović, G.: Govor mržnje (Hate speech). Političke analize 2(6), 68–70 (2011). https://hrcak.srce.hr/175715
17. Čolović, N.: O govoru mržnje (About hate speech). Politička misao 54(3), 147–158 (2017). https://hrcak.srce.hr/186457
18. Klain, E.: Psihoanalitičko razumijevanje govora mržnje (Psychoanalitical understanding of the hatred speech). Govor 20(1–2), 191–204 (2003). https://hrcak.srce.hr/179372
19. Marković, J.: Silences that kill? Hate, fear, and their silences. Etnološka tribina 48(41), 122–143 (2018). https://doi.org/10.15378/1848-9540.2018.41.03
20. Munivrana Vajda, M., Šurina Marton, A.: Gdje prestaju granice slobode izražavanja, a počinje govor mržnje? Analiza hrvatskog zakonodavstva i prakse u svjetlu europskih pravnih standarda. Hrvatski ljetopis za kaznene znanosti i praksu 23(2), 435–467 (2016). https://hrcak.srce.hr/177439
21. Roksandić Vidlička, S., Mamić, K.: Zlouporaba društvenih mreža u javnom poticanju na nasilje i mržnju i širenju lažnih vijesti: potreba transplantiranja njemačkog Zakona o jačanju provedbe zakona na društvenim mrežama? (Abuse of social networks in public incitement to violence and hatred and in the spreading of false news: the need for the transposition of the German Act on improving law enforcement on social networks?). Hrvatski ljetopis za kaznene znanosti i praksu 25(2), 329–357 (2018). https://hrcak.srce.hr/218951
22. Kocijan, K., Požega, M.: Building family trees with NooJ in formalising natural languages with NooJ 2014. Selected papers from the NooJ 2014 International Conference, Ed. by J. Monti, M. Silberztein, M. Monteleone, M. Pia di Buono, pp. 198–210. Cambridge Scholars Publishing, Newcastle upon Tyne (2015)
23. Silberztein, M.: Formalizing Natural Languages: The NooJ Approach. Cognitive science series. Wiley, London (2016)

Dealing with Producing and Consuming Expressions in Italian Sentiment Analysis

Nicola Cirillo[✉]

Università degli Studi di Salerno, Salerno, Italy
n.cirillo9@studenti.unisa.com

Abstract. To perform aspect-level sentiment analysis, in the context of customer reviews, it is necessary to deal not only with subjective opinions, that are well covered by literature, but also with fact-implied opinions, that are less examined since they are less common and harder to handle. This work focuses on a specific type of fact-based opinion called producing and consuming expression. For example, expressions like "this printer consumes a lot of ink" and "this washing-machine makes a lot of noise" are instances of this type of opinion. This research aims to build a tool that can identify these expressions, classify their sentiment polarities and determine their opinion targets. To achieve this task, we started analyzing these expressions from a linguistic point of view. Then we developed a set of linguistic resources using the Nooj software. This set consists of one dictionary and one grammar. The dictionary contains verbs that express usage and production; adjectives and determiners that modify quantity, size, etc. and some generic nouns of resources and wastes. The grammar can recognize and tags simple and complex sentences that are producing and consuming expressions. This grammar produces a tag that allows to determine the sentiment of the expression simply by applying the rules of sentiment composition.

Keywords: Sentiment analysis · Natural language processing · Nooj

1 Introduction

The field of study called sentiment analysis, is attracting a lot of attention among the researchers in computational linguistics. This phenomenon is mainly due to the increasing need to retrieve and summarize valuable information from the enormous quantity of written opinions existing on the web.

In order to summarize these written opinions, it is necessary to deal with the ways in which opinions can be expressed. The most common way to express opinions is with adjectives. For example, in the statements "this pen is good" and "I bought a good pen" the adjective *good* expresses a positive opinion about the entity *pen*.

Since this is the most common opinion as well as the simplest, some sentiment analysis systems, especially the earliest, were able to identify only this type of opinion. However, there are a lot of ways in which an opinion can be expressed. For example, it can be expressed through verbs (e.g. "I like this pen") as well as through adverbs (e.g. "this pen writes badly"). The words that express opinions are called sentiment words.

H. Fehri et al. (Eds.): NooJ 2019, CCIS 1153, pp. 198–208, 2020.
https://doi.org/10.1007/978-3-030-38833-1_17

There are also constructions that modify the sentiment expressed by a sentiment word, one of them is the negation. For example, in the sentence "this pen is not good", the negation *not* invert the sentiment expressed by the adjective *good* (that is positive) and so the overall sentiment expressed by the sentence is considered negative.

Indeed, there are also some constructions that imply opinions nevertheless they do not contain any sentiment word. For example, the sentence "this washing machine is noisy" clearly implies a negative opinion in the context of customer reviews.

This type of constructions can be very complex, and the more complex they are, the more difficult to treat them. However, the difficulty should not represent a justification to avoid their treatment. An effective sentiment analysis system must identify and treat properly as many opinion types as possible, even complex and infrequent ones.

To recognize and classify properly complex opinions, researchers have developed lexicon-based approaches that describe the composition of opinions with sets of explicit rules.

These models are valuable from both theoretical and practical point of view: they represent theoretic models of the language constructs that express opinions while they can also be used to retrieve and summarize these opinions automatically.

Our aim is to build a lexicon-based model that is able to treat a complex type of opinion: the producing and consuming expressions [1, 2].

A producing or consuming expression expresses an opinion through a statement about the production (or consumption) of resources (or wastes). For example, sentences like "this printer consumes a lot of ink", "my new torch emits an intense light" and "the washing-machine makes a lot of noise" can be considered producing and consuming expressions.

In this paper, we will present the main lexicon-based approaches proposed in the literature in Sect. 2. In Sect. 3, we will discuss some limitations of these approaches, especially focusing on their application on Italian sentences. In Sect. 4, we will propose our methodology to represent the rules of sentiment compositions. In Sect. 5, we will describe our system and in Sect. 6 we will discuss the results of the application of our system on three corpora of reviews.

2 Related Works

Research about sentiment composition began with the idea that sentiment words are not sufficient by themselves to determine the sentiment of some opinions. The context, in which the sentiment words appear, needs to be considered.

One contextual element that can modify the sentiment expressed by a word is *not*. If *not* precedes a sentiment word, it inverts the sentiment polarity of that word. This fact has been considered since early works [3, 4]. Words like *not* are called negatives [5]. But the negatives are not the only elements that can modify the sentiment polarity, there are also other constructions that can do the same: intensifiers, modal operators and connectors. These constructions are called contextual valence shifters [5].

Besides the idea of a modifier, that modifies a sentiment word, as well as the idea that the sentiment of complex syntactic constituents can be considered as a function of their sub-constituents was proposed by Moilanen and Pulman [6]. This idea is based on the principle of compositionality [7].

Following this idea, a set of sentiment composition rules was developed by Liu [1, 2]. Every rule of this set represents a linguistic construction that implies an opinion [1]. Some of these rules are as simple as single opinion words while some others can be complex. The set of sentiment composition rules is composed of top-level rules that are expanded by subsequent rules up to lists of lemmas. For example, a top-level rule is represented by *POSITIVE = PO* where *POSITIVE* is the final sentiment and *PO* is a positive sentiment expression. A subsequent rule is *PO = CONSUME SMALL_LESS RESOURCE*, each element of this rule is a list of lemmas: *CONSUME = to consume | to use | to deploy | [...]*; *SMALL_LESS = few | little | smaller | [...]*; *RESOURCE = water | gas | oil | fuel | [...]* [1].

With regard to the applications of NooJ [8] in sentiment analysis, it has already been used by researchers to develop lexicon-based sentiment analysis systems. Merkler and Agic [9] used NooJ to build a sentiment analysis system that analyzes daily horoscope in Croatian. NooJ has also been used to develop Doxa [10]: an Italian sentiment analysis system that takes contextual valence shifting into account.

3   Problems of Sentiment Composition Rules

Because of the complexity and diversity of the sentiment composition rules, a good way to represent them formally in a grammar framework is still needed [1]. The representation scheme proposed by Liu [1] (that is based on regular expressions) presents two issues.

The first issue is that it cannot represent a linguistic phenomenon that is involved in the correct identification of the target opinion in some Italian sentences such as the agreement in person and number between subject and verb. This phenomenon contributes to determine which is the subject between a noun that precedes the verb and another noun that follows it. For example, in the sentence "il cane odia il gatto" (the dog hates the cat) *il cane* (the dog) is the subject of the verb *odiare* (to hate) while *il gatto* (the cat) is its object. In the sentence with an OVS (object-verb-subject) order "il cane odiano i gatti" (the cats hate the dog), *il cane* is the object of the verb and *i gatti* (the cats) is the subject because *odiano* (they hate) is the third person plural of the verb *odiare* and so it agrees in person and number with the noun *i gatti* (third-person plural) but not with the noun *il cane* (third-person singular).

The second issue is that the representation scheme proposed by Liu [1] cannot represent the fact that some syntactic constructions express information just like words. For example, in the domain of producing and consuming expressions (in Italian), the right (or left) dislocation can express information about the quantity like adjectives do. It should be noted that the sentence "ne consuma di batteria" (it consumes a lot of battery) has a meaning closer to the sentence "consuma molta batteria" (it consumes a lot of battery) than to the meaning of the sentence "consuma batteria" (it consumes battery).

4 Proposed Approach

Our approach is lexicon-based since it relies on a lexicon and on a set of rules to identify the producing and consuming expressions, classify their orientations and identify their opinion targets. The proposed system is composed of three main linguistic resources:

- a sentiment lexicon
- a set of syntactic grammars
- a set of semantic composition rules.

In order to develop the sentiment lexicon and the syntactic grammars, we started from the semantic components that compose consuming and producing expressions (taken from the rules proposed by Liu [1]) and then we analyze each component to describe the ways in which it is expressed in text.

4.1 Analysis of Semantic Components

The semantic components are six, divided into three pairs:

- *PRODUCE* and *CONSUME*
- *LARGE_MORE* and *SMALL_LESS*
- *RESOURCE* and *WASTE*.

Each producing or consuming expression must contain one and only one component for each pair. Their combination determines the sentiment orientation of the expression. For example, the sentence "questa torcia emette una luce intensa" (this torch emits an intense light) contains the component *PRODUCE*, expressed by the verb *emettere* (to emit); the component *LARGE_MORE*, expressed by the adjective *intensa* (intense); and the component *RESOURCE*, expressed by the noun *luce* (light). So, the sentiment of this expression, according to the rules of sentiment composition [1], is *POSITIVE*.

PRODUCE and CONSUME

Verbs. The *PRODUCE* and *CONSUME* components are usually expressed through verbs. For example, verbs like *produrre* (to produce), *fare* (to make), *creare* (to create) express the *PRODUCE* component; while verbs like *consumare* (to consume), *usare* (to use) and *adoperare* (to deploy) express the *CONSUME* component.

Nouns. A noun that is a nominalization of a *PRODUCE* or *CONSUME* verb expresses its same semantic component. For example, the noun *consumo* (consumption) that is a nominalization of the verb *consumare* (to consume), expresses the *CONSUME* component.

Adjectives. We expected that what happens with nominalizations, must happen also with adjectivizations, but we were able to find only one case: the adjective *bisognoso* ("needful") that is an adjectivization of the verb *abbisognare* (to need) and expresses the *CONSUME* component.

LARGE_MORE and MORE_LESS

Adjectives. The *LARGE_MORE* and *SMALL_LESS* components are usually expressed through adjectives. For example, adjectives like *grande* (big), *largo* (wide), *intenso* (intense) express the *LARGE_MORE* component while adjectives like *piccolo* (small), *stretto* (narrow), *scarso* (scarce) express the *SMALL_LESS* component.

Compound Determiners. The *LARGE_MORE* and *SMALL_LESS* components are also often expressed through compound determiners. We identified two types of determiners:

- Fixed determiners, e.g. *un sacco di* (a lot of).
- Free determiners, e.g. *una grande quantità di* (a great quantity of).

Fixed determiners are non-compositional and must be listed in the sentiment lexicon while free determiners are composed by an article, by a *LARGE_MORE* or *SMALL_LESS* adjective and by a noun of quantity like, for example, *quantità* (quantity) or *numero* (number). They basically express the semantic component expressed by the adjective that they contain.

Verbs. In some cases, the verb that expresses the *CONSUME* or *PRODUCE* component, can express by itself also the *LARGE_MORE* component. This is the case, for example, of the verb *mangiare* (to eat) as in the sentence "la stampante mangia cartucce" (the printer eats cartridges).

Right (or Left) Dislocation. There is also another way to express the *LARGE_MORE* component that is not a lexeme but a sentence structure: the right (or left) dislocation. In this construction, there is the partitive pronoun *ne* (of it), the verb, and a prepositional phrase that usually follows the verb (but it can also appear at the beginning of the expression). An example of this construction is the sentence "la stampante ne consuma di inchiostro" (the printer consumes a lot of ink).

RESOURCE and WASTE

Nouns. RESOURCE and WASTE components can only be expressed through nouns. These two components differ from the others for the fact that they are domain-dependent: a noun that expresses the component *RESOURCE* in a domain may not do the same in another domain. For example, the noun *rumore* (noise) expresses the *WASTE* component in the domain of the appliances and the *RESOURCE* component in the domain of the air horns. However, there are some generic *RESOURCE* and *WASTE* nouns that can be considered domain-independent as, for example, the nouns *carburante* (fuel) and *spazzatura* (garbage).

4.2   System Structure

Figure 1 shows the structure of the system. The system takes in input a corpus of reviews and performs a lexical analysis by using the sentiment lexicon. Then a syntactic analysis is performed by using the syntactic grammars. During the lexical analysis, the system performs a general lexical annotation and it also tags every word that expresses a semantic component with the component expressed (semantic component annotation). During the syntactic analysis, the system identifies the producing and consuming expressions, tags the semantic components expressed with syntactic structures, extracts the semantic components contained in each expression and performs the target extraction. Once extracted the semantic components contained in each expression, the rules of sentiment composition are applied to the expressions in order to classify their sentiment polarity. The final output of the system is the set of producing and consuming expression contained in the corpus and tagged with their polarity and their opinion targets.

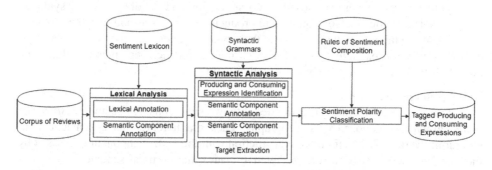

Fig. 1. Structure of the system

We developed only the sentiment lexicon and the set of syntactic grammars because, once the semantic components have been extracted, it is possible to apply, as set of semantic composition rules, the rules proposed by Liu [1] to perform the polarity classification.

5   Linguistic Resources

The system was built using Nooj [8]. The sentiment lexicon consists of a domain-independent Nooj dictionary and in a set of domain-dependent Nooj dictionaries that store the domain-dependent *RESOURCE* and *WASTE* nouns. The set of syntactic grammars is composed of one Nooj syntactic grammar organized in smaller sub-grammars.

5.1   Domain-Independent Dictionary

The domain-independent dictionary (Prod_cons.dic) is manually compiled. It contains 342 lexemes divided as follows:

- 157 adjectives: 91 are tagged with +L_M (*LARGE_MORE*), 65 are tagged with +S_L (*SMALL_LESS*) and 1 is tagged with +*CONS* (*CONSUME*).
- 11 fixed compound determiners with the +L_M tag.
- 82 verbs: *31* are tagged with +*CONS* (*CONSUME*) and 51 with +*PROD* (*PRO-DUCE*); 7 of these verbs are also tagged with +L_M.
- 72 nouns: 31 are nominalizations of *PRODUCE* verbs and so they have the tag +*PROD* and 22 are nominalizations of *CONSUME* verbs and so they have the tag

+*CONS*. The dictionary contains also 8 nouns tagged with the tag +*RES* (*RESOURCE*) and 6 nouns with the tag +*WAST* (*WASTE*). The last 5 nouns are the nouns used to identify the compound determiners that are not fixed. They have the tag +*Quan* (*Quantity*).

5.2 Syntactic Grammar

The syntactic grammar is composed of 63 subgraphs and handles different syntactic structures. It identifies the consuming and producing expressions and tags the semantic component contained in them. It tags the opinion target and the second term of comparison in comparative opinions. Furthermore, it handles negatives by adding the tag +*INV* to the expressions when a negative is present.

Description of the Grammar

The main graph of the grammar is divided into two subgraphs: *active* and *passive*. The *active* graph is composed of 6 subgraphs. Each graph represents a syntactic construction: the right dislocation, the construction with the *L_M* component expressed by the verb, the standard sentence, the relative clause, the nominal sentence, the nominalization, and the adjectivization.

The *passive* graph is divided into 4 subgraphs, they handle the following constructions: the right dislocation, the construction with the *L_M* component expressed by the verb, the standard sentence, and the nominal sentence.

These third-level graphs recognize and tag the expressions that have the specified syntactic structure or that are permutations of these structures.

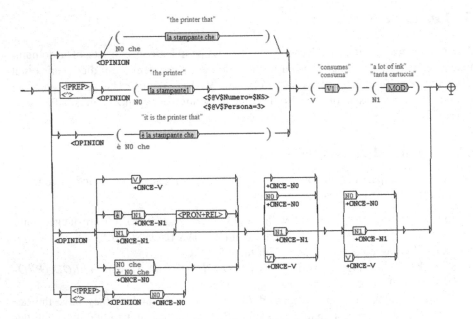

Fig. 2. Standard sentence subgraph

To give an idea of how these grammars work, the standard sentence subgraph is shown in Fig. 2. The upper part of the grammar is divided into three elements: the subject (N0) that is the opinion target, the verb phrase (V) that express the *CONSUME* or *PRODUCE* component, and the object (N1) that express both the *LARGE_MORE* or *SMALL_LESS* component and the *RESOURCE* or *WASTE* component. The lower part of the grammar recognizes permutations. All the other subgraphs that handles the various syntactic structures were made following the same approach.

5.3 Tag Produced

After the syntactic analysis, each identified producing or consuming expression is tagged in the Nooj TAS [8] with the tag *<OPINION>* followed by the tags of the semantic components contained in the expression (the tags appear in the order in which the components appear in the expression). For example, the sentence "questa stampante consuma molta cartuccia" (this printer consumes a lot of ink) is tagged with *<OPINION +CONS+L_M+RES>*. The opinion target is tagged with *<TARGET>* and the second term of comparison is tagged with *<COMPARISON>*. Both these two tags must appear inside the tag *<OPINION>*. Figure 3 Shows an example of these tags.

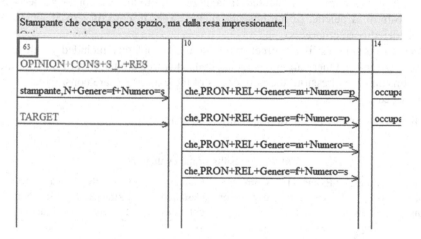

Fig. 3. Example of the tag produced by the grammar

6 Evaluation and Discussion

To evaluate the system properly an Italian corpus is needed where consuming and producing expressions are manually annotated. We have neither been able to find a corpus with this feature nor to compile it. So, we didn't evaluate the recall of the system. However, we evaluated the precision of the system and the errors that it commits by applying it on three unannotated corpora and then we judged the tag produced.

The three corpora of reviews were extracted from Amazon. The first corpus is composed of 762 reviews of an inkjet printer. The second is composed of 450 reviews of a led torch and the third is composed of 282 reviews of an ice maker machine.

The corpora were imported in Nooj and annotated using some linguistic resources from the Italian module of Nooj [11] (_Sdic_it.nod, Dnum.nom, ElisioniContrazion. nom, tronche.nod, DNUM.nog). Together with these linguistic resources, the producing and consuming dictionary (Prod_Cons.nod), a manually compiled RESOURCE and WASTE dictionary for every corpus (res_printer.nod, res_torch.nod, res_ice.nod) and the producing and consuming grammar (Prod_Cons.nog) were used in the annotation.

Once tagged the corpora, every expression tagged by the system is judged by the author of this paper with regard to the following factors:

- Producing and consuming expressions identification: if an annotated expression belongs to the category of the producing and consuming expressions, even if it falls partially out of the tag <OPINION>, it is considered a correct expression.
- Polarity classification: if the extracted semantic components of a correct expression, (once applying the rules of sentiment composition) lead to the correct polarity of that expression, the polarity is considered correctly classified.
- Target extraction: if the extracted target of a correct expression is correct, that target is considered correctly extracted (anaphora resolution has not been performed. A pro-form, a deictic, or the absence of the target in case of zero anaphora were considered correct targets).
- Opinion boundaries: if a correct expression is completely included inside the tag <OPINION> and there are no elements in this tag that are not part of that producing or consuming expression, the boundaries of the expression are considered correctly identified.

The results of this evaluation are shown in Table 1.

Table 1. Results of the evaluation

Domain of the corpus	Number of reviews	Extracted expressions	Correct expressions	Correctly classified polarities	Correctly Extracted Targets	Correctly Identified Boundaries
Printer	762	12	10	10	9	8
Torch	450	41	36	35	34	29
Ice maker	282	23	12	12	9	9
Total	1494	76	58	57	52	46

6.1 Expression Identification

58 out of 76 expressions extracted by the system are correct (precision 0.76). Analyzing the incorrect expressions, we can identify two main types of errors: expressions that are not opinions and errors due to lexical ambiguity.

In the first type of errors, the extracted expressions had all the features of consuming and producing expressions except for the fact that, because of their context, they did not express opinions. Take for example the sentence (taken from the ice maker corpus) "lo consiglierei per chi ha bisogno di un po' di ghiaccio al volo" (I would recommend it to those who need some quick ice). Here, the expression "chi ha bisogno di un po' di ghiaccio" (who needs some ice) does not express any opinion. To solve this problem, it is possible to discard the extracted expressions that have as target the personal pronoun *chi* (who).

Whereas, the errors due to lexical ambiguity occur since no disambiguation was performed before applying the system. These errors may be significantly reduced with the disambiguation of frequent items, such as the preposition *in* (at | to | into) that can also be an adjective and the relative pronoun *che* (that) that can as well be an adjective and a noun.

6.2 Polarity Classification and Target Extraction

The polarity classification has been performed correctly on 57 out of 58 expressions (precision 0.98). The only expression that was classified incorrectly is the following: "credevo che facesse più luce" (I thought it made more light). It was classified as positive, but it was negative. This happens since, in this sentence, the modality (that the system does not treat) shifts the sentiment polarity of the expression.

The targets have been extracted correctly in 52 out of 57 expressions (precision 0.91). The errors made by the system were mainly due to two factors: the lexical ambiguity and the lack of punctuation. Especially the lack of punctuation represents a challenging problem. Let's consider that, in corpora of customer reviews, the opinion target is usually omitted when it is the product reviewed. It is hard to formulate rules that can deal with syntactic constructions with a VOS (verb-object-subject) order. Our system, when an expression without a target is followed by a noun that agrees with the verb of the expression, extracts that noun as opinion target. However, it is not the opinion target since it is part of another sentence that is not separated from the expression with a punctuation mark.

7 Conclusions and Perspectives

In this paper, we presented a system that uses Nooj to extract and tag producing and consuming expressions. The results of our evaluation show that our system is precise in extracting producing and consuming expressions, in classifying their sentiment polarities and in extracting their opinion targets.

In the future, we plan to improve the system by expanding our sentiment lexicon and improving our syntactic grammars. We will also try to apply the methodology used to develop this system in order to develop other systems that identify other types of opinions.

References

1. Liu, B.: Sentiment Analysis: Mining Opinions, Sentiments, and Emotions. Cambridge University Press, New York (2015)
2. Liu, B.: Sentiment analysis and subjectivity. In: Indurkhya, N., Damerau, F.J. (eds.) Handbook of Natural Language Processing, pp. 627–666. Chapman and Hall/CRC, Boca Raton (2010)
3. Das, S., Chen, M.: Yahoo! for Amazon: sentiment extraction from small talk on the web. Manag. Sci. **53**(9), 1375–1388 (2007)
4. Pang, B., Lee, L., Vaithyanathan, S.: Thumbs up? Sentiment classification using machine learning techniques. In: Proceedings of the ACL-2002 Conference on Empirical Methods in Natural Language Processing, vol. 10, pp. 79–86. Association for Computational Linguistics, Stroudsburg (2002)
5. Polanyi, L., Zaenen, A.: Contextual valence shifters. In: Proceedings of the AAAI Spring Symposium on Exploring Attitude and Affect in Text (2004)
6. Moilanen, K., Pulman, S.: Sentiment composition. In: Proceedings of the Recent Advances in Natural Language Processing International Conference, pp. 378–382. INCOMA, Shoumen (2007)
7. Montague, R.: Formal Philosophy: Selected Papers of Richard Montague. Yale University Press, New Haven (1974)
8. Silberztein, M.: NooJ manual (2018). http://www.nooj-association.org
9. Merkler, D., Agic, Z.: Sentiscope: a system for sentiment analysis in daily horoscope. In: Donabedian, A., Khurshudian, V., Silberztein, M. (eds.) Formalizing Natural Languages with Nooj, pp. 173–181. Cambridge Scholars Publishing, Newcastle upon Tyne (2013)
10. Pelosi, S.: Sentita and Doxa: Italian databases and tools for sentiment analysis purposes. In: Bosco, C., Tonelli, S., Zanzotto, F.M. (eds.) Proceedings of the Second Italian Conference on Computational Linguistics CLiC-it 2015, pp. 226–231. Accademia University Press, Torino (2015)
11. Vietri, S.: The Italian module for NooJ. In: Basili, R., Lenci, A., Magnini, B. (eds.) Proceedings of the First Italian Conference on Computational Linguistics, CLiC-it 2014. Pisa University Press (2014)

Rule Based Method for Terrorism, Violence and Threat Classification: Application to Arabic Tweets

Wissam Elahsoumi[1]([⊠]), Ines Boujelben[2], and Iskander Keskes[3]

[1] Miracl, University of Sfax, Sfax, Tunisia
wissamelahsoumi@gmail.com
[2] Higher Institute of Computer Science and Multimedia of Gabes,
Gabes, Tunisia
boujelben_ines@yahoo.fr
[3] Higher Institute of Business Administration of Gafsa, Gafsa, Tunisia
iskandarkeskes@gmail.com

Abstract. In this paper, we present a rule based method to classify Tweets under three main categories; terrorism, violence and threat classes. Given that Arabic is a morphologically complex language, we build a linguistic module to identify a set of patterns for each class. Our proposed method requires three fundamental steps: First, we create our reference corpus collected from Arabic tweets. From the study of this corpus, we identify a set of linguistic rules. Finally, these patterns will be rewritten into local grammar within the linguistic platform NooJ. The evaluation of our system achieved encouraging results to obtaining 84%, 86.8% and 84.7% in terms of recall, precision and f-score respectively, when applied to test corpus.

Keywords: Pattern · Local grammar · Terrorism · Threat · Violence · Tweets

1 Introduction

Nowadays, the term of social networks is becoming prevailingly ubiquitous following the prominently famous applications such as Facebook, Twitter and Instagram etc. Social networks are not exclusive for the major or elite class of society. In fact, some statistics were made in 2019 showing that 50% of children between the ages of 12 and 13 have used a social media application at least once. With the growth of these social networks such as Facebook and Twitter, some mindful users are starting to share and report occurrences and cases of cyber harassment such as terrorism, violence, and threats that may pose a potential danger to other social network users. These acts entail the abuse of these applications especially when they allow the amplification of these phenomena which can be threatening to the society itself.

In this context, a study that was conducted in 2019 by the "Anti-Defamation League" shows that more than 30% of American Internet users in 2018 who use these social networks have declared that they have been victims of a severe form of hatred or harassment such as physical threats, compulsive follow-up, etc. This number has

© Springer Nature Switzerland AG 2020
H. Fehri et al. (Eds.): NooJ 2019, CCIS 1153, pp. 209–219, 2020.
https://doi.org/10.1007/978-3-030-38833-1_18

increased to 68% in 2019. Thus, several works have been proposing to deal with this problem while eliminating acts of harassment in social networks, and especially the detection of terrorism. Although, the extraction of harassment acts has been widely treated in the literature for English, French and other Indo-European languages whereas the Arabic language is abandoned in this area. Infact, a review of literature shows that very limited efforts have been made for this task in Arabic.

For these reasons, we had the incentive to tackle this issue that falls within the domain of NLP, analysis, extraction and classification of acts of harassment from the tweets and apply it to the Arabic language.

In this framework, two main approaches emerge: the language-based approach and the learning-based approach. The main objective of this work is: First, the construction of our own corpus that contains the harassment acts such as Terrorism, Violence and Threat. Then the proposition of a rule-based method for the classification of these harassment acts. Thus, the process of the identification of these acts relies concretely on the identification of the significant and representative terms of terrorism, violence and threat.

The remainder of this paper is organised as follows; We survey firstly the prior studies on terrorism or harassment identification. Then, we explain the harassment task as well as the different challenges. The next section illustrates the architecture of our process, in which we detail the three main steps of our proposed method. Finally, we present the experimentation of our system from which we discuss and analyse the reported results. Indeed, the detection of these acts of harassment represents now a new challenge in Natural Language Processing through NLP.

2   Related Work

In literature, several methods have been proposed to identify harassment acts from text. These methods can be classified into two broad categories: the rule-based approach and Machine Learning-based approach.

The linguistic approach rely on handcrafted rules as it focuses on linguistic information through the extraction of relationships between terms that present the language phenomenon. This kind of method takes the form of extraction patterns allowing the description of possible sequences of events. Among the studies that rely on the rule-based method in the field of terrorism, we cite [1] who extract terrorism acts from Arabic tweets using local grammars created in the linguistic engine NooJ [2]. The evaluation of their system obtained a precision of 90% and a recall of 70%. In the same context, [3] aimed to extract terrorist events to recognize named entities. Their proposed method is divided into 4 phases. The first phase is the pre-processing phase which consists of classifying articles with XML tags. The second phase is the selection of linguistic features, this phase is divided also into 3 parts: (i) the creation of geographical repertoire of terrorism using a GATE GUI tool, (ii) The creation of terrorist nomenclature compliant list, terrorism ontology and the Thai terrorist event extraction system which is developed using the GATE GUI tool, (iii) The elaboration of terrorist grammar rules (TGR). This study uses the JAPE (Java Annotation Pattern Engine) grammar of the GATE tool to develop the rules of the terrorist's grammar. The third phase is the application of the ANNIE system which relies on finite state algorithms and the JAPE language. For the classification the authors used a TF-IDF similarity calculation algorithm finally, the last phase is the extraction of information.

For the machine learning approach, we distinguish the supervised learning which requires annotated learning data, associating the input data with the desired results. Among works used supervised techniques, we mention [4] who used 3 automatic classification techniques on articles to support the categorization of events: Naïve Bayes, Support Vector Machine and the network of propagation propagation neurons. The evaluation of their system reported that the Naïve Bayes and SVM classifications provided a stable improvement (from 47% to 68%), while the neural network had the highest precision with 70 characteristics used.

And finally, the unsupervised learning which refers to a form of learning based on raw data (non-annotated corpora). It aims to highlight relationships linking events, without prior knowledge of their type and number. Thus, the relationship classes must be identified automatically from the texts.

Among the works that rely on unsupervised learning, we mention [5] who worked on web content for the detection of hate and violence to revisit the problem of Web classification through a new method and technique of textual content analysis. The authors used an unsupervised LDA learning method to improve the accuracy and reduce false positives of the system at the classification level.

3 Challenges of Identifying Harassment Acts from Arabic Tweets

Before enumerating the different challenges of our task, it is mandatory to explain each area of harassment acts. Firstly, the terrorism presents the unlawful use of intimidation, especially against civilians in the pursuit of political aims like for example the sentence:

[أبو إيفانكا الواشنطني بالذبح أتيناكم.]

[Abu Ivanka Alasantini we are coming to slay you.]
The violence is the behavior involving physical force intended to hurt, and morally damage. To illustrate this act, we can take this example:

[بشار يا خنزير.]

[Bashar is a Pig.]
Finally, the threat act which presents a statement of an intention to inflict pain, injury, damage or other hostile action on someone in retribution for something done or not done. For example, consider the following tweet:

[سأقتلك واشرب من دمك هل اوضح اكثر؟]

[I will kill you and drink of your blood do you want me to explain further.]
The identification of these harassment acts from Arabic tweets poses various challenges. Some of these challenges are related to the specificities of the Arabic language. In fact, Arabic is a Semitic language that presents interesting morphological and

orthographic challenges that could complicate the identification of the terms of the field of harassment. These challenges are added to the general problems of the identification task as presented in the following Table 1.

Table 1. Challenges of terrorism, violence and threat identification.

Problems	Examples
Presence of negation	ليس القتل هو الحل بل الذبح يا بشار
	Killing is not the solution, but slaughter, Bashar
Implicit expression of violence	بشار يا خنزير
	Pig Bashar
Tweet expresses two classes similarly (Violence and threat).	أبو إيفانكا الواشنطني بالذبح جيناكم
	Abu Ivanka Alasantini we are coming to slay you
Ambiguity between classes	سأقتلك واشرب من دمك هل اوضح أكثر
	I'll kill you and get closer to your blood, it's clearer
Tweet does not express terrorism act although the presence of terreorism trigger.	الارهاب لا دين له
	terrorism has no religion

The challenges listed above should be considered to achieve an efficient system for harassment's identification that includes Terrorism, Violence and Threat.

4 Proposed Method

Our goal is to classify Arabic tweets into three broad classes of harassment which are: Terrorism, Violence and Threat. To reach this goal, we propose a linguistic method based on linguistic patterns. Our method uses a representation of linguistic rules by means of transducers.

Figure 1 shows our method's of a working model divided into three general steps. The first step involves a construction of our reference corpus. The second step concerns the identification of linguistic patterns. These patterns are deduced from the study of our reference corpus referring to a linguistic expert to resolve some of the problems that were cited previously. Finally, in the third step, we transform these patterns into a set of finite-state transducers using the linguistic platform NooJ.

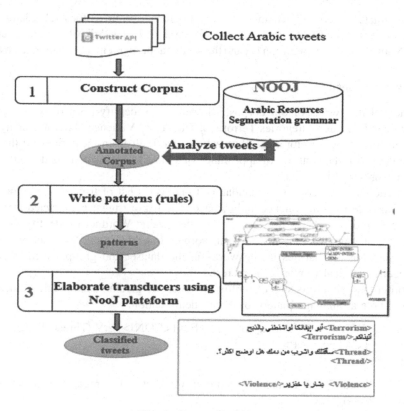

Fig. 1. Proposed method

4.1 Construct Corpus

The majority of prior studies treats only one or two areas at least for harassment events. To our knowledge, there is no available Arabic corpora in the literature that similarly treat the three acts of harassment which are Terrorism, Threat and Violence. Moreover, today twitter application is one of the most used social media in the world. For these reasons, we drive to build our own corpus collected from Tweets in Arabic language.

To collect tweets, we have created an account at Tweeter to have access to data shared on this application. After the automatic collection of Tweets, we created an algorithm with the R language using the RStudio software. This algorithm allows the search to Tweets through a given string that works in real time, which allows to extract the Tweets that are published with the most recent dates.

The R language is a programming language and a mathematical environment used for data processing and statistical analysis. It is commonly used in the field of Big Data for data mining and processing.

Our final corpus is composed of 1,998 tweets, 89 text digits, 21,332 of tokens, 18,956 words.

To annotate our corpus, we apply a set of linguistic resources for Arabic language. Indeed, we reused the Electronic Dictionary for Arabic "El-DicAr" [6], the grammars of Arabic Named entities recognition [7] and the grammar of segmentation elaborated by [8].

4.2 Write Patterns

The study of the tweets of our corpus, allowed us to identify a set of rules used to classify them into three categories Terrorism, Threat and Violence. After this analytical study and following the empirical observations, we built from these rules all the patterns dealing with the contexts of appearance of a class of harassment its dependencies on other words and its syntax.

To write these patterns, it is mandatory to collect a list of trigger words for each relevant class, terrorism, violence and menace. The list of trigger is extracted from our reference corpus. To enrich this list, we use the Arabic Wordnet to identify the synonyms of each trigger identified from our corpus. Indeed, Arabic Wordnet is used to identify semantic similarities in the words in the dataset and groups words that are semantically identical to words of interest.

In order to explain this step of writing patterns, we give an example that illustrates how to rewrite a language pattern of threat identification.

Pattern 1: {<WF>} * <V_Threat_Trigger + F > {<CONJ>}[<V_Threat_Trigger + F > <PRON>] * {<WF>} * <P>

With:

– <WF>: (Word Form) means any word in the dictionary, regardless of its grammatical category.
– [..] *: the cardinality of a word {0..n}
– {..}: Optional component
– <V_Threat_Trigger>: The triggering words of the threat class taking the category of a verb.
– <CONJ>: Conjunction
– <V + F >: Verbs conjugated in the future tense.
– <P>: punctuation mark.

This pattern can treat the following examples:

I'm going to kill you	سأقتلك
Today I'm going to kill you	اليوم سأقتلك
I'm going to kill you today	سأقتلك اليوم
Today, I'm going to kill you and drink your blood	اليوم، سأقتلك وسأشرب من دمك
I'm going to kill you and drink your blood today	سأقتلك واشرب من دمك اليوم

This step aims at formalizing the patterns identified in the study corpus using the formalism of the transducers via the linguistic platform NooJ. We opted for the use of finite state transducers because they allow us to easily represent the generic aspect of the patterns through recursive calls of sub graphs and the use of dictionaries and symbols representing different categories such as words <WF>, the punctuation marks <P>... Also, the graphical representation of the transducers facilitates the tests, revisions and updates.

The implementation of the proposed rule-based method is carried out using the NooJ platform. For the classification of tweets, we have reused the different Arabic resources available in this platform such as dictionaries (nouns, verbs, adjectives, etc.) and grammars (morphological and syntactic) as well as the grammars for Arabic Named Entities recognition [6].

Given that we focus on three classes terrorism, violence and threat, each class requires a set of patterns. These patterns are represented in the following grammar. We obtain the main transducer of Fig. 3. As illustrated, we elaborated three sub_graphs. Each graph contains the pattern of harassment classes.

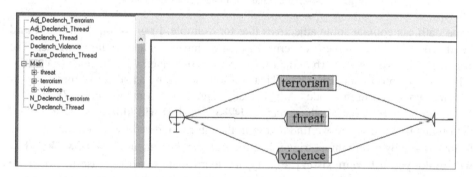

Fig. 2. Transducer of different graphs related to acts Terrorism, threats and violence

Figure 2 shows the main graph allowing the classification of tweets as threat, terrorism or violence. Each path in this graphic represents one or more than one pattern. The grammar is composed of three sub-graphs. in order to understand this main graph, an explanation of the sub-grammar, Threat is provided.

In order to identify a threat acts in the tweet, we need firstly to extract Trigger words. These trigger words can take various grammatical categories. For each category, we propose a set of patterns. As presented, in figure (Fig. 3) the Threat grammar is composed of many paths. The first path treats the case, in which we find a trigger verb of the threat class in the future form like for example: [سأقتلك] **[I will kill you]**. These triggers are listed in the sub-grammar labelled "V_Threat_Triggers". This grammar contains about 70 threat triggers. To be sure that these trigger verbs are in the future, we add to each entry of node (V + F). This same path can be enriched by another threat trigger verb like for example: [سوف اقتلك و اهينك] **[I will kill you and insult you]**. The

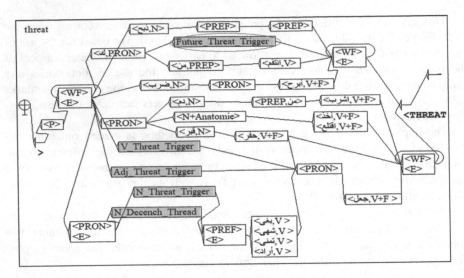

Fig. 3. NooJ grammar for threat act identification

same path can contain some adjectives like for example: [سأقتلك بيدي] [**I will kill and insult you**]. The second path concerns the case we have an adjective threat trigger. The case, in which we have a verb in the future which is presented with the node (<V + F>) followed by a pronoun (<**PRON**>). That is also followed by an adjective threat trigger which is presented in the node "Adj_Threat_Trigger" that contains about (78 entries). This path treats for example the sentence: [سوف اخطفك] [**I will kidnap you**]. The third path treats the case where we find a verb in the future followed by a pronoun which is followed also by a verb threat trigger like for example the sentence: [سأجعلك تقتل أختك] [**I will make you kill your sister**]. Finally, the fourth path treats the case in which we have the same verb in the future followed by a pronoun followed by a set of trigger verbs followed by a prefix (<**PREF**>) which is attached to a noun threat trigger. These nouns triggers are presented in the node <N_Threat_trigger> which may or may not be related to a pronoun. This path can treat the example: [سأجعلك تحب الموت ، سأجعلك تحب موتك] [**I will make you love death, I will make you love your death**]. We have added other paths to treat some complicated threat expressions like for example: [أنا لن أقتلك لكن سأذبحك] [**I'll not kill you but slaughter you.**]. For the annotation of this grammar, we add the tag ("Threat") for each tweet identified by this grammar.

5 Experimentation and Evaluation

For the evaluation of our relation extraction method, we built another test corpus different from the training corpus. Our test corpus is composed of social media sentences in Arabic standard. In Table 2, we summarize the characteristics of both the reference and test corpus, mentioning the final number of tweets, tokens, digits and words forms that compose our corpus.

Table 2. Training and test corpora.

	Training corpus	Test corpus
Number of tweets	1998	294
Number of words forms	18956	3504
Number of tokens	21332	3884
Number of digits	89	34

To evaluate our system, we analyze firstly our reference corpus in order to extract manually the tweets expressing terrorism, violence and threat. The application of our local grammar obtains the following results.

Fig. 4. A sample of concordance obtained from the evaluation corpus

Following the application of our grammar, our system categorized the tweets into three different classes: Threat, Violence and Terrorism.

After that, we compared the obtained results with the manually obtained extraction. The evaluation metrics we used for the classification task are recall, precision and f-score. Table 3 presents the results of the evaluation of our grammar when applied to our test corpus.

Table 3. Obtained results on the evaluation corpus.

	Recall	Precision	F-score
Threat	89.2%	89.2%	89.2%
Terrorism	80.1%	79.2%	79.6%
Violence	84%	86.8%	85.3%

Table 3 shows that our system gets promising results compared to recall, precision and f-score.

When visualizing the obtained results presented in Fig. 4, we can mention the following analysis: First of all, we can note the influence of the effectively employed Arabic Wordnet on our work which gave a significant richness to our grammar. Indeed, some Tweets were not ranked well due to the non voyellation of texts that composed our corpus. And finally, some terms are not recognized due to that some of tweets of our corpus are written in Arabic dialect besides being heterogeneous and extracted from various resources.

6   Conclusion and Future Work

In this paper, we presented a rule-based method for tweets classification using the NooJ platform. We described two different approaches for identifying terrorism, violence or threat: rule-based approach and machine learning approach. Moreover, we have enumerated various problems related to the terrorism identification task besides the problems related to the Arabic language. While some problems are resolved, others need specific treatments that must be considered to ameliorate the results.

We have conducted experimentation on a test corpus which resulted in satisfying findings with an average of 85%.

Concerning perspectives, we have to orient our work towards new challenges. First, We intend to add new rules or patterns to detect implicit harassment acts from tweets. Additionally, we plan to integrate our system to other NLP applications such as text classification, automatic summarization and web mining. Finally, we intend to add machine learning model to enhance the overall recall of our system.

References

1. Chenny, H., Mesfar, S.: Generating alerts from automatically-extracted Tweets in Standard Arabic. In: Barone, L., Monteleone, M., Silberztein, M. (eds.) NooJ 2016. CCIS, vol. 667, pp. 145–154. Springer, Cham (2016). https://doi.org/10.1007/978-3-319-55002-2_13
2. Silberztein, M.: The Formalisation of Natural Languages: the NooJ Approach, p. 34. Wiley, Hoboken (2016)
3. Inyaem, U., Phayung, M., Choochart, H., Dat, T.: Ontology-based terrorism event extraction. In: First International Conference on Information Science and Engineering, pp. 912–915, Nanjing, China (2009)
4. Chung, W.: Categorizing Temporal events: a case study of domestic terrorism. In Intelligence and Security Informatics (ISI), pp. 159–161, Arlington, VA, USA (2012)
5. Liu, S., Forss, T.: New Classification models for detecting hate and violence web content. In: 7th International Joint Conference on Knowledge Discovery, Knowledge Engineering and Knowledge Management (IC3K), Lisbon, Portugal (2015)
6. Mesfar, S.: Analyse morpho-syntaxique automatique et reconnaissance des entités nommées en arabe standard. Ph.D. thesis, Franche-Comte University, France (2008)

7. Mesfar, S.: Named entity recognition for Arabic using syntactic grammars. In: Kedad, Z., Lammari, N., Métais, E., Meziane, F., Rezgui, Y. (eds.) NLDB 2007. LNCS, vol. 4592, pp. 305–316. Springer, Heidelberg (2007). https://doi.org/10.1007/978-3-540-73351-5_27
8. Keskes, I., Benamara, F., Belguith L.: Discourse segmentation of Arabic texts using cascade grammars. In: NooJ 2012 International Conference, pp. 231–233, Paris (2012)
9. Arabic Wordnet. http://globalwordnet.org/resources/arabic-wordnet/. Accessed 21 Feb 2019

Author Index

Printed in the United States
By Bookmasters

Lecture Notes in Mathematics 2250

More information about this series at http://www.springer.com/series/304

Anna Skripka • Anna Tomskova

Multilinear Operator Integrals

Theory and Applications

 Springer

Anna Skripka
Department of Mathematics and Statistics
University of New Mexico
Albuquerque, NM, USA

Anna Tomskova
School of Computer Science and
Engineering
Inha University in Tashkent
Tashkent, Uzbekistan

ISSN 0075-8434   ISSN 1617-9692   (electronic)
Lecture Notes in Mathematics
ISBN 978-3-030-32405-6   ISBN 978-3-030-32406-3   (eBook)
https://doi.org/10.1007/978-3-030-32406-3

Mathematics Subject Classification (2010): Primary: 46L51, 47B49, 47A60, 47A63, 47B10, 47C15, 47A55, 15A60; Secondary: 46N50, 58J30, 46L87, 46G12, 46H10, 47L25, 26A16

This Springer imprint is published by the registered company Springer Nature Switzerland AG.
The registered company address is: Gewerbestrasse 11, 6330 Cham, Switzerland

Preface

A multilinear operator integral is a powerful tool in noncommutative analysis and its applications. Theory underlying multilinear operator integration has been developing since the 1950s, with a number of amazing advancements made in recent years. The field has accumulated many deep theoretical results and important applications, but no book on this beautiful and important subject appeared in the literature. This book provides a brief yet comprehensive treatment of multilinear operator integral techniques and their applications, partially filling the gap in the literature. The exposition is structured to be suitable for both a topics course and a research aid on methods, results, and applications of multilinear operator integrals.

We survey on earlier ideas and contributions to the field and then present in greater detail the best up-to-date results and modern methods. The content includes most practical, refined constructions of multiple operator integrals and fundamental technical results along with major applications of this tool to smoothness properties of operator functions (Lipschitz continuity, Hölder continuity, differentiability), approximation of operator functions, spectral shift functions, spectral flow in the setting of noncommutative geometry, quantum differentiability, and differentiability of noncommutative L^p norms. We demonstrate ideas and include proofs in simpler cases, while highly technical proofs are outlined and supplemented with a list of references. We also state selected open problems in the field.

Albuquerque, NM, USA
Tashkent, Uzbekistan
September 2019

Anna Skripka
Anna Tomskova

Acknowledgements

The authors thank Fedor Sukochev for inspiration to write an overview of multilinear operator integration, which has ultimately grown into this book. The authors are also grateful to the three referees for their valuable comments and suggestions. In particular, Theorems 5.1.12 and 5.1.13, Sects. 5.1.6 and 5.3.7, and the example after Theorem 3.3.11 were suggested by the referees.

Research of the first author was supported in part by NSF grant DMS-1554456.

Contents